ROCKPOOL

NEIL PERRY

ROCKPOOL

NEIL PERRY

THE ICONIC RESTAURANT REDEFINING
MODERN CUISINE

NEW
HOLLAND

This book is dedicated to the memory of my father, and to my mother, who started all of this.
To my business partner, Trish, who allowed me to get the best out of myself.

First published in Australia in 1997 by
New Holland Publishers Pty Ltd
Sydney • Auckland • London
www.newholland.com.au

This edition published 2016

The Chandlery Unit 704 50 Westminster Bridge Road London SE1 7QY United Kingdom
1/66 Gibbes Street Chatswood NSW 2067 Australia
5/39 Woodside Ave Northcote, Auckland 0627 New Zealand

ISBN 9781742578828

A record for this book is available at the National Library of Australia

Managing Directorr: Fiona Schultz
Publishing manager: Lliane Clarke
Editor: Jessica McNamara
Designer: Andrew Quinlan
Production manager: James Mills-Hicks
Printer: Printed in Malaysia by Times Offset (M) Sdn. Bhd.
Cover image: Earl Carter

ACKNOWLEDGEMENTS

This book is really the collaboration of four people with the same vision, all adding the parts to make the whole stronger. I would like to thank the other three: Petrina Tinslay for the photography that brings the book to life, Colin Rowan for his beautiful design for the original book that captured the essence of Rockpool, and Sue Hines who kept pushing me back on track when I'd start to wander.

The ideas and philosophies behind Rockpool and its group of restaurants emanate from Trish and I, but it's our staff that bring these ideas to life and give them real meaning. It is their professionalism and belief, the extent of blind faith, in those philosophies that is the strength of Rockpool.

Greg Frazer, Lorraine Godsmark, Ross Lusted, Michael McEnearney, Susan Cunningham, Terry Higgins, Narelle Kellahan Melissa Lamb, Christian Denier, Kylie Kwong, Tippy Heng, Howard Morris, John Keddie, Mark Stapleton, Dean Gibson, John Low, Michael Schmidt, Ian Farquharson, Ken Huth, Carolyn Glover, Natalie Keon, Suzi Kuti, Nichole Light, Julie Little, Glen Langley, Kate Neeson, Rebecca Carroll, Daniel Moran, Amanda Gale, Gabrielle Goldshaft, Emma Woods, Anjela Fletcher, Mathew Snare, Jacinta Byrne, Kim Lockyer, Jason Green, Tolan Dyer, Hamish Watt, Amanda Fincham, Andrew Evans, Claudette Napper, Louise Holland, Megan Edwards, Aboobu Zainul, Ohid Ahmed, Frid Razalee Yanis, Mau Hai Ngo, Barnaby Smith, Courtney Bracks, Phillip Rose, Georgina Becher, David Mackintosh, Paul Angwin, Todd Cumins, Simon Shannon, George Hatzimihail, Scott Martin, Christian Green, Nicholas Harris, Jocelyn Harris, Sophie Read, Seamus Dinnigan, James Hemmings, Pern Choo, Lisa Saunders, David Titsha, Minna Hutchings, Tim Lion, Jennifer Collits, Merylyn James, Kate Millard, Cassandra Heke, Kylie Harrington, John Pletzer, Gary Martin, Tracey Fordham, Matthew Webber, Georgini Russel, Robert Bolt, Levi Rabuli, Ian Parkinson, Stephen Ward, Carl Bentley, Eric Forschinger, Brently Reid, Joshua Ireland, David Hollis, Joanne Tonkin, Tania Cusack, Tiffany Rivette, Kevin McGreal, Apollonia Saulekaleka, Jenny Quy, Antony Neeson, Rachael Doyle, Richelle Bambling, Marlon Lambert, Sarah Trant, Alan Murray, Vadim Gotovsky, Thomas Stack, Bao Zhong, John Hanley, Matthew Richards, Raquel Ramos, Elizabeth Willis-Smith, Jane Collins, Brigitte Hafner, Chris Miller, Adrian Durrant, Megan Scott, Inge Stainley, Linley Wilks, Richard Lindell, Tim Eastwood, Amelia Donald, Danielle Baker, Harriet Graham, Adam Gilbert, Barney Fallows, Eleni Georgiadis, Shari Henderson, Matthew Lee, Brent Sheriden, Alison Smith, Hanofi Achmat, Sam Crawford, Desmond Kalka, Mohamed Salihy, all the others in the past and those in the future who help us realise the dream.

CONTENTS

INTRODUCTION

Rockpool is the culmination of all the things that have influenced my career and my life, a reflection of my experience and thoughts on cooking and food. It's not only about the restaurant, but about the origins and inspirations of years of eating, and the joy to life that the pursuit of good food can bring. I had hoped, with my restaurant Rockpool, to create a special place for a special time. This book recounts much of the thrills and spills of its creation and refinement through the years.

My initial instinct about writing a book was 'Who needs it? What more can I add to the millions of words already written?' I figured I should let my food speak for itself, not my words. However, after much thought and discussion, my close friends convinced me that part of the responsibility of a cook is not just to create new recipes for cooks to follow, nor to show the world new food never seen in any other cookbook, but rather, to distil the hits and misses that come out of the thousands of hours that I have cooked, the thousands of words that I have read, and the many great meals I have enjoyed around the world. I had an obligation to pass it on.

While globalisation has ensured that cooks around the world can lay their hands on the same variety of produce that I use in my kitchen in Sydney, I'm convinced that we produce quite different creations out of those same ingredients in Australia. Because of the very nature of our culinary beginnings — or rather, the lack of one — Australian cooks can think laterally without being held back by a strong food tradition. Anyone coming from a strong food culture — be it French, Chinese or Italian — often seems to attempt to dominate new produce introduced into that country. For example, nearly every French cook who writes cookbooks I've read fetishises ethnic produce, or worse, tries to render the produce French, and makes it perform unnatural acts. I don't know how you feel about it, but I'm sure the lemongrass hates it. The tightness of some aspects of Old World culture makes it hard for some of its practitioners to relax with unfamiliar produce. Accordingly, not enough attention is paid to how the best is seduced out of the produce in its native land, where it has been used to its fullest advantage for centuries.

I'm quite sure that it would have been impossible for me to cook in the style I do if I had been born in another country, at the very least if born in an Old World country. Born of the New World and a truly multicultural society, it has been easier for me to learn from the many diverse food cultures that make up my cooking style. This involves respecting and blending with sympathy produce from its origins. You'll notice that I happily borrow from each culture a myriad of threads that I weave into a dish that I believe is uniquely Australian. It is heartening that as we move into the new century Australia is becoming more and more confident with its own identity, and creating food that is distinguishable, and recognisibly Australian.

Writing this book has also been to tell the story of a place that has influenced my career and my life —

Sydney. I can think of no better place in the world to cook and live in. It is also the story of growing up in a family that cared about food. My father was a butcher and a keen fisherman who cared enough about authentic food to make up his own curry spice blends. My mother was a good cook, too. When I was younger I took for granted that everyone ate sweetbreads and lambs' brains on toast for breakfast, and enjoyed liver, kidneys and tripe. Indeed, I found it quite amusing when I discovered many Australians' squeamish eating habits. From a young age, I was taught the meaning of freshness, and the importance of developing a keen eye for produce. If my father caught a fish it was always consumed the same day; if we went to the market produce was pulled at, poked and smelt — nothing was taken at face value. As he used to say, 'You know son, these blokes will try to put one over you, if you let them.' Pretty good advice that applies as well today.

When I was about six or so our family befriended two young Chinese boys, Ken and Jensen, who over time became part of our extended family. We used to head off to the Mandarin Restaurant in George Street in those days — long since gone — for supper. No gwailo (foreign devil) food for us, we ate what they ate: red-braised dishes, abalone braised in oyster sauce, white-cut chicken, jellyfish, and my favorite, stir-fried mudcrab with black bean and chili sauce. What a treat it was to grow up without copping sweet and sour pork every time. I'm sure that this grounding in good food started my love affair with Chinese food and all things Asian.

I hope you see the recipes in Rockpool as more than a collection of instructions. They should excite you and instil confidence and competence in your cooking, and promote skills that add to your experience. They are not meant to take the fun and spontaneity out of cooking, however, and definitely not to be followed slavishly.

You will see recipes that you may think are complicated. Usually they are not difficult at all but long; many dishes are made up of a number of small recipes. You just need to break the various components down and organise yourself accordingly. Viewed in this fashion, the recipes can be seen as a group of tasks coming together in one dish. Don't take for granted that all you have to do when enlarging a recipe is to increase the volume of the ingredients; very often certain elements go out of balance on a large scale, and it is necessary to readjust the proportions. Time after time I still go back to my favorite cookbooks, not for reference, but for companionship and a warm feeling that one gets when seeing an old friend. These are the books that teach you to cook, they make you think about food, they make you dream of it.

It's my hope that this book will grow to be your companion, through all your days of cooking and eating. May it inspire you to cook, and think a little more about the food you put in your mouth, and about eating well.

THE ROCKPOOL STORY

People often ask me, 'What made you cook?' and 'Why open a restaurant like Rockpool? These questions have their answers in what has made me, and where I came from. The story of my life is, in a way, the story of Rockpool.

Rockpool opened its doors for the first time in March 1989. I still remember our first meal with fondness. It was a special dinner for friends of the restaurant. The gas couldn't be connected until around 4 p.m., and we'd been hard at work all day, preparing. It wasn't until I'd finished cooking later that night that I realised I hadn't really seen the restaurant with all the lights on from the outside. We'd pushed so hard to open our doors that the scaffolding had only come down the day before, and the painting had only been finished two days previously. As I looked into the restaurant I felt like crying; it was more beautiful than I had imagined, with its gleaming stainless-steel surfaces, white-coated waiters rushing up and down the ramp, cooks cleaning the shiny new kitchen that was visible from the street and most importantly, friends drinking, eating and enjoying themselves.

If I wanted to cook and run a restaurant it had to be the best I could possibly make it. This was one thing I had learnt from the Great Chefs of France, one of the first cookbooks I read and still revisit constantly for comfort and inspiration. When you set out to create a restaurant you're not doing it for fame in a guide, probably not even for the customers, but for yourself. If you've worked and inspired others to work with you to the best of their ability then you've succeeded in your goal. In a fine restaurant good management, staff training, housekeeping and financial planning are as important as good food; only when all these things exist together do we achieve greatness. It's my feeling that too often, restaurateurs have forgotten that they're in the hospitality industry. A restaurant is, in the end, a house, a meeting place, and a place for enjoyment. It's the restaurateur's job to make people feel at home, to instil a sense of belonging to the patron, and to provide them with the complete dining experience. This was what I had in mind when I created Rockpool.

The Rockpool philosophy is quite simple. We set out to do everything to the best of our ability today, then try even harder tomorrow. This approach has enabled Rockpool to improve throughout its history, and will continue to push us forward into the future. The philosophy is maintained not only in the kitchen, but is the driving force behind the entire restaurant.

The Rockpool philosophy can be easily taken into your kitchen. It's about care. Care about what you eat. Care about the quality of your produce. Talk to, and form good relationships with, your suppliers. Be relaxed and happy when cooking — you can't cook well when you're in a bad mood. Keep yourself and your work space tidy and organised. Think about what you've just cooked and look for ways to improve on both the dish and your skill. Always taste for flavor and seasoning. The most important lesson about cooking is to learn to season properly, that's the key to harnessing flavors from food. If you season food after you cook you'll never bring out the rich flavors that cooking with salt will allow you. Adding salt at the end of the cooking process will produce a predominantly raw, salty flavor. In some cases that may be what you are looking for, as with salads. However, if harmony and balance are desired don't be afraid to use salt at the beginning of allow it to work its magic.

If you're a novice cook, don't hurry, and learn to do your tasks properly. If you hone a task again and again, it becomes a skill you can take with you always. Don't invent dishes for the sake of it — we must have sanity in this business. Instead, work on your best ones and always strive to refine them over the years. Try to pick up all-round skills; so few cooks today, for example, know how to break a side of meat.

Is life really worth living without quality food and wine? I'm convinced that moderation is the key to all healthy diets, and if this is practised throughout your life you'll not only live healthily but happily.

Going to the kitchen and cooking with wonderfully fresh produce is obviously one way of ensuring a good diet, but the demands of modern life often make that impossible. However, there is no excuse for eating the sort of rubbish that is pushed at us. The best that can be said about junk food is that it's cheap and convenient — so convenient you don't even have to think or taste it while you're eating. Processed foods usually have little nutritional value and are high in sugar and fats.

Flavor, nutrition and good living ought to go hand in hand. The irony is, while New World fast foods seem to have taken off, it's the Old World foods that present much better taste and nutritional options. The cooking doesn't necessarily take a long time, either. They've been at it for a longer time and regard flavor, not gimmicks and profit, as the most important part of their make-up. Many restaurants, produce stores and take-away bars these days produce quality authentic food preparations that are ideal for cooking with or used to build a dinner party around. In Sydney, for example, you can easily obtain Greek, Italian, Lebanese, Vietnamese, Thai and Chinese products without too much trouble, for a meal that is easy to prepare and not quickly forgotten. This is the way to eat convenience food and enjoy flavor.

The art of dining too, is frequently lost these days. I remember sitting at the table and enjoying a glass of wine with the family at fifteen. I'm sure this was critical to the development of my fascination with food and flavors, and my understanding of the enjoyment of fine food, good wine and good company. Food was our entertainment, not the television.

There are two important phases in my development as a chef. Damien Pignolet and Stephanie Alexander influenced what I call the first half of my cooking life, and gave me very important grounding in not my cooking style, but philosophy. Steve Manfredi and David Thompson are the main players behind my second stage, and instrumental in the maturation and definition of Rockpool cuisine. I gravitated towards the food industry upon leaving school, and started out not cooking but waiting. I received valuable all-round training in restaurant management and, coming to cooking late, had a firm grasp of what good restaurant food was about, what constituted good service, and an understanding of how customers felt about what was happening in the dining room.

In this time my greatest influence was Ross Hartman. He owned Sails at McMahons Point and taught me all about running a restaurant: percentages, margins, and working with, and being responsible for, staff. This experience first sparked off my dream of being a professional restaurateur. At Sails Rose Bay I decided o change my career path slightly and head for the kitchen. The chef at the time loved parachuting and one Monday morning, mistimed his landing and hurt his back. I spent the next two weeks in the kitchen as replacement cook and fell in love with the excitement, the pressure and the buzz of calling a service for two hundred people during a Sunday lunch.

But I knew I still had a lot to learn, and so went to see Damien and Josephine Pignolet, then of Claude's about some advice. I was starving for knowledge and wanted to learn everything. They asked me to read widely, especially everything by Escoffier, Elizabeth David and Jane Grigson, and read them again and again. They also invited me to work with them on a semi-regular basis, and what an education I received! Damien especially made me acutely aware of taste and texture, and reinforced what my father had always stressed about freshness. The period with them, in and out of the kitchen, and especially the time I spent cooking with Josephine over one winter, was to me a real time of serenity and fulfilment.

Another important experience was working with Stephanie Alexander in Melbourne. From Stephanie I learnt that if you concentrated on every job — however small, be it cleaning mussels or washing lettuce — you'll only do it better the next time. When you've performed a task a hundred or a thousand times, you have a skill. In hindsight I think I failed to appreciate my time there partly because I missed doing service. The other reason was the cold of the Melbourne winter.

When I returned to Sydney, I did a brief stint in the kitchen with Jenny Ferguson at You and Me, a stay that I look back on with fondness. I think Sydney was the loser the day that restaurant closed. It was also here that I met a good friend, Steve Manfredi.

I then waited at Berowra Waters Inn for Gay Bilson, and was once again frustrated and desperately unhappy because I wanted to be in the kitchen. When I left Berowra, I worked on the fryers and pans at the Bayswater Brasserie. I learnt so much during this period. In any evening at the Bayswater, we would do up to 350 covers, valuable lessons in timing and organisation. Working with and for Tony Pappas was a delight and we have remained friends in the ensuing years. By the end of 1982 I had decided it was time I started looking for a job running a kitchen; I felt I had absorbed enough and needed to expand on all these ideas. Service was my buzz, my drug, and I really need it to feel satisfied at the end of the day.

I then moved to work with Michael and Judy McMahon at Barrenjoey House in Palm Beach, and formed a working relationship that was to last for three years. From Barrenjoey House we moved to Perry's in the city.

I went to France towards the end of 1985, and it was around this time that my own style started to develop. I had had a meal at a restaurant called L'Archestrate, owned by a chef called Alain Senderens. The food was a marriage of flavors and textures between meat, fish and vegetable, with no secondary sauces. I decided to pursue this approach with my food, and eliminate the use of all fats apart from those that came naturally with the meat or fish, relying instead on the pan juices. Somehow I also wanted to integrate my knowledge of Chinese food with this.

Over the years I've come to realise that my cooking wasn't just a matter of not using butter, or turning my back completely on sauces. Rather, it had to do with balance, and doing what was needed to bring out the best flavor in food. My food today is therefore a product of Asian and European produce and techniques. There is a balance and a harmony that exists between the past, present and future, and that, I think, is what makes my cooking unique. As my food has matured so has Rockpool as a restaurant.

At the beginning of 1986 a site came up in Bondi. It was huge and pretty ugly but it had everything I needed for a simple, inexpensive, buzzy restaurant that served spanking-fresh grilled food with Asian influences. The Bluewater Grill, as it was called, offered the most amazing view over Bondi Beach and down the coast; at night the city skyline glistened. In two weeks we were off and flying, doing 2000 covers a week. The Bluewater menu also started becoming really eclectic. It seemed natural, in this breathtaking setting, that the food should display the multicultural style that was becoming more evident in our lifestyle. The business partnership, however, failed to work.

In the end I left for London, Paris and New York, and toyed with the idea of opening a fine-dining restaurant, the Rockpool, in New York. At around the time I was to decide if I would be staying in New York or coming home, I was told about a site in Sydney that would become Rockpool. I only had to see the bridge as we were landing to know where I belong. I'm Australian. I cook Australian food and I want to do it here, in the birthplace of modern Australia.

That was in 1988. Bill McMahon, Steven Roberts and Michael Scott-Mitchell of D-4 Design were engaged to refit Rockpool from the ground up. I was there everyday during the design and fit-out stage, making sure that everything was designed specifically for the needs of the restaurant. I would have terrible arguments with Steven over the design of things, who would want to put in beautiful but totally impractical things, warning me that the finished restaurant will look like a fucking milk bar. To which I'd say, 'Well, it won't fucking work like that!' We did compromise, and the result, was a design that was beautiful and functional.

Banks were as dubious as everyone else about our ability to make it, and the recession was starting to make its presence felt. The refit was nearly complete, but the budgets were blowing out, and the owner of the building developed cold feet and wanted out. Thankfully my cousin Trish, who had been working on the finances for Rockpool with me, stepped in and put her money where her mouth was. We went into partnership and it is she who keeps the dream happening, and makes every work day a joy.

That night I looked back into the restaurant, I knew it was the first day in the life of a restaurant that would one day be a great one. The first staff booklet, produced some seven-and-a-half years ago, stated that it was imperative that not only the restaurant, but the staff attitude be vibrant, not only after the first ten days but after the first ten years. I'm very pleased to say that I'll have to amend that to twenty years.

The Rockpool menu at the beginning displayed the eclecticism that I had started at the Bluewater Grill. I continued to explore dishes that did not rely on butter or demi-glace as a sauce. I also moved further and further down the path of integrating not just Asian flavors, but more importantly, Asian techniques in my cooking.

Most of my Asian influences were Chinese until I met David Thompson, who was then cooking in a hotel in Newtown. David had lived in Thailand for a couple of years, and so fallen in love with the culture, food and language that he decided to show Australians what real Thai food was all about. The first meal David cooked for me blew all my preconceived ideas about Thai food out of the water — this was food that displayed complexity, balance of flavor and texture, and real style. It was through David that I discovered the essence of Thai technique, and it has changed the way I cook forever.

Another culinary stimulus is Steve Manfredi, whose food is an inspiration. We virtually grew up side by side in the Sydney food scene. Steve's cooking is simple and direct, with an uncompromising attitude to flavor, texture and freshness. He also shares my obsession with quality produce. We make a stack of fresh pasta everyday at Rockpool, and it was Steve and his mother, Franca, who set the benchmark for what pasta should be.

From a flying start we have continued to flourish and grow; we now have three successful restaurants and a catering company, further expansion on the horizon and 150 young Australians working for us. No doubt, there were many years of struggle. I have always strived for what Rockpool is all about, and in a way, I have made it. In the final analysis, however, I believe it's Rockpool that has made me.

Trish often tells me that she has never lost that thrill of dining chez Rockpool, and I'm convinced that we're such good partners because we've never stopped loving being in the restaurant or being involved in it. I love what I do, I have a great wife, a beautiful daughter and a business partner to die for. So when people ask why I decided on a cooking career, I just say it was fate.

ROCKPOOL THEN

ROCKPOOL NOW

WINE

For me wine is as integral a part of dining as food; it is the enjoyment of both that makes dining such a civilised pastime. It has always been my belief that chefs, and home cooks, should have a sound understanding of wine to allow them to cook to the best of their ability. It's all part of understanding flavor and aroma, which are invaluable in cooking. Your palate is your guide, and must therefore be tuned at every opportunity. Try taking the time to think about what you eat and drink. All things have taste and aroma, and if you commit them to memory, they'll help you develop a finely tuned palate. Food is no different to wine this way; the length and intensity of flavor play a part in determining quality.

People who say wine and Asian food don't mix are quite mad, I think. Most of them would be just as happy eating lamb cutlets and mashed potato with their precious wines. Dining should be a fun experience, and the wine should be allowed to relate to the dinner, and not be the pinnacle. That the majority of the people in the great wine-producing countries of the Old World sit down and talk about food marriages all the time, or even go through the trouble of drinking different wines with different food is a myth. Nine times out of ten they'll drink the local wine with, and throughout, a meal. How can four people sit down in a restaurant and marry their food with the wine? They'd all have to order the same dishes, and that would be boring, not only for them, but for those of us in the kitchen. Dining is eating and drinking what gives you pleasure. Any restaurateur or chef who thinks otherwise should perhaps rethink his or her role.

Are winemakers being influenced by the chefs? Is the type of food being prepared influencing decisions at the winery? I'd suggest the process is symbiotic: we inspire each other to ever-greater heights. Consumers are drinking wine they enjoy with the food that's being offered at restaurants, and the availability of resources and books has allowed many households to cook a version of contemporary restaurant food at home. So it would seem that the market forces are affecting some of the wine-making decisions. The general consensus in the industry is that attitudes in wine-making have been affected by consumers' desire to drink younger wines, meaning that there are few wines bought today at retail level that are destined for cellaring or consumption in ten years' time. For the winemaker, there's an obvious economic need to turn the wines around as quickly as possible. Not only is cash flow a priority, but many small wineries lack the space to hold onto the current vintage once the next is arriving. These winemakers have also realised that if their wine is to be consumed younger than before, they'll have to tread that fine line between generosity at a young age, and staying power as the wine matures.

New World wine styles, with their generous fruit and robust flavors, were made to go with New World multicultural food. We're very fortunate in Australia to be turning out well-made and very inexpensive wines that complement all the wonderful food we produce here, be it curry, roast duck or the myriad flavors of Asian food. Enjoyment of food with wine is not only possible but paramount, as we become more civilised and cultured in our attitude towards dining. I was having lunch one day with Donlevy Fitzpatrick, who ran the Melbourne Wine Room and George Hotel in Melbourne. He had two pinot noirs to taste. One was more expensive, three years older and a much bigger wine with great structure and a nice balance of fruit and acid. The second had a rich color, opulent silky fruit, wonderful intensity and length of flavor. Donlevy asked which I would rather drink, and I chose the second. The moral of the story is, drink the delicious wine every time, go with your tastebuds, and not the label or price. Drink the wine that gives you pleasure.

Don't get me wrong, I love an old bottle of wine, one that has slept through a world war or two, or one that may have seen my birth, or at the very least, a teenager. For me old wine is about romance and taste. I love to see these special wines during special occasions, but we want memories from them, not headaches.

Before I started the Rockpool I knew I wanted to develop a house wine list, so that wine would be available by the glass. The intention was not to produce cheap wines for the list, but to have wines with the same style and integrity as the restaurant, wines that customers could feel have a real relationship with the Rockpool. To achieve this I had to convince some of Australia's best winemakers to believe in the concept, and, with Greg Frazer, who handled the wine list, we went about achieving just that.

Jeffrey Grosset was the first to be persuaded, and in December 1989 we put the first Rockpool Riesling on the list. There were more than twelve wines available under the Rockpool label. I would suggest to any restaurateur to do the same; it's wonderful looking at rows of vines knowing that they are destined for your restaurant, or taste wine from a barrel that's going into your blend. I would like to thank the Rockpool winemakers who made this all possible, especially Jeffrey Grosset and Joe Grilli, who stuck through the tough times and made the good times even better.

All the aromatic styles of white wine work well with Asian-flavored foods, as do medium to light-bodied reds. Look for good seductive aromas, length, intensity and balance of flavor. A wine that fills these four criteria will be a quality wine. It's easy to stop and think quickly about a wine, and your enjoyment will increase as you pay a little more attention to what's going on.

The Australian wine industry has grown dramatically from the early 1970s. We now produce some of the best wines in the world, and some of the best value. Concern for quality has risen dramatically, and for that we can all be pleased.

The service side of the hospitality industry has also been enhanced. It's all well and good to produce quality wines, but they are improved out of sight if you have service staff who know how to deal with them. It's very important that your staff know about the wines that you have on your list, and that they are served with respect.

MUSEUM OF CONTEMPORARY ART AND CATERING

During the building of the Rockpool in 1989 I would walk down George Street, thinking of things that had to be done, things we hadn't addressed so far, such as the 300-odd drawings, plans for staff and staff rule books and all the other important stuff. Out of the corner of my eye I'd see people playing handball one level down from George Street against a beautiful old building that was at that time the Maritime Services Board building. I have always loved the way that it stood out from across the quay of the Opera House, like something from the city of Metropolis; as you looked back across the vista I've always expected Superman to leap off and fly to the rescue of some fair maiden. As Rockpool began life, the beautiful building seemed to die when the Maritime Services left for a more modern — one suspects more computer friendly — building. It lay dormant and seemed to disappear in the minds of most Sydneysiders. It was still there, reflected in the windows of the Rockpool, but it was as if a mysterious force had shadowed it from view.

I first became aware that the Museum of Contemporary Art (MCA) was going to open across the road from Rockpool in this very site later that year. Rockpool had only been open a year, and I didn't think we seriously thought that our destiny would take a turn not only down a different road, but across the road. We had no idea that we would play a part in making the Museum a place that fast wove itself into the cultural fabric of Sydney.

They were open to suggestions and opinions on how to use the space, and seemed receptive to the idea of a café within the site. Trish and I walked over late one January afternoon and were shown around. The sun was setting, and the washed light reflecting off the buildings at East Circular Quay cast a beautiful glow into the room that reminded me of La Coupole in Paris, a big, bustling brasserie. Trish and I just glanced at each other, no words were needed.

We were finally granted the lease at the end of September, and in five weeks, had to raise the money and set up the kitchen in time for the Museum's official opening on 11 November 1991. We were very lucky to be able to secure finance in such a poor climate, with the recession well and truly on. Again, it was due in no small part to Trish.

At the site, however, all manner of hell was breaking loose — workmen were hanging over each other and he plumbers were screaming at electricians, who were in turn screaming at the painters. We were caught in the middle, trying to get in to do some work among all this madness.

Come 11 November — what a nightmare! The kitchen was in, but the gas wasn't on so we had no ovens and a lunch to prepare for 300. We had decided previously to do a roast Illabo leg of lamb and lemon tart. If I had had four years catering experience behind me I wouldn't have even broken a sweat, but back then, had no idea how many serves 300 serves really were, or how much time it would take to put out that many meals. Put simply, I had 60 legs of lamb and no ovens. Rockpool was flat out, and Lorraine was busy cooking the lemon tarts in the convection oven anyway. I ended up ringing Serge Dansereau at the Regent, my friend and neighbour. He asked me to send up the lamb which he proceeded to cook in the banqueting department. The sight of six chefs carrying big white tubs full of roasted lamb legs running along George Street is amusing now, but chaos reigned in the kitchen that day. By the time the last of the 300 plates went out we all stood in the kitchen looking at each other, shell-shocked, and just a little disillusioned. Worse, it wasn't over yet we had to cater a cocktail party for 1500 patrons, members and guests for the opening of the museum that evening. Was this to be the next edition of my nightmare?

We set up a 'kitchen' in the back alley — the fire escape — and out the front of the museum, and had barbecues and gas ovens going flat out. We prepared in the vicinity of 18,000 pieces of food that night, from a kitchen with no gas. Everyone has memories of looking out into the back alleyway that night and seeing the cooks completely smoked out, frantically barbecuing seafood sausages, satays and murtabak dough wrapped around pork and peanut curry. At twelve-thirty that night, with a glass of wine in hand, I thought about the cleaning up and the cafes opening the next day. I prayed that the gas would be on; I suspected it would make things much easier.

One of the really rewarding things about catering is that occasionally you are asked to take part in history and we have been privileged to be a part of many such moments. We closed the catering side of Rockpool Consulting down in 2001 to concentrate solely on our restaurants once again, but the great memories live on

COCKTAIL FOOD

Here are some ideas for cocktail food which we found work very well at the MCA. The most important thing is to keep them small, neat, and easy to eat. Don't forget the person eating will probably have a drink in one hand and most probably be trying to hold a conversation. Nothing is worse than wearing half your canape when you're trying to impress.

SALTCOD TARTLETS WITH FRESH TOMATO SAUCE

For the Saltcod Puree, soak a piece of saltcod in fresh water, changing the water every half-day for 24 to 48 hours, depending how salty you like the dish. I prefer it with a pronounced salt flavor. Cook the saltcod in a court-bouillon for 25 minutes. As it cools remove the flesh. Heat up some olive oil in a pot and gently fry the saltcod with the crushed garlic, stirring with a wooden spoon to crush the cod. Once the saltcod starts to form a purée add the mashed potato in about one-half proportion to the saltcod. Add some milk and continue to stir, drizzling in sufficient olive oil to make a purée. Season to taste with lemon juice and cracked pepper. Remove from the heat and set aside until ready to use. For the Tartlets: Use your favorite puff pastry to make small tartlet cases, or buy them from good pastry shops. For the Tomato Sauce: Sweat the onions and garlic in olive oil until soft. Add salt to taste and the blanched, peeled, seeded and diced tomatoes. Reduce for a further 10 minutes, add the chopped anchovies and capers. Take the sauce off the heat, grind over some pepper and add the chopped flat-leaf parsley. To assemble, warm the puree and put a small dollop in a pastry case. Add a splash of fresh tomato sauce and serve immediately.

YAMBA KING PRAWN AND SUN-DRIED TOMATO RICE-PAPER ROLLS

Peel and devein the fresh king prawns, and put a skewer through the centre to straighten them. Grill on a barbecue until just cooked, leaving the centre slightly translucent Remove the skewer. Dice good quality dried tomatoes with small amount of chopped red shallots, fresh garlic, flat-leaf parsley and coriander. Blanch some cos lettuce in boiling water. Refresh immediately in cold water and pat dry. Open out a cos leaf so it lies flat. Lay a prawn along the leaf, add the chopped tomato mixture and roll up into a small parcel.

Moisten the rice-paper in warm water until pliable. Remove from the water and place on a tea-towel. Put the prawn, wrapped in the lettuce leaf on the bottom and roll up. Tuck in the corners and continue rolling until you have a nice spring roll. Place on a tray and cover with a damp cloth until needed. They last well for up to 3 to 6 hours. When ready to serve slice each roll into four and serve on a banana leaf.

POLENTA WITH PEA AND ARTICHOKE AND PROSCIUTTO SALAD

Make your favorite polenta (mine always has cheese and plenty of butter). Spread it out on a flat dish to about 1.5 cm thickness. Refrigerate to set overnight.

For the Salad, peel and blanch the peas in plenty of salted, boiling water. Refresh and set aside. Peel off the tough out leaves of the artichokes, cut off the top and remove the choke. Brush with lemon juice and cool n salted boiling water for 25 minutes until soft. Tip upside-down on a tower to drain. To assemble, fry the sliced red shallots and garlic julienne some good-quality olive oil. Add the sliced prosciutto and until slightly crisp. Add the artichoke julienne and peas, a stir in some lemon juice, salt, freshly ground pepper, chopped flat-leaf parsley and tarragon. Cut the polenta into 4 cm squares and, with a small carrot baller, remove the centre. Crisp or fry the squares, put on a tray and top the pea and artichoke salad. Serve immediately.

BLUE SWIMMER CRAB FRITTATA

Whisk some eggs together and add salt, pepper and grated Parmesan. Sweat some onions, garlic and tarragon in some olive oil and add to the picked and cooked crabmeat. Mix these into the egg mixture. Melt a knob of butter in a pan on the stove and once it bubbles pour in the crabmeat mixture Continue to stir and once the bottom starts to set let the egg mixture from the centre spill over into the bottom of the pan. When the frittata is half set, place in an oven at 140°C (290°F) for about 10 minutes to allow the top to set properly. Remove, turn out, and when at room temperature, cut into small squares for serving. Serve just above room temperature.

SUGAR-CURED SALMON WITH WASABI ON TOASTED BRIOCHE

Place a side of salmon in a mixture of sugar, sea salt, crushed ginger, picked thyme and cracked black peppercorns to cure for between 4 and 6 hours. Wash off when the salmon is cured and cut into nice thin slices as for smoked salmon. Shred and salt the cucumber. When it's soft rinse off the salt, and mix with a little sugar and rice-wine vinegar. Mix some powdered wasabi with hot water, and whisk into a vegetable-oil mayonnaise. Make sure the mayonnaise is hot and spicy. Cut some brioche (page 219) into small squares and toast. To assemble, place a slice of cured salmon on the brioche, spoon on some cucumber and finish with a dollop of wasabi mayonnaise. Serve immediately.

STICKY RICE AND CHINESE SAUSAGE BALLS

Soak the glutinous rice overnight. Spread on a damp cloth and place in the steamer for 1 hour. Sprinkle with water from time to time during cooking to stop a crust from forming. Chop up the reconstituted shiitake mushrooms, Chinese sausages and spring onions. Fry in the sesame oil for a few moments. Take the rice from the steamer and mix with the other ingredients. Add some chopped coriander and, if you like, chopped coriander roots. Form into small balls and serve with a soy dipping sauce.

PORK AND PEANUT CURRY TARTLETS

Mince some belly pork finely. Crush equal amounts of red shallots, garlic, coriander roots, blackened chilies and white peppercorns to a fine paste. Fry some peanuts and crush. Julienne some lime leaves and basil. In a large frying pan, heat the peanut oil and coconut cream together until the coconut cream splits. Add the paste and fry until fragrant (about 8 minutes). Add the mince and continue to fry for another 10 minutes or until well browned. Add the palm sugar and caramelize, then the fish sauce. Top with coconut milk and simmer for 10 minutes. Add the crushed peanuts, basil and lime leaves, cook for another minute, and remove from the heat. The curry reheats very well and can be put into little puff pastry tartlets for a canapé. Serve immediately.

TEA-SMOKED OYSTERS AND GREEN MANGO SALAD ON FRIED WONTONS

Make your own wanton skins (or buy them from Chinatown) and deep-fry until crisp. Make a Nam Jim (page 106). Julienne some green mango. Add some crushed peanuts, coriander, mint, fried and raw shallots and fried garlic to the mango. Tea-smoke oysters on the half shell (see instructions for tea-smoking on page 48). Place some of the mango salad and a smoked oyster on top of the wonton skins. These are a delicious starter to a meal or canapé.

PRODUCE: THE CORNERSTONE OF GOOD COOKING

Good food starts with fine fresh produce, and if you want to cook well you must first pay attention to the quality of your produce. The front page of the Rockpool menu lists our suppliers; I recognise that without their support and commitment to the finest, all our efforts in the kitchen would be in vain. Build up a good relationship with your butcher, baker, fishmonger and vegetable supplier. Don't be afraid to ask for the best and to complain if the produce is not up to scratch. Producers will soon realise it's easier to look after you in the first place than earn your wrath. Suppliers who are interested in quality will welcome your enthusiasm, and those who don't are best ex-suppliers. If chefs work closely with their suppliers they can help change things for the better. It's all a matter of supply and demand — if you demand the best all the time, the message will finally get through. Chefs, suppliers and growers or producers have worked together in Australia to make available a wide variety of quality produce in a very short span of time in our culinary history.

An example of this is John Susman, then from the Flying Squid Brothers, who started servicing the domestic market with quality products that are usually reserved for the export markets. His unrelenting push for quality has led to a re-examination by the suppliers at the Sydney markets of what quality seafood is, and they have in turn lifted their game. The process has taken years but the attitude has changed, and I firmly believe it's because of John's efforts.

Tony Lehmann was also among the new breed of Australian producers who understood what the market required and has delivered, in no uncertain terms, a quality product that is now available not only to restaurants but at a retail level to Sydneysiders. He's one of the many suppliers who recognises quality and an individual product. We met sometime in 1989 and discussed the impossibility of procuring good quality lamb outside spring, and raved about the exquisite milk-fed lambs of Europe — in other words, real lamb! Tony took these thoughts and slipped off into the night. Six months later he called up and delivered the first of those delicious Illabo lambs into Rockpool's coolroom. Others who have been instrumental in the supply of quality produce include Barry McDonald, who first brought us good Australian cheeses; Simon Johnson, who picked up where Barry left off and now provides us with some of the best imported and local produce imaginable; Matt Brown who, with Barry McDonald, is a purveyor of quality fruit and vegetables; Ian Milburn of Glenloth Farm for the beautiful pigeons and free-range chickens; Luv-aDuck for ducks only dreamed of after trips to Europe; Frank Marchand of Heidi Farm, and Gabrielle Kervella, two of Australia's greatest cheesemakers, who set the benchmark for the industry. In the following section I have outlined the fresh and preserved produce that you'll need for the recipes in this book. Some of them may be unfamiliar, but most are readily available from gourmet food shops and delicatessens. Remember when using ethnic spices to look very closely at the culture it comes from (or dominates), and try to learn how to balance the various spice flavors within a dish.

SEAFOOD

When it comes to fish, fresh is best, so if you are going to the market, buy fish only for that day or the next, at the most. Fish deteriorates at such a high rate that one or two days really makes a difference in the quality. The bacteria and enzymes in seafood work at a much lower temperature, and break down much faster than meat Two or three hours at room temperature can age a piece of fish three days. To choose the freshest fish just follow your nose; fresh seafood and fish shouldn't smell fishy. You should look for bright color, closely knit scales, firm flesh, sparkling eyes and a very fresh smell of the sea. If the fish has an ammonia or very strong smell, concave eyes or soft flesh they should be avoided. I recommend that you buy fish whole, and have your fishmonger fillet them for you, or fillet them yourself at home.

Crayfish, yabbies and crabs, where possible, should be bought live as the flesh starts to deteriorate the minute they die. Mussels and oysters should be heavy and tightly closed. To store fish in the refrigerator for the next day keep it on ice with a drip tray underneath. This helps lower the temperature and retard the deterioration of the fish. Keep it off the water.

Sea urchins are about the size of a tennis ball, and have a hard shell covered in prickly spines. They are sometimes available live, and the roe is at its best when eaten raw. Trays of pre-shucked roe are sometimes available at fish markets. Avoid fish that has already been filleted and lying on ice at the markets. The water seeps in and takes away the flavor, color and texture from the fish. Never buy frozen seafood — I cannot be convinced that it's anywhere near as good as fresh — and as it defrosts the crystals puncture the cells of the fish, making it soft and mushy.

BEEF

Beef should be a bright red color and well marbled with fat so that the cut is lubricated while cooking. The younger the animal the more tender it will be. As it ages, however, the meat develops a better flavor, so the choice is between tenderness and flavor. Try to find a butcher who will hang your meat for you. If meat is hung for between 14 and 20 days it develops a tenderness and flavor much superior to a freshly killed animal.

VEAL

The best veal comes from a young milk-fed animal up to four months old that has been fed on either cow's milk or milk substitutes. Once the animal starts to eat grass the flesh will darken. Meat from the milk-fed animal stays a much paler, milkier color, and the muscles will be creamy and pink. This type of veal is very expensive to produce but the quality is far superior and you'll get a tenderness and flavor that surpasses normal veal fed on grass or grain. Veal is a fairly lean cut so it must be cooked carefully over medium heat as there isn't any internal fat to moisten the meat during cooking. If possible wrap the meat in caul fat or cover it in back fat before roasting to give the meat additional moistness.

LAMB

The best lambs are those up to 3 months old. Most lamb in Australia is killed between 3 months and 12 months and I find a lot of it too strong in flavor. The young milk-fed Illabo lamb is 6 weeks old, and one of the most beautiful meats you'll ever eat. Tender, full of flavor, subtle and clean, it cooks up to a beautiful pinkish-white. It's really worth locating a butcher who will get you that quality of lamb. All the parts of the smaller lamb — the shoulder, neck, skirt, breast and shank— are marvellously tender and flavorsome, so there is little waste.

PORK

This delicious and versatile meat is the major meat in Chinese and South-east Asian cooking. Its flesh should be a pale pink color with a layer of pure white fat. The cuts most used in Chinese cooking are the shoulder, belly and loin. The best place to buy the highest quality pork at very reasonable prices is in Chinatown.

OFFAL

When buying offal remember that it deteriorates very quickly and starts to go downhill two or three days after slaughter. Sweetbreads, brains, liver, hearts and kidneys should all be bought very fresh or, at a pinch, frozen. They should be vibrant-looking, glossy and bright. Avoid those with a milky or pale sheen. The best place to buy tripe is in Chinatown, where it's usually sold unbleached (unbleached tripe will be a sandy, slightly brown to green color). The flavor is well worth it.

CHICKEN

Use only good-quality, free-range chickens. Most specialty shops will carry a corn-fed or free-range chicken of some kind, but they must be taste-tested — the branding doesn't always ensure quality. One of the best places to buy chickens is at Chinese markets, where they are usually sold with the heads and feet left on. These birds also tend to be plump, and have a more defined flavor. Avoid the battery-reared supermarket chicken. Once you've found a good chicken supplier stick with them.

DUCK

The most important thing about ducks is to make sure that they're not too fatty. The larger, 2 kg duck is a perfect size for most Chinese-style dishes. A smaller wild Barberry or Muscovy duck of about 1.6 kg is ideal for roasting and served rare in the French style. Make sure that the skin isn't damaged and the duck hasn't been frozen. In Chinese cooking duck is cooked in much the same way as pork.

PIGEON

Pigeon or squab, the young bird with the larger breasts, is suitable for roasting. Only pigeon is good for braising, and it's delicious roasted and served very rare, as the French do. Its tender, almost melting, very game-like flesh also sits well with the Chinese technique of first cooking the bird in a master stock and then wok-frying. I find that the best is somewhere in-between, when the skin is crisp, but the flesh still pink. King pigeons work best with this particular cooking technique.

OLIVE OIL

Along with wine and bread olive oil is a staple in the Mediterranean, and like wine, it's revered, tasted and debated over. Good oils all have their own flavor and character, and will vary in taste from season to season. It's possible to have an extra-virgin olive oil for every salad mix, meat or fish. I find Colonna from Tuscany a good all-rounder. Virgin olive oil is the first pressing by physical means only and produces four grades of oil. Pure olive oil is produced from successive pressings of the leftover pulp by heat or chemical methods. Extra-virgin olive oil has less than 1 per cent oleic acidity (acidity being an index of spoilage). Virgin olive oil has less than 4 per cent acidity, and the superfine and fine olive oils fall somewhere in-between at 2 and 3 per cent respectively. Extra-virgin olive oil should be stored away from heat and light, and consumed as soon as possible after opening. Don't leave an opened bottle near the stove for too long as it will deteriorate. When a recipe calls for olive oil I mean pure olive oil.

NUT OILS

Walnut, hazelnut and almond oils are pressed in much the same way as olive oil. They are usually used in salad dressings, and once opened, should be refrigerated and consumed reasonably quickly as they turn rancid easily.

BUTTER

Always use unsalted butter of the finest quality. Cultured butters have long been available in Australia, and these work for the table as well as the kitchen.

AROMATICS AND GREENS

BAMBOO SHOOT

Fresh bamboo shoots are available during spring and autumn in Sydney, and they are truly wonderful — their texture and mild straw-like flavor is beyond compare. Peel back to the shoot, slice finely and blanch three times in salted boiling water to get rid of any bitterness before using in Chinese stir-fries.

BASIL

see Thai sweet basil

BOK CHOY

Also known as pak choy or Shanghai bok choy. They have varying degrees of green leaf and pale milky stems and are ideal accompaniments to main courses. They are delicious either stir-fried or steamed, and are readily available from Chinatown. See also Chinese broccoli and mustard greens.

CHILI

Chilies are thought to have originated from Mexico ten thousand years ago. They are fruits of the New World and it's amazing how closely the cuisines of Thailand, Indonesia and India, who didn't have the fruit until the Portuguese introduced it to Asia in the seventeenth century, are linked to chilies. Imagine Thai food without chili! The heat in many of the hot dishes in Thailand before the introduction of chilies were thought to have come from peppercorns and ginger. The chilies mostly used in this book are the long red variety and the small, wild green chilies of Thailand known as 'heavenly rat droppings' or 'bird's eye chilies'. These chilies have a wonderful immediate heat and citrusy lime-like flavor, which is more complex than the small red chilies that the Chinese use. Both fresh and dried long red chilies are used in curry pastes, and are readily available from Asian food stores.

CHINESE BROCCOLI

Also known as gai lan. They are usually green all the way through, and the stems, leaves and white flowers can be eaten. They have a slightly bitter flavor, and a pleasant texture and crunchiness. They are delicious stir-fried with garlic, ginger, and oyster sauce.

CORIANDER

Also known as cilantro or Chinese parsley, coriander is a member of the parsley family and treated as a herb or garnish in Western dishes. In many Asian dishes it is used as a vegetable for flavoring and bulking out a dish. Coriander is very aromatic and has a wonderfully clean, uplifting flavor with a slight aniseed quality. I tend to add coriander at the end of cooking as it imparts a slightly bitter flavor when overcooked. The root is widely used in Thai curry and stir-fry pastes. It's also a good flavoring agent for salad dressings.

DILL

Dill has a very strong aniseed flavor, so use it sparingly as it can easily overpower a dish. Dill works very well with seafood and adds a wonderful intensity of flavor to salads and soups.

EGGPLANT

A native of South-east Asia, and many varieties are used throughout the book. Japanese eggplants are thinner and slightly paler than European eggplants. Apple eggplants are green, yellow-orange or purple in color, and about the size of golfballs. Pea eggplants grow in clusters and are somewhat bitter. All can be added to stir-fries, are very good in curries, and the apple and pea eggplants are known to form the basis of several nam priks.

GALANGAL

Galangal is quite often known as 'lesser ginger' and is a rhizome used in curry pastes and soups. It's an integral part of Thai cooking, with a very aromatic quality and uplifting flavor that gives Thai curries part of their charm. It is simply peeled, sliced, crushed and added to soups.

GINGER

It's almost impossible to imagine Chinese cooking without ginger. Ginger, garlic and spring onions come to mind as the main seasonings for most Chinese dishes and stir-fries. Ginger is not actually a root but a rhizome that grows on an underground stem. Buy young ginger with a shiny tight skin and is heavy for its size. Avoid wrinkled ginger that's been sitting around for too long and looks dehydrated. Scrape off the pale-brown skin before use. Dried powdered ginger isn't a substitute at all. See also pickled ginger.

KAFFIR LIME

Both the skin of the fruit and the leaves are used extensively in soups and curries in Thailand and many South-east Asian countries. The rind has a lime-like uplifting flavor and is an integral part of curry pastes. The juice is rarely used as it has an overwhelming perfumed flavor reminiscent of dishwashing liquid (Thais are known to wash their hair with it). The leaves have two distinct sections, and are used in curries and soups. When crushed, they give off a wonderful lemon–lime aroma. Be careful not to use too many — they can impart a bitter flavor. Kaffir limes and leaves can be bought fresh in most Asian food stores and are far superior to the dried or frozen product.

LEMONGRASS

An aromatic herb that is used to flavor Thai and Vietnamese food. It has a slight lemony perfume and long, grass-like leaves. Lemongrass is usually sold in long stalks but use only the white part, the bottom 10 cm (4 in) of the stalk. Peel off the tough outer leaves and chop the inside finely for curry pastes. Or, bruise to release its flavor into soups and braises Along with spring onions, garlic, coriander and galangal, lemongrass is a popular flavoring for Thai food.

MANGO (GREEN)

This is unripe mango, which is very sour. It's generally used in salads, and is available, when in season, from Asian food stores.

MINT

This is used extensively in soups and salads in South-east Asia, and especially in Vietnam and Thailand. Large quantities are used in salads for its fresh aromatic flavor. It can be substituted for basil in pesto and, with the addition of chili, makes a really interesting dressing for meats.

MINT, VIETNAMESE (RAU RAM)

This herb is used fresh in Vietnamese salads, spring rolls and fragrant soups. It has a very aromatic, uplifting quality, and a little heat with a subtle underlying mint flavor.

MITZUNA

This is a Japanese herb. Its long, pointy leaves can be used in much the same way as rocket or arugula.

MUSHROOM, BLACK AND WHITE WOOD

Also known as wood-ear or cloud-ear fungus. Both are now available fresh and, as far as texture goes, they are far superior to the dried tree mushrooms. Their texture is silky and crunchy, and the Chinese believe they are a very good digestion aid. If you're using the dried variety soak in hot water until they have expanded to several times their original size.

MUSHROOMS, ENOKI

These are becoming more readily available in Australia. They are grown in little punnets and come in clumps. Enoki mushrooms are delicious in salads but even better when cooked for a few moments in soup or used as a garnish with stir-fries. They are reasonably fragile and only keep for 3 to 4 days in the refrigerator. Ideally they should be used very fresh.

MUSHROOM, SHIITAKE

Fresh shiitake mushrooms have become more widely available in Australia over the last few years, and are often used in mushroom salads and ragouts by European cooks. Although they are quite delicious the Chinese wouldn't think they are a substitute for the dried at all — the texture, quality, and intensity of flavor of the dried mushrooms are unsurpassed. The mushrooms need to be reconstituted in hot water before use, and the stems should always be removed as they stay hard and are indigestible.

MUSTARD GREENS

Also known as gai choy or mustard cabbage, this dark-green vegetable has a slightly bitter mustard flavor when used fresh. It is often found pickled in earthenware jars in Chinese shops, and a welcome addition to soups and stir-fries. I love it stir-fried with ginger and garlic.

PAK CHEE FARANG

Another coriander-style herb. Its Thai name actually means 'foreign coriander' and it's also sometimes called 'sore tooth herb'. It's used to flavor broths and, in Vietnam, with fresh rice-paper rolls and different phos.

PANDANUS LEAF

Pandanus leaves are used quite extensively in Thailand and Indonesia in desserts and some savoury dishes. Meat or fish can be wrapped in the leaves and deep-fried. The juice from the pounded leaves are used to color desserts, and impart a lovely floral dimension when cooked with things like coconut rice or glutinous (sticky) rice.

PAWPAW (GREEN)

This is basically unripe pawpaw. The flesh is pale yellow to whitish, and usually finely shredded and added to salads for texture. The enzymes in pawpaw make a good tenderiser for octopus and meats.

POMELO

A large, grapefruit-like tropical citrus. The very thick pith peels back to reveal either pink or white flesh that is sweet, tangy and crunchy. Remove the tough membrane and use in salads or as a fruit.

SHALLOTS

These are formed more like garlic than onions, and have a head composed of several small cloves. The cloves are covered with a thin, papery skin that, when peeled away, yield pale-purple to reddish flesh. They have a distinctive but not overpowering onion taste. Very popular in South-east Asian cooking.

SPRING ONIONS

Also known as scallions, and often incorrectly referred to as shallots in Australia. Spring onions have a white bulb that is not fully developed and long, straight, green leaves. Both the tops and white part are used in Chinese cooking.

THAI SWEET BASIL

Also known as Asian basil, and is thought to be the original basil. The Italian basil was imported from South-east Asia and developed into the herb we know today. The two varieties of Thai basil that we use are the sweet, which is more closely related to the Italian basil, and the hot, which is used for frying, garnishing and flavoring different braised and curry dishes. Sweet basil is used for garnishing soups, stir-fries and, with mint and coriander, in Thai salads. It has a wonderful aniseed flavor that is less pungent than Italian basil, and lends a rich, subtle flavor when used in large quantities in soups. The same quantity of Italian basil would overpower the dish.

TURMERIC

Another relative of the ginger family, with a wonderful deep-orange centre, usually peeled, crushed and added to flavor and color curries. It has an earthiness that reminds me of truffles. If possible it should only ever be used fresh.

WATER CHESTNUT

Once you've eaten a fresh water chestnut it's very difficult to go back to the canned. Fresh water chestnuts have a black skin that, when peeled, reveals a white disk. Simply rinse under cold water and it's ready for use. If you're keeping them overnight store them in lightly salted water to prevent fermentation. They add a sweet, crunchy flavor and texture to Chinese stir-fries, soups and salads.

DRIED AND BOTTLED PRODUCTS

BEAN PASTE

A seasoning made from fermented soybeans. It is possible to get sauces that have been flavored with chili, garlic and so on. They make terrific flavorings and also impart body to stir-fries and stews. See also hoisin sauce.

CASSIA BARK

This is quite often called 'false cinnamon' or 'Chinese cinnamon', and is the bark from the laurel or Indian bay tree. True cinnamon comes from Sri Lanka and Indonesia. The curled, paper-thin quills add a robust taste to Chinese red-braised dishes, and are an important ingredient of five-spice powder

CHINESE RICE WINE

see Shaohsing wine

COCONUT MILK

Coconut milk is not the liquid inside the coconut, that is coconut juice. To prepare fresh coconut milk chip away at the hard outer shell with a cleaver and break it up into small pieces for easier handling. Grate the white flesh with a coconut grater (available from Chinatown). Add about 2 cups of hot water to the grated flesh and steep for 20 to 30 minutes, then squeeze hard through muslin or cheesecloth. This is called the first pressing. More hot water can be added to obtain second and third pressings. The quality and thickness of milk depends on whether it comes from the first, second third pressings. The fat or cream that rises to the top of the first pressing is known as coconut cream. The second and third pressings can be used for either poaching or curries. Tinned coconut milk will never be as good; its flavor is stronger and more pervasive. However, if you don't have time, it's a reasonable substitute. Dilute the big coconut flavor by adding water. When you open a tin of coconut cream be sure not to shake the can; scoop out the firm top part of the coconut, fill up the rest of the can with water, and pour over the top part to bring the flavor back in line with the other ingredients.

FISH SAUCE

Nam pla or fish sauce is the run-off from salted anchovies or squid. The best varieties come from Thailand and Vietnam. They are highly prized and used to make dipping sauces (nam jim or nuoc cham). The stronger sauces are used in cooking. Three Crab brand is one of the best for salads and sauces, and Squid brand is a good all-rounder for cooking. Refrigerate after opening.

HOISIN SAUCE

This is a bean paste made from soybeans with a sweet, garlicky flavor. The texture is usually quite firm and jam-like and it's generally used in stir-fries and as a sauce for Peking or Sichuan duck. My favorite variety is from Korea and is seasoned with chili. It has a deep and mysterious flavor, and when mixed with sesame oil, sugar and soy sauce makes a great sauce for oysters. It's available in tins and jars from Chinese grocers and supermarkets.

JELLYFISH

The Chinese and Japanese use jellyfish simply for its bland, crunchy texture. Only the top or head of the jellyfish is used, the tentacles have been removed. The best ones come packed in salt rather than dried like beancurd skin. The Japanese produce a very good jellyfish packed in salt.

MIRIN

Mirin is sake (Japanese rice wine) boiled with sugar. It's readily available from Asian food stores and Japanese shops.

NORI

This is Japanese seaweed that has been compressed and dried into thin sheets. It ranges in color from a deep-green to dark purple, and is usually used to make sushi rolls. I also use it to feed marine fish. Available from Asian food stores and supermarkets.

NORI, OGO

A delicate seaweed that's available from Japanese specialty shops, at its best salted, rinsed and used in salads.

OYSTER SAUCE

This is a sauce made from oysters, water, salt, cornflour and caramel. Many of the varieties sold are actually imitation oyster sauce, go for the ones labelled 'oyster sauce' instead of 'oyster-flavored sauce'. Oyster sauce is ideal in stir-fries and as an all-purpose seasoning. It works well with seafood and meat as well as vegetables. The more expensive the sauce, the better the quality.

PICKLED GINGER
This is young ginger preserved in rice-wine vinegar. After several months of marination it takes on a pinkish hue. It can be used as a condiment, seasoning or garnish. Widely used in Japanese and some Chinese cooking.

PRESERVED CUCUMBERS
These are little cucumbers that are first salted and boiled in sugar syrup. They are readily available in jars from Chinatown.

PRESERVED LEMONS
Preserved lemons give a wonderful lift to many dishes. The best time to preserve lemons in Australia is around May and June, when the thin-skinned Lisbon lemons are in season. Recipes vary slightly from book to book and quite often you will see the addition of different spices such as cinnamon and bay leaves. I prefer them plain. You'll need a preserving jar, lemons, sea salt and freshly squeezed lemon juice.

Wash the lemons in cold water, and pat dry with kitchen paper. Cut into quarters, leaving the last centimetre uncut. Place a tablespoon of sea salt in the middle and close the lemon. Fill up the jar with the lemons, pushing down to fit as many as possible. Add more salt and top with lemon juice. Make sure all the lemons are covered, or they'll go mouldy. Seal the jar and put in a cool, dark place for six weeks.

To use, wash the preserved lemon and remove all the pith with a sharp knife. Discard. Dice the peel finely, and add chili powder, paprika and cumin powder to the lemons in a bowl. Add chopped flat-leaf parsley and coriander, olives, lemon juice and extra-virgin olive oil, and you'll have a sensational dressing for grilled fish. Or, cook some chickpeas, make half of them into hummus, and dress the other half with this dressing. Place the hummus in the middle of a plate and push it out to the sides to form a well. Put the chickpea salad in the middle and top with quarters of vine-ripened tomatoes. This can be turned into a sophisticated entrée with the addition of either grilled prawns or sea scallops. Try putting the same dressing on pasta and throwing on some shaved Parmesan.

RICE, ARBORIO
The only rice that can be used to make a good risotto is Arborio rice, the short round-grained rice of Italy.

None can match its absorption powers and creaminess. In the restaurant we use the grade known as superfini, the longest of the grains and readily available from good food stores. Make sure your rice is fresh and that the packet is not broken or the grains crushed, as the rice absorbs aromas easily.

RICE, GLUTINOUS

Glutinous or sticky rice is delicious with spicy fresh salads and things like sausages, kim chee (preserved vegetables) or raw beef. It's usually steamed to give a lighter result. Boiled sticky rice is heavier, and more pudding or cake-like. Both methods are delicious. Soak the rice overnight in water, line a steamer with muslin and steam for 20 minutes.

RICE, JASMINE

I serve rice with all my Asian dishes, usually Thai jasmine rice, which is a long-grain rice. Wash the rice well to remove any dust and dirt and put in a pot with a tight-fitting lid. Place your index finger on the surface of the rice perpendicularly and cover with water to the first finger joint. Bring to the boil and lower the heat. Simmer for 18 minutes, remove from the heat and allow to stand for 2 minutes. If you're keeping the rice cover with a damp cloth to stop the top from drying out. Please don't ever salt rice for Asian food, it is a staple and supports the dishes at the table, and therefore needs to be pure of taste. Around 80 g to 90 g of rice is enough for one person.

RICE-WINE VINEGAR

The one we use most at Rockpool is Japanese vinegar, which is much softer and less acidic than normal wine vinegars from Europe. Chinese black rice vinegar or 'Chin Kiang' vinegar is not made from rice but sorghum and millet, and sometimes, wheat. They have a very rich, complex flavor somewhat reminiscent of balsamic vinegar but not as sweet, with a more bitter finish. This vinegar works well in some Western dishes. It's available from Asian supermarkets.

SESAME OIL

Sesame oil is one of the great Chinese flavors. Nutty and fragrant, it gives a lift to any dish when a few drops are, added at the end of cooking. It can also be successfully used to make dressings.

SESAME-SEED PASTE

This Chinese paste is made from roasted sesame seeds and is therefore a lot richer and darker than the Middle-eastern tahini. It's used in marinades and has a pleasing affinity with chicken and spinach. Sold in jars at Chinese food stores.

SHRIMP, DRIED

These tiny red dried shrimp of Asia should always be a nice pink to red color. Don't buy them as they go brownish or if they are hard — these would have lost their flavor and have obviously been on the shelf for too long. Dried shrimp are good in stir-fries and are also used in chili and sambal pastes. Refrigerate after opening.

SHRIMP PASTE, DRIED

Dried shrimp paste from Malaysia, or belacan, is generally used for laksa pastes and other Indonesian and Malaysian dishes. The dark brown blocks are usually sliced, grilled and crumbled before being added to dishes. They are also used extensively in Nyonya cooking. Store in the refrigerator in a tightly sealed container after opening. Fermented shrimp paste from Thailand is much softer and more fragrant, and adds a pungent flavor to many of the curries and soups of Thailand. The fermented and dried pastes cannot be substituted for each other as they are totally different flavors.

SHAOHSING WINE (CHINESE RICE WINE)

This is fermented water and glutinous rice. It has a lovely dark straw color and very unique flavor. Dry sherry is a popular and reasonable substitute. Never use other rice wines such as sake as they are not similar at all. Shaohsing is used quite extensively in stir-fries, braised dishes such as red-braised pork hocks, and used often in 'drunken' dishes. It's available from Asian supermarkets.

SOY SAUCE

Soy sauce is the fermented juice of the soybean and a staple of Chinese and Japanese cooking. Light soy is used in most cooking and is saltier than dark soy. It's always labelled 'Superior Soy'. Dark soy sauce is labelled 'Soy Superior Sauce', and is much stronger and maltier, with a thicker pouring consistency. It is suitable for braising. Both are readily available from Chinese food shops and supermarkets.

STAR ANISE

This is the eight-pointed pod of a tree related to the cassia. It has a robust aniseed flavor but isn't related to the aniseed family at all. In Chinese cooking it's quite often used with cinnamon and is one of the components of five-spice powder and a must for braised dishes. Check the aroma before buying; as it gets older it loses its aroma and takes on an almost rancid flavor. Store in a tightly sealed jar.

SICHUAN PEPPERCORNS

These are not peppercorns at all but little berries from a Chinese shrub. They are reddish brown in color, with a strong, pungent odour that gives your mouth a wonderful numbing sensation that's quite warming. Buy them whole from Chinese stores and grind as you need them. To make Sichuan salt and pepper, combine three parts sea salt and two parts peppercorns and roast in a heavy-based frying pan over medium heat until the mixture starts to brown. When cool, grind to a powder and seal tightly in a jar until ready to use. This gives roasted foods an incredible lift. It can also be sprinkled on crisp wok-fried dishes.

SUGAR, PALM

A staple of South-east Asia, with a wonderful dark, deep flavor that is reminiscent of golden syrup. There is no substitute for palm sugar when preparing Thai curries. It also makes a wonderful caramel and works very well in desserts.

SUGAR, YELLOW ROCK

This is a crystalized mixture of sugar and honey, and is essential for red-braised dishes. It also imparts a deep mellow flavor to other dishes. Crush the larger crystals in a mortar and pestle before using.

FROM EAST TO WEST THE HARMONY OF THE TWO

To understand what makes Rockpool cooking is to first understand the two worlds of food thought that have made it, and to accept that it is a child of multicultural heritage. For that very reason I have broken this section of the book into two main sections: Eastern and Western. The divisions are more to do with cooking techniques specific to both the East and West; the ideas for the dishes could have been born from either. Each of the recipes uses a basic technique that can then be used in different ways when cooking Asian or New World multicultural food. I have also included a few of my favorite foods (and stories) that belong together. At the end of trying out these basic recipes I hope you will have the confidence to cook from experience.

My style of cooking could not have eventuated without the blend of cultures that have influenced me. Asian cooking even determines the way we make the house salad at the Rockpool. Cooking is no different to travel, as you go down the road you learn from your experiences, both good and bad, and at the end you can choose to use those experiences to become a better person and cook. I hope your journey through these recipes and thoughts will have some influence on your future considerations towards food.

My main Eastern influences have been Chinese and Thai, and more recently, a little Vietnamese. These three countries approach food in different ways, but with the same underlying philosophy. In this chapter I'll explain how I see their approach to food, and the basic techniques used. Of course this is by no means a definitive study of Chinese, Thai or Vietnamese culture and cuisine; they are by themselves worth many books. Rather, the recipes collected here display how these influences have worked their way into Rockpool food.

With most Asian cultures food not only fuels the body but the soul as well, and it is always linked and interwoven with their philosophy on life, love and medicine. To that end each ingredient has its own properties, and a relationship to another ingredient. In Chinese this is known as yin and yang, not two opposites, but two interrelated parts of a whole. To live together in harmony, one cannot be without the other. This approach can be seen right through Asian cooking. This section of the book may also introduce you to some ingredients that the Chinese believe not only work well together but belong together. Most of them are explained in the Produce section.

My influences from the West include France and Italy, two countries that inspired much of my early cooking style. When I read Elizabeth David's wonderful *French Country Cooking* and *French Provincial Cooking* it was impossible not to fall in love with the simple French approach to food, which marries beautiful sauces and meat with simple vegetables, braises, confits, terrines, soups and delicious pastries. You get a real feel for the food and culture of France from her books, and I'll recommend them not only to cooks, but to anyone who enjoys travelling and culture.

The more I read into French food, the more excited I was about the offerings from three-star chefs the likes of Michel Guerard and Paul Bocuse. Each book was a step into an enchanting new world of cooking. Even after many trips I still look forward to my visits to France. I've fallen madly in love with Paris in particular, and it's probably the only place apart from Sydney that I could happily live in.

My other major influence is Italy, with its charming food, from simple first plates (antipasto) to pastas, risottos and polenta to simply cooked meats beautifully paired with vegetables. The wonderful richness of Italian-style tomato sauces and braised vegetables, served with roasted or pot-roasted meats is hard to top

EASTERN COOKING

This section of the book is a very brief outline of the techniques used and recipes inspired by Chinese, Thai or Vietnamese cuisine.

Underpinning all Chinese cooking is the yin–yang theory, which is related to Chinese beliefs about health and food. Remembering which is yin and yang may sound like a nightmare, but it's actually quite simple. Yin are the cooling foods, yang the heating foods, and the idea is to achieve harmony and balance between the two within a meal. If you follow Chinese recipes from start to finish it will all start to unfold. Suddenly you'll see the color, taste and texture of Chinese food and, without realising it, you'll be stir-frying broccoli, ginger and garlic, adding soy sauce, sesame oil, stock and a dash of sugar, creating simple and delicious delights.

Many Chinese dishes require more than one cooking procedure. Each cooking method adds another taste or texture to the dish; it is not unusual for two, three or even five different cooking stages to come together for one dish.

Here are the main methods of Chinese cooking: steaming, roasting, poaching and frying. Once you're proficient in each technique, Asian flavors will be at your fingertips.

STEAMING

Steaming is one of the most delicate cooking methods to be used in either Eastern or Western cooking. The true flavor of the ingredient is kept intact, and the texture of the cooked food is soft and delicate if properly done. The Eastern method of steaming in a broth or with other liquids in a bowl inside the steamer is a particularly ingenious way of cooking fish especially the leaner varieties. It's also a convenient way of heating up simple meals or garnishes for a more elaborate dinner.

The best way to set up a Chinese steamer is to first measure a large pot at home, then leg it down to your local Chinatown to buy a bamboo steamer and lid that fit the rim of your pot. If you have a gas stove at home you may even opt for a wok as a steaming base. Stainless steel and aluminum steamers are also available. If you can't get hold of any of these implements, an upturned bowl with another, bowl placed the right way up in a large pot with boiling water all around will suffice. Once you put the lid on you have a modified steamer.

Steaming is a great way to cook whole birds and fish, and textures can be changed by pouring hot oil over the steamed food or by stir-frying. The juices that are release during cooking will usually make a terrific sauce. Steaming is also ideal for cooking crabs, crayfish and lobsters as there is no way the poaching liquid will get into the meat, as it is prone to when you cook them in a court-bouillon.

When steaming don't let the boiling water come over the food, this ruins the texture. Always have enough water in the steaming base for the duration of the steaming time or you'll end up with a burnt steamer pot. Make sure the water is boiling before the food goes in, this helps seal the food and cook it more quickly.

WHOLE STEAMED FISH WITH GINGER AND SPRING ONIONS

SERVES SIX AS PART OF A SHARED MEAL

This really is an ingenious way to steam fish. Cooking in a bowl in stock allows the juices released during steaming to add the finished sauce. To finish, hot oil is poured over to crisp the skin and bring another level of fragrance to the dish. This dish is designed like all other Asian dishes in this section the book — to be shared — so if the number of diners grows, so should the selection of dishes. If you have over eight diners you would probably need to double the recipe to allow each guest a proper taste. Most reef fish work well. The fish should be gutted, scaled and the head left on; the Chinese consider it the best part. You'll need to find a bowl big enough to fit the fish and its cooking broth, and a steamer large enough to fit the fish. My advice is to head straight for Chinatown.

INGREDIENTS
- 1 x 1 kg (2.2lb) whole fish, such as snapper, dory and seabass
- 1 leaf Chinese cabbage, left whole
- 4 spring onions (scallions), left whole
- ½ teaspoon sea salt
- 100 ml (3.5fl oz) Chicken Stock (page 122)
- 60 ml (2fl oz) light soy sauce
- 30 ml (1fl oz) sesame oil
- 30 ml (1fl oz) shaohsing wine
- 30 g (1oz) castor sugar
- 1 large knob ginger, peeled and cut into very fine julienne
- 4 spring onions (scallions), finely shredded with some green left on
- 80 ml (3fl oz) peanut oil
- a good handful of coriander (cilantro)

METHOD
Pat the fish dry with a tea-towel and place on a chopping board. Make three slits into the fish from head to tail at an angle, and repeat, in the same angle, in the opposite direction to create a diamond pattern. Repeat on the other side of the fish; this helps the fish cook more evenly.

Place the cabbage leaf and whole spring onions on the bottom of the steaming bowl. Rub the fish with the salt and put it over the vegetables.

Mix together the stock, soy sauce, sesame oil, shaohsing wine and castor sugar. Pour this mixture over the fish and top with the ginger julienne.

Place the bowl in the steamer over rapid boiling water, and steam for between 10 and 15 minutes. (The time will vary depending on the amount of circulation the steam can achieve.) The fish should be just setting on the bone. Be careful not to overcook, as it will be covered in hot oil.

Once you have removed the bowl from the steamer place the sliced spring onions on top. Heat up the peanut oil in a small pot until it is smoking and douse the oil over the fish. Top with the coriander and serve. The fish can be served in the bowl it has been cooked in, or replated just before the oil is poured on.

...MED PACIFIC OYSTERS
...H MIRIN AND SOY SAUCE

...OUR TO SIX AS PART OF A SHARED ENTREE

...n this dish should be shared between a
...e, but I can understand the desire to eat
...f these beautiful oysters as possible. The
...be easily increased, just buy more oysters
...se the dressing proportionately. This dish
...ade with large Pacific oysters. Be careful
...rcook them, they are at their best when
...The sauce is also delicious on fried food
...ed fish.

...NTS

...je unopened Pacific oysters
...l (5fl oz) mirin (sweet sake)
...2fl oz) rice-wine vinegar
...2fl oz) light soy sauce
...o ginger, finely diced
...g onions (scallions), finely diced
...g onions (scallions), sliced, with some
...eft on (garnish)

METHOD

Shuck the oysters and reserve the juices.

In a small bowl, mix the reserved juices,
wine vinegar and soy sauce with the di
and spring onions. Stir well to incorporate
slightly in a small pot. Set aside.

Place the oysters in a steamer basket ar
minutes to heat through. Arrange on a
plate and pour over the sauce. Sprinkl
spring onions and serve.

STEAMED WHOLE MUDCRAB WITH BLACK BEAN AND CHILI

SERVES ONE OR FOUR AS A SHARED MEAL

Mudcrabs are something I always think of as being uniquely Australian. They are not, of course, but having eaten them all over Asia I believe Australian mudcrabs have the finest flesh. Never buy a dead crab, there is nothing more disappointing than mushy crabmeat when you're expecting sweet, crunchy flesh.

I first made this sauce at the Bluewater Grill in Bondi, in an attempt to avoid using cornflour as a thickener. I can't for the life of me understand why the texture of thickened sauces is so appealing to the Chinese, when reduction or the addition of other thick flavoring components does the job better. The texture of this sauce is more like a dressing, and the thickening is done by adding hot bean paste, which gives a richness and heat to the sauce.

This dish serves one devoted crab eater or can be shared among four with other dishes. The sauce will give enough for six serves, so if you wish you can buy more crabs and put on a feast.

INGREDIENTS
- 1 x 1–1.5 kg (2–2.5lb) live mudcrab
- leaves from 1 bunch coriander (cilantro)
- 4 spring onions (scallions), shredded

Black Bean And Chili Sauce
- 60 ml (2fl oz) peanut oil
- 1 large knob ginger, peeled and cut into fine julienne
- 1 Spanish onion, peeled and cut into small cubes
- 150 g (5oz) salted black beans, lightly crushed, unwashed
- 1 red capsicum (pepper), seeded and cut into small cubes
- 4 tablespoons hot bean paste
- 500 ml (1 pint) sake
- 250 ml (8fl oz) mirin
- 125 ml (4fl oz) rice-wine vinegar
- 30 ml sesame oil

METHOD
To make the Black Bean and Chili Sauce, heat up the peanut oil in a wok over high heat. When the oil is smoking, add the ginger and onion, and stir-fry for a few minutes. Add the black beans, capsicum and bean paste. Stir for 1 minute. Add the sake, mirin, rice-wine vinegar and sesame oil and simmer for 30 minutes until the mixture has reduced by about a third.

Turn the crab upside and push a chopstick through from the vee in the tail and straight out between the eyes to kill it. This is by far the quickest way of rendering it so. Pull off the top shell, discard the brown lungs and wash. Pull off the claws, chop the body in half, and crack the hard shell on the claws with the back of a cleaver.

Place the crab in a bamboo steamer and steam for 8 minutes. The flesh should be white and firm when done. Remove the crab from the steamer and place in a bowl. Pour over the dressing, sprinkle over the coriander and spring onions, and toss to coat the crab. Serve immediately.

ROASTING

There is a Chinese barbecue shop in Sydney called BBQ King that I've called home for many years. I was very young when my father first took me there for plates of roast duck, suckling pig, Empress chicken, soy sauce chicken and barbecued pork, eaten with garlic spinach, Chinese broccoli with oyster sauce, rice and noodles. I still go there regularly and enjoy the same dishes. Washed down with a nice cold beer and in the company of good friends, it is still a heavenly experience. For those of you who don't live in Sydney, bad luck! In my opinion BBQ King is the best roast-food shop the world.

This section of Chinese cooking includes some the most magnificent-tasting meats you can imagine, and you will not believe how easy it is to produce such things as Peking-style duck in an oven at home.

Roasting in the Chinese style involves circulation of dry heat around an oven that looks more like a kiln, with a fire that used to be mostly fuelled by coal in past. More and more households, however, are turning to gas. The food is hung vertically in the oven, and the effect can be recreated, though not as well, in a domestic oven. It can be confusing when meats that come out of this oven called roasted or barbecued, when birds like pigeons, which are poached in stock and fried till crisp, are also `roasted'. I suspect this is really a translation problem brought about by the fact that very few homes in China would have an oven, and these meats and poultry are almost always bought from the local barbecue shop.

Dry heat is also used for tea-smoking, a wonderful style of cooking that is a Chinese favorite. It involves burning tea, rice and sugar to impart a seductive, smoky aroma and gives a wonderful mahogany lustre to the food. This method is used often at both Rockpool, and it won't take you long to get into the swing of things at home. Just make sure the exhaust fan is switched o kept on during the duration of the smoking until all the smoke is gone. Don't give up the first time the house smells like the fire brigade should be called

Salad of roast duck, sea scallops and Sichuan pickled cucumbers

SALAD OF ROAST DUCK, SEA SCALLOPS AND SICHUAN PICKLED CUCUMBERS

SERVES SIX

This is one of the Rockpool signature dishes, and my favorite entrée when I dine at the restaurant. It is pure Asian in its preparation, very Western in its presentation, and has sumptuous taste with an elegance that makes it a very complete dish. The marriage of crispy duck and silky scallop is one made in heaven; the other ingredients are in supporting roles to lend texture to the dish. If you're buying the duck from a shop, ask them to pack up the juices for you as well.

The recipe for Sichuan Pickled Cucumbers is inspired by Bruce Cost's book on ginger. They are spicy, hot, crunch, and silky all at the same time, and are particularly good with all manner of cold cuts, not just Asian-inspired ones. Thy recipe provided yields 6 to 8 cups, so keep any leftovers for up to 2 weeks in the refrigerator. This is a classic example of each mouthful of food preparing the tastebuds for the next. To me there's nothing more boring than a dish that offers the same flavors and textures spoonful after spoonful — on might as well stop after the third and save the waistline!

INGREDIENTS
- peanut oil
- 18 large sea scallops
- about 250ml (8fl oz) juices from the cavity of the duck
- 3 tablespoons hoisin sauce
- 20 rocket leaves
- 6 wing beans, blanched and sliced
- 1 Roast Duck (page 50) or store-bought, reserve the juices
- 500g (1lb) Sichuan Pickled Cucumbers

Sichuan Pickled Cucumbers
- 8 continental cucumbers
- 60 g (2oz) sea salt
- 250 ml (8fl oz) peanut oil
- 10 small dried chilies
- 2 large knobs ginger, cut into fine julienne
- 8 long red chilies, seeded and cut into fine julienne
- 20 dried black shiitake mushrooms, soaked, rinsed well and sliced
- 150 ml (5fl oz) rice-wine vinegar
- 125 g (4oz) yellow rock sugar
- 1 tablespoon Sichuan peppercorns, roasted and ground

METHOD

To make the Sichuan Pickled Cucumbers, cut the ends off the cucumbers and halve Scrape out the seeds and cut each half into 4 cm (2in) blocks, then into batons. Place in a bowl, sprinkle with salt, and leave to stand for an hour. Squeeze the water out of the cucumbers and pat dry with a paper towel. Heat the oil in a wok and add the dried chilies. Once they blacken, remove from the heat. Add the ginger, chilies, shiitake mushrooms, vinegar, sugar and ground Sichuan peppercorns, and stir. Add the cucumber. Stir to incorporate, then place in a sterilized jar.

Heat some oil in a frying pan until smoking and sear the scallops. Do it in two or three lots, it is very important that the scallops seal properly and don't stew. They should have a firm crust but still be rare inside. Rest them in a warm place.

To make the dressing, place the juices from the cavity of the duck and the hoisin sauce in a small saucepan. Stir to mix, and reduce by half. Allow to cool slightly. Put the rocket and wing beans in a bowl, and toss with some of the dressing.

Slice the meat off the duck breast and legs, leaving it in large diamonds of about 2 cm square.

To serve, place the pickled cucumbers on the base of each plate. Place the wing beans and rocket on top of the cucumber. Place 2 pieces of duck on top of the mound then place three scallops around the outside. Pour the remaining dressing over the scallops, and serve. There should be lots of dressing and it's great mopped up with good sourdough bread.

TEA-SMOKED QUAIL

SERVES TWO

Tea-smoking yields one of my favorite flavors, and it is easy to achieve as long as you use a powerful extractor fan until all the smoke has dissipated. The quail in this recipe is first steamed, then smoked, and finally, wok-fried. Each of the steps changes a part of the taste or texture, adding a completeness to the final dish. I serve this with a simple steamed eggplant dressed in bean paste sauce as a starter at Wockpool. This dish again is designed to be part of a shared table; however, it can be easily converted into an entree for four or six people by simple doubling or trebling the ingredients.

You will need a wok with a lid, and a rack that looks like a small cake rack. These are readily available from Chinatown. Or you can improvise with two baking trays, one turned upside-down on the other.

The Eggplant Salad is delicious with smoked, poached and roasted meats. It is similar to eggplant caviar from the Middle East in texture but is pure Asian in flavor.

The recipe for the Tea-smoking Mixture makes more than needed for one smoking. Store in a screwtop jar.

INGREDIENTS
- 2 large quails
- 1 teaspoon sesame oil
- 60 ml (2 fl oz) peanut oil
- Sichuan salt and pepper

Tea-Smoking Mixture
- 200 g (7 oz) jasmine tea
- 200 g (7 oz) brown sugar
- 200 g (7 oz) long-grain rice

Eggplant Salad
- 2 large eggplants (aubergine), peeled and cut into small cubes
- sea salt
- 1 quantity Bean Paste Sauce (page 55)
- leaves from 1 bunch coriander (cilantro)

METHOD

For the Tea-smoking Mixture, combine the tea, brown sugar and rice, and put in a jar until needed.

To make the Eggplant Salad, salt the eggplant cubes and allow them to stand for 1 hour. Rinse and dry the eggplant with a paper towel. Place in a steamer over boiling water and steam for 30 minutes, or until soft. Allow to cool and squeeze out the moisture. Toss with the dressing and coriander.

Place a steamer over a pot of boiling water on the stove. Put the quails on a plate and steam for 8 minutes. Remove and allow to cool. Rub the quails all over with sesame oil.

Place a wok on the stove. Cut out a small circle of aluminum foil about 20 cm (8in) in diameter. Scrunch the sides until you have a container of about 12 cm in diameter. Put 8 tablespoons of the Tea-smoking Mixture in the container and place it on the bottom of the wok.

Turn up the heat to full and once the tea starts smoking, add the rack and place the quails on top. Cover with the lid and leave the heat on for 5 minutes, then remove the wok from the heat. Don't lift the lid. Allow the wok to cool and the smoke to slowly dissipate.

Lift the lid after about 20 minutes and remove the quails. Heat the peanut oil in a wok and stir-fry the quails on all sides until they are crisp and deep mahogany color.

Debone the quail and serve with Sichuan salt and pepper and the eggplant salad.

ROAST DUCK

SERVES SIX TO EIGHT PEOPLE AS PART OF A SHARED MEAL OR TWO AS A MAIN COURSE

This dish is again a classic example of understanding and experience removing the mystery from the process. At first glance many will think this method of cooking duck is difficult, but once you realise how simple it is, it will arrest fears of other recipes that seem long. In reality most only need little bursts of attention over a period of time. This doesn't mean they are time-consuming and will tie you up for a day; rather, you only need to start the proceedings earlier on and re-fit your schedule to suit. This roast duck will take four hours' cooking from start to finish, but of your actual preparation time, only about 30 minutes.

There are a few steps to creating a good roast duck. Once you understand why all of the steps are necessary, they will seem like a series of small, easy steps instead of one long recipe.

Loosening the skin from the flesh by inflating the duck allows the fat under the skin to melt away and helps crisp the skin. The duck is then scalded with boiling water mixed with maltose, soy sauce and vinegar to tighten and glaze the skin. This results in crispy skin that will turn a dark mahogany color when cooked in the oven.

Air-drying the skin after the scalding is usually done in front of a fan. This step is extremely important and must be carried out. The skin will feel like parchment when it is ready, and will be the final step that ensures crisp skin.

Before the duck goes into the oven fill the cavity with flavored stock, close the duck and slide it into the oven. The liquid steams the duck from the inside as the oven crisps it from the outside. The result is a glamorous, crispy exterior with meat of melting consistency perfumed with star anise.

I serve this duck with stir-fried spinach and either rice or steamed buns.

INGREDIENTS
- 1 x 2 kg (4 lb) Peking duck
- sea salt
- 3 star anise
- 2 sticks cinnamon
- 200 ml (7 fl oz) Chicken Stock (page 122)
- 60 ml (2 fl oz) light soy sauce
- 30 g (1 oz) yellow rock sugar
- 30 ml (1 fl oz) sesame oil
- 1 teaspoon Sichuan salt and pepper

Maltose Mixture
- 5 litres (10.5 pints) water
- 200 ml (7.5 fl oz) maltose
- 150 ml (5 fl oz) light soy sauce
- 100 ml (3.5 fl oz) rice-wine vinegar

METHOD

Remove the fat from the cavity of the duck and place it on a chopping board with the neck facing you. Massage the skin of the duck over the breast and legs for about 5 minutes. This helps to loosen the connecting tissue between the meat and skin. Make a slit in the skin about halfway down the neck. Slide a sharpening steel or dowel into the hole and carefully work it down to the breast and legs of the duck. This is the simplest, but the most dangerous way to loosen the skin for easy inflation, so be careful.

Once the skin is loose, rub the inside of the duck with the salt and place the star anise and cinnamon sticks in the cavity. Put a metal or bamboo skewer through the back cavity to seal it, as if you were sewing cloth together. Tie a piece of string at the top of the neck, this will help you hold the duck over the boiling maltose and hang it up to dry. Place another loop of string down past the cut around the duck neck.

Place a bicycle pump with a football inflator into the cut in the neck and inflate the duck. When it is fully inflated draw the string tight, slip the pump nozzle out and tie a tight knot. You can also do this by blowing through a straw as the skin has been so well loosened by the steel.

To make the Maltose Mixture, bring all the ingredients to a boil in a large pot. Boil the mixture for 5 minutes.

Submerge the duck, breast-side down, into the liquid for 20 seconds, pull it out and continue to baste until the skin has tightened up. Don't expect the glaze to be dark; if it is, it will burn in the oven before the duck is cooked. Remember not to leave the duck in the boiling liquid for too long or the oils will start coming out of the skin, and it will not crisp evenly. Place the duck in front of a fan for 3 hours to dry. The skin should feel like parchment.

Preheat the oven to 200°C (400°F) and put a roasting dish full of boiling water on the bottom of the oven.

Bring the stock, soy sauce, sugar and sesame oil to the boil. Pull the skewer slightly from the duck, just enough to slip a funnel in. Pour in the liquid and push the skewer back to seal the duck. Slide the duck into the oven with its legs to the back. Make sure it sits straight on the rack to allow the heat to circulate well around the duck. Close the oven door and cook for between 45 and 60 minutes.

When cooked, remove from the oven, and allow to rest for 10 minutes. Pull out the skewer and drain the duck. Chop up Chinese style, pour over the juices, and serve.

POACHING

Poaching or cooking in liquid is one of the great arts of Chinese cooking. There are many different poaching styles, and once you've mastered them you will not believe the different textures and flavors you can tempt out of poultry, meat and fish. Many of the poaching liquids can be kept and reused, or reduced to make a luxurious sauce. The four main techniques used in this book are master-stocking, red-braising, white-cut and salt-watering. Each method produces different textures and tastes, in some cases from almost the same ingredients.

The recipes that follow for Master Stock Chicken and Saltwater Pork will provide you with a really good grounding in this art. The simplest things are usually the best, but remember they are also the easiest to stuff up!

Master stock is a sauce in which the ingredient is first cooked and allowed to cool in. This allows the flavor to start permeating the skin, but not to reach deep into the flesh; the result is a silky texture and meat with just a hint of flavor. Chicken is usually used but pork and gizzards are often used by the Chinese. In China some master stocks are generations old by virtue of the fact that the old base is boiled and added to the next use. We do the same at the restaurant. I wonder if someday my daughter Josephine will inherit the Master Stock and pass it on to her children? I pity the poor apprentice who kicks over the stock in the coolroom and has to hose history down the drain.

MASTER STOCK CHICKEN

SERVES EIGHT AS PART OF A SHARED MEAL

Master Stock Chicken is to me the Chinese equivalent of a beautifully roasted chicken with garlic. I find the best thing to do with the chicken the next day is to fry it.

INGREDIENTS
- 1 x 1.6 kg corn-fed chicken, left whole
- 1.5 litres water
- 250 ml (8 fl oz) light soy sauce
- 250 ml (8 fl oz) shaohsing wine
- 150 g (3.5 oz) yellow rock sugar
- 1 large knob ginger, peeled and sliced
- 3 cloves garlic, sliced
- 4 star anise
- 2 sticks cinnamon
- 3 pieces dried mandarin peel

Three Dipping Sauces
- Ginger and Shallot Oil (page 57)
- Black Vinegar and Ginger Sauce (page 57)
- Bean Paste Sauce (page 57)

METHOD
Remove all visible fat from the chicken and wipe down the cavity with paper towels.

Bring all the ingredients except the chicken and dipping sauces to the boil in a pot just big enough to fit the chicken. Turn down and simmer for 20 minutes. Submerge the chicken in the stock, breast-side down, and bring back to the boil. Lower the heat to a strong simmer for 20 minutes.

Turn the chicken and allow to simmer for another 3 minutes. Put a lid on and remove the pot from the heat. Allow the chicken to cool in the stock.

Once the stock has cooled, remove the chicken. The master stock should then be strained, brought up to the boil, cooled and refrigerated. It can then be added to the next time it is needed. As the stock gets older will grow in strength and its flavor will intensify. Add water if necessary to dilute the stock

The chicken is now ready for use in a salad or chopped up Chinese-style and reformed on a plate. It is delicious served with coriander and any of the three dipping sauces. You will find this chicken silky and delicious and I'm sure it will change your mind on boiled chook from now on.

To make a simple Chinese roast chicken, heat 4 cup of peanut oil in a wok and fry the chicken on all sides until golden brown and the flesh is heated through. Serve with Sichuan salt and pepper and lemon juice.

THREE DIPPING SAUCES

The Ginger and Shallot Oil is very good on boiled and fried dishes, and a great dressing for grilled scallop salad.

You'll find the Black Vinegar and Ginger Sauce easy to make but very effective on boiled meats. The Bean Paste Sauce can be used as a cold dipping sauce or heated up and tossed with steamed vegetables.

INGREDIENTS
Ginger And Shallot Oil
- 50 ml (2 fl oz) peanut oil
- 6 dried chilies
- 3 spring onions (scallions), white part, with small of green left on, finely sliced
- 1 large knob ginger, finely diced
- 2 cloves garlic
- 1 teaspoon shaohsing wine
- 1 teaspoon rice-wine vinegar
- 2 tablespoons sea salt
- 2 tablespoons castor sugar

Black Vinegar And Ginger Sauce
- 100 ml (3 fl oz) Chinese black rice vinegar
- 2 large knobs ginger, finely diced

Bean Paste Sauce
- 30 ml (1 fl oz) peanut oil
- 4 spring onions, sliced into rounds
- 2 large knobs ginger, finely diced
- 3 cloves garlic, finely diced
- 2 red chilies, sliced
- 60 ml (2 fl oz) bean paste
- 60 ml (2 fl oz) shaohsing wine
- 60 ml (2 fl oz) rice-wine vinegar
- 4 tablespoons crushed yellow rock sugar

METHOD

Heat the peanut oil in a wok and fry the chilies until they blacken. Discard the chilies and allow the oil to cool. In a mortar and pestle crush all the other ingredients lightly. As the oil cools add to the mortar and mix well. Leave for a little while to allow the flavors to marry.

Mix the diced ginger with the vinegar and allow stand for 1 hour before serving.

In a wok, heat up the peanut oil and fry the spring onions, ginger, garlic and chilies for 3 minutes. Add all the other ingredients and reduce the sauce by half. Remove from the heat and cool.

LOBSTER, SOY CHICKEN AND MANGO SALAD

SERVES SIX

This dish is in this section because it uses not only the Master Stock Chicken, but other Asian ingredients. It is a blend of both Asian and Western techniques and flavors, and has been refined over a period of time. My objective was to end up with a layering of textures and flavors that built up from firm and sweet to soft and creamy. If there was one thing Eastern cooking has taught me, it is the balance and interplay of flavors from strong to subtle.

This recipe also uses extra-virgin olive oil alongside tamarind, soy sauce and palm sugar to achieve a full-flavored dressing that melds all parts of the composite salad together. When cooking Thai and Chinese food it is imperative not to use olive oil as it masks the authentic flavors, but once you understand the balance of these flavors you can start to blend with sympathy, and to create dishes that is in harmony with both their roots. The key to this salad is the same as with any composite salad; all the parts must be of the highest quality. The mangoes should be ripe but not overly sweet and soft. The chicken cannot be compromised, it must be fresh to achieve the right texture. Ensure that all the ingredients are at room temperature. It is ideal if all the preparation is done on the same day, but if that's impossible make sure you take everything out of the fridge well beforehand.

INGREDIENTS

- 2 x 750 g (1.5 lb) live lobsters
- 10 litres (21 pints) boiling water
- a handful of sea salt
- 2 tablespoons water
- 4 heaped tablespoons palm sugar
- 50 ml (2 fl oz) tamarind juice
- 30 ml (1 fl oz) light soy sauce
- 125 ml (4 fl oz) extra-virgin olive oil
- 150 g (3.5 oz) fresh fine egg noodles, cooked
- 30 g (1 oz) fresh black wood fungus
- 30 g (1 oz) fresh white wood fungus

- 30 g (1 oz) enoki mushrooms
- 1 to 2 ripe mangoes, for 6 nice slices
- 6 slices breast meat from Master Stock Chicken
- (page 54), skin removed
- freshly ground white pepper

Pickled Cucumber

- 1 continental cucumber
- sea salt
- 60 ml (2 fl oz) rice-wine vinegar
- 30 ml (1 fl oz) castor sugar

METHOD

To make the Pickled Cucumber, slice the cucumber lengthwise on a mandolin or slice very thinly. Add the sea salt and allow to stand for 30 minutes. Wash the cucumber in water and dry with a paper towel. In a small bowl, mix the vinegar and sugar together and add to the cucumber. Set aside until ready to use.

Drown the lobsters in fresh water, this will take about 30 minutes. Boil the water and sea salt together vigorously in a pot large enough to fit the lobsters. Add the lobsters and cook for 6 minutes. Remove from the pot and allow to cool to room temperature. Do not refresh.

Remove the lobster tails and peel off the shell by cutting down each side and pulling away the shell.

Crack the shells and remove the meat from the legs.

To make the dressing, put the 20 ml (1 fl oz) water and palm sugar together in a small pot and cook until the sugar has caramelized. Add the tamarind juice and soy sauce, and allow to cool to room temperature. Add the olive oil and stir vigorously.

In a large bowl mix the noodles, black and white wood fungus, and enoki mushrooms together. Add half of the dressing and toss to coat.

Divide the salad between 6 large plates. Place a slice of mango on each plate, top with a slice of chicken, lobster and some leg meat. Top with a slice of pickled cucumber, and grind over some pepper. Drizzle over the remaining dressing, and serve.

RED-BRAISING

The term red-braising comes from the process where shaohsing wine, yellow rock sugar and dark soy sauce combine to form a lovely reddish-brown sauce and is one of the most luscious and sumptuous stews of any cuisine. Once tasted, one can only lust for the next encounter. Red-braised Pork Hock is a constant on the Wockpool menu. The cooking time is extended enough so that the aromas of the red-braising ingredients can penetrate and flavor the meat. This technique works best with pork and duck, both of which can withstand long cooking. Fish is also delicious cooked this way.

A reduction of chicken stock and other red-braised ingredients makes a mellow and mysterious sauce.

As with all braising, the more gentle the process, the more tender and integrity of flavor the ingredient will retain. When I say simmer, I mean the barest of simmers, with the liquid only just moving.

RED-BRAISED PORK HOCK
WITH SHIITAKE MUSHROOMS

SERVES SIX TO EIGHT AS A SHARED MEAL

In the early days, this dish was a regular on the menu at the front section of Rockpool. This section of the dining room had been there since the very beginning of Rockpool, and I have always intended it to be cheaper and simpler than the main dining room. It didn't take long before the room took on its own identity, and after the first couple of years, it turned completely Asian. This was where we did our authentic Asian cooking, where technique was followed to the letter, and the real flavors of Asian cooking were understood. In reality it was the breeding ground for many of the dishes that would marry both Eastern and Western food together, so I guess you could say it was integral to what Rockpool is now and what it will be in the future. By 1994 I knew we could not become the restaurant we could be while we were doing two menus out of the same kitchen. On any given day we would cook as many as 60 different dishes for 250 people. It was impossible to spend the time required on each dish. Trish and I finally decided that the most important thing was Rockpool, so we closed the front section and made plans for a bar sometime in 1995. An easy decision for me, a brave one for Trish as it contributed 20 per cent of our weekly income. The outcome is, Rockpool is now a better restaurant, and we have the opportunity to make it even better. The front section is now Wockpool, a separate restaurant in Darlinghurst. It's the completely Asian side of Rockpool, and we now have the opportunity to make it as good a restaurant as it can be.

However much you love pork hocks, don't sit down to a whole one by yourself, they are far too rich. Big bowls of steamed jasmine rice and steamed bok choy are great accompaniments to this dish.

INGREDIENTS
- 2 pork hocks
- 6 litres (12 pints) water
- 250 ml (8 fl oz) shaohsing wine
- 1 large knob ginger, finely sliced
- 6 cloves garlic, finely sliced
- 6 spring onions
- 100 ml (3 fl oz) light soy sauce
- 40 ml (1 fl oz) dark soy sauce
- 200 g (7 oz) yellow rock sugar
- 4 star anise
- 3 sticks cinnamon
- 3 pieces dried mandarin peel
- 24 dried shiitake mushrooms, soaked, rinsed and stems removed
- peanut oil for frying
- 60 ml (2 fl oz) sesame oil

cold stock. Place it back on the stove and l
boil. Add the shiitake mushrooms.

e pork hocks, place the hock on a chopping
the side where the skin is closest to the
g up. With a sharp boning knife cut into
l the way to the bone and along the hock.
knife right around the bone until the meat
ome off; you will have a rectangle of meat.
uld ask your butcher to do it and save the
you.

Unwrap the hocks carefully. Place a wok o
with enough peanut oil in it to cover the ho
frying. Fry the hocks for about 10 minutes u
brown, then place them in the simmering s
gives the skin unbelievable texture, and is
the effort.

ectangles of muslin twice the size of the
place them on the bench. Place the pork
he middle of the muslin, skin side down. Roll
rk hocks to form a sausage, then roll them
huslin. Tie in four places with kitchen string.
cks and bones in a pot (ensure a snug fit).
e water over the top and bring to the boil.
r 30 minutes and skim the surface regularly
of the scum.

Simmer the hocks for a further 25 mi
remove. Reduce the stock to 500 ml (1 pin
the sesame oil. Place the whole hocks in a
bowl and pour the sauce over or slice th
serving. In any case you should be able t
with a spoon.

inutes add the shaohsing wine, ginger and
simmer for a further 30 minutes. Add the
ons, both soy sauces, yellow rock sugar,
cinnamon sticks and mandarin peel, and
o simmer for a further 1½ to 2 hours, or until
are tender.

When cooking Eastern dishes remembe
are usually designed to be part of a sh
The number of people who serve Eastern
a Western sense never ceases to amaze
like screaming when I get a dish that obvic
to be shared, or at the very least needs to
with rice, only to be told that the chef do
rice. I then start to seriously worry about th
in, and already I've formed an opinion abo
Bear in mind that when making authentic
you'll have to adjust the flavors, or add a
side dishes to balance and round off the m

he pork hocks and bones from the stock.
e the hocks and stock overnight. Discard
. The next day skim off all the fat from the

Y SMOKED OCEAN TROUT
TH SPRING ONION CAKE

S SIX AS A MAIN COURSE

d ocean trout has been a regular on the menu and is one of Rockpool's signature dishes. Th together three of my favorite elements of Chinese cuisine: the rich smoky flavor from tea-smo ous, salty, sweet and spicy sauce inspired by the red-braising broth, which would have to be m aste; and a crisp-fried spring onion cake to soak up the juices. Ocean trout works well in this oily enough to take being cooked twice. The flesh retains its integrity and the richness of the s the steamed bok choy and crisp spring onion cake. After the first smoking the trout is usually it a firm crust and a melting medium-rare centre. It can be easily roasted in an oven for the or, better still, barbecued.

DIENTS

1.6 kg to 1.8 kg (2.5–3 lb) ocean trout, whole
same oil
ablespoons Tea-smoking Mixture (page

lices prosciutto
aby bok choy, blanched in boiling water
2 minutes and refreshed

uce

ml (8.5 fl oz) shaohsing wine
arge knob ginger, sliced
loves garlic, sliced
tres (6 pints) Chicken Stock (page 122)
tar anise
arge piece cassia bark, broken in half

- 6 spring onions (scallions), with 2 cm o green left on
- 100 ml (3 fl oz) light soy sauce
- 24 dried black shiitake mushrooms, so and stems removed
- 150 g (5 oz) yellow rock sugar

Spring Onion Cakes

- 2 tablespoons spring onions, green top
- ½ teaspoon peanut oil
- 180 g (6 oz) plain flour
- 100 ml (3 fl oz) boiling water
- ½ beaten egg
- plain flour for rolling
- peanut oil for rolling
- sea salt

OD

fish on a chopping board. Hold the head
and slip a sharp thin-bladed knife into the
ust under the head. Take the knife to the

To remove the skin, place the fillet skin-side on the board. Remove the side bones, and your knife between the skin and the flesh. the knife and, with a sawing motion, pull t

Place one fillet on a board, skinned side down, and top with the other fillet, with its head to the other fillet's tail, skinned side facing you. Roll the top fillet under the bottom fillet a little so that they form a cylinder when tied up. Place the prosciutto lengthwise down the two sides of the fish, this not only adds a nice flavor to the overall dish, but stops the string from cutting into the flesh. Starting from one end tie the fish with butcher's string every 2 cm (1in) You should now have a cylinder of fish. Cut the fish in half and the halves into 3 pieces to give you 6 portions.

To smoke the fish, rub each portion with sesame oil and put on a rack that will fit in a wok with a lid. Cut out a small circle of aluminum foil about 20 cm in diameter. Scrunch the sides until you have a container about 12 cm in diameter. Put the Tea-smoking Mixture in the container and place it on the bottom of the wok Turn up the heat to full and once the tea starts smoking, add the rack and place the fish on top. Cover with the lid and leave the heat on for 5 minutes. Remove the wok from the heat and don't lift the lid. Allow the wok to cool and the smoke to slowly dissipate.

To make the sauce, combine the shaohsing wine with the ginger and garlic in a small saucepan, and reduce by a third. Add the chicken stock and reduce the volume by half. Add the star anise, cassia bark, spring onions, soy sauce, shiitake mushrooms, and yellow rock sugar, and reduce by half. Keep warm.

crust needs to form on the outside of the fish, and the centre has to be warm, but don't overcook. Remove the string from the trout and grill on one side for 3 minutes. Turn and grill the other side for 2 minutes. Rest in a warm place.

To make the Spring Onion Cakes, stir-fry the spring onions in peanut oil for about 15 seconds. In a small bowl add the boiling water to the flour and stir to combine. Add the egg and mix until smooth. Rest for 20 minutes. Take the dough and knead on a floured bench for 10 minutes until smooth and elastic. Roll the dough into a long strip and cut into 6 pieces. With a rolling pin roll out each piece of dough to a 10 cm (5in) circle. Brush lightly with peanut oil, sprinkle with salt and divide the spring onions between the 6 circles. Fold in 2 sides of the circle so they overlap slightly. Roll each piece into a pipe and flatten slightly. Roll each one into a snail and flatten again. Heat the peanut oil in a heavy-based frying pan and shallow-fry the cakes, a couple at a time, until golden brown. Turn and cook the other side. Drain on kitchen paper.

Put the bok choy in the sauce to warm through.

In a large white bowl place a serve of trout, next to it a piece of bok choy, and spoon some sauce over the top. Place a spring onion cake between the fish and bok choy and serve immediately. There should be quite a bit of sauce.

WHITE CUT

White-cut is a cooking process that works especially well with chicken and pork. This method of cooking gives the meat a firm texture and renders the skin firm but silky. The meat is immersed in a stock and allowed to steep, then cooled in the poaching liquid. It is then plunged into ice-water, which traps the juices and fats under the skin. The result is the most sumptuous cold-cut chicken you can imagine. Chicken prepared in this way is perfect when combined with jellyfish for a salad.

WHITE-CUT CHICKEN

SERVES SIX TO EIGHT AS A SHARED MEAL

I remember my first run-in with white-cut chicken years ago at BBQ King with my father. They would chop it and serve it with a sauce of ginger, spring onions and a little chili, all floating in a pool of stock, soy sauce and sesame oil. Even more heavenly is Empress Chicken, which sits cloaked in a green sauce, the chicken itself virginal white. BBQ King still serve the dish like that, and I suspect it will still be on the menu when my daughter Josephine takes her children there. This is a measure of a terrific restaurant, whether grand or simple — their specialties are kept on, and refined, over many, many years.

The first thing that struck me about this dish was the firmness of the flesh. There was no resistance, it was in fact meltingly soft, and yet the skin was firm and silky, almost slippery. The leg bone still had visible signs of blood, but the meat was cooked through. How could it be raw and tender at the same time? In fact the chicken wasn't just cooked, it was cooked to perfection. Both Master Stock Chicken (page 56) and this are effectively boiled chickens, but the cooking method produces totally different tastes and textures.

INGREDIENTS
- 1 x 1.6 kg to 1.8 kg (2.5–3 lb) corn-fed chicken
- 3 litres (6 pints) water
- lots of ice

METHOD
Rinse the chicken in cold water, remove any fat from the cavity and pat dry with a paper towel.

Bring the water to the boil in a heavy-based pot in which the chicken will fit snugly. Place chicken in the pot and bring back to the boil.

Skim for 5 minutes and turn down to a strong simmer. Place a lid on the pot, and simmer for 15 minutes more. Remove the pot from the heat and steep the chicken for 20 minutes. Don't lift the lid or the heat will dissipate faster.

Remove the lid and take out the chicken. Drain the cavity, and plunge the chicken into ice-water. Leave it there to cool for 15 minutes. Drain the chicken and chill in the refrigerator to completely set the juices.

This chicken can be cut up and served with any of the Three Dipping Sauces (page 57). It is also delicious in salads, not just Asian ones. Try this chicken shredded, tossed in mayonnaise and made into club sandwiches.

CHICKEN AND JELLYFISH SALAD

SERVES SIX AS A SHARED STARTER

Don't let the thought of eating jellyfish turn you off this salad, it has no flavor other than the one given to it by the dressing, but its texture is unsurpassed for crunch and resistance. The most important thing to remember is not to put hot water on the jellyfish or it will toughen up. You'll find the creamy silkiness of the chicken a match for the crunch of the jellyfish.

INGREDIENTS

- 1 medium carrot
- 1 small daikon
- 4 spring onions
- 150 g (5 oz) salted jellyfish
- 1 small knob ginger, crushed with the back of a cleaver
- 1 spring onion (scallion), left whole
- 20 ml shaohsing wine
- 1 breast from a White-cut Chicken (page 71)
- 3 tablespoons sesame seeds, toasted

Sesame Dressing

- 15 ml Chinese sesame-seed paste
- 20 ml light soy sauce
- 15 ml rice-wine vinegar
- 1 tablespoon finely diced ginger
- 2 cloves garlic, crushed
- 15 ml castor sugar
- 60 ml sesame oil

METHOD

To make the Sesame Dressing, in a bowl mix the sesame paste and soy sauce together. Add the vinegar and, while stirring, add the ginger, garlic and sugar. Stir until the sugar dissolves, add the sesame oil, and allow to stand for 30 minutes to let the flavors mingle.

Cut the carrot, daikon and spring onions into fine julienne and soak them in ice-water for half an hour.

Place the jellyfish in a sieve and rinse really well under tap water. Transfer to a bowl with a lid or use a plate as a lid. Add the crushed ginger, spring onion and shaohsing wine. Run the hot-water tap until it is just warm, not much hotter than blood temperature, and pour enough water over the jellyfish to just cover. Leave for 10 minutes. Remove the jellyfish and discard the seasoning.

Shred the chicken breast finely and place in a bowl with the jellyfish, carrot, daikon and spring onions. Add the dressing and toss. Place the salad on a large plate and sprinkle with sesame seeds. Serve immediately.

KOREAN-STYLE TUNA TARTARE

SERVES FOUR AS A STARTER

This dish has nothing to do with White-cut Chicken, but it uses the exact same dressing, so I've followed one with the other. The dish is a take on a Korean salad of raw beef with a sesame-oil dressing, raw egg yolk, Chinese cabbage and a combination of sesame seeds and pinenuts. The beef is almost frozen, and the crisp texture is offset by the silkiness of the egg yolk and the creaminess of the pinenuts. This dish is so good that in the old days Greg Frazer, Barry McDonald and I have been known to start with one and have another for dessert at the end of a meal. I decided to do a tuna dish inspired by this, and since it was raw and used an egg yolk, I called it Korean Tuna Tartare. The times I have taken it off the menu have been met with firm resistance from regular customers.

INGREDIENTS

- 1 medium carrots
- 4 spring onions
- 1 x 400 g (14 oz) piece fresh yellowfin tuna
- 1 small Chinese cabbage heart, finely shredded
- leaves from 1 bunch coriander (cilantro)
- 3 tablespoons roasted pinenuts 2 quantities Sesame Dressing (page 72)
- 4 egg yolks
- 2 tablespoons sesame seeds, toasted freshly ground white pepper

METHOD

Cut the carrot and spring onions into a fine julienne and soak in ice-water for half an hour.

Place the tuna on a chopping board, and remove the skin. Cut it into rounds of 0.5 cm thickness, then cut it lengthwise into strips of about 0.5 cm square.

Place the tuna, carrots, spring onions, cabbage, coriander, pinenuts and dressing in a bowl. Toss to dress and divide between 4 plates. Make a little well in the centre of each and place an egg yolk on top. Sprinkle with sesame seeds and grind over some pepper. Serve immediately.

SALT WATERING

As the name implies, salt-watering is curing in salt and spice for a number of hours, or even days, depending on the size of the cut of meat. The meat is then boiled and pressed when cold. The result is clean flavors and a surprisingly balanced-tasting meat that isn't overwhelmingly salty. The texture is fine and firm. Once you've tasted Saltwater Pork with Relish I'm sure it will be your favorite cold cut. The process also works well with duck, and with pickled summer fruits such as cherries or peaches.

SALTWATER PORK SHOULDER WITH RELISH

SERVES TEN AS A SHARED STARTER

This was a very successful starter at Wockpool, and more often than not is ordered by the Chinese customers. Along with Red-braised Pork Hock, this is one of my favorite pork dishes. In a way this is Chinese cooked ham, and anything you do with ham applies; they work especially well as sandwiches for an Asian-style picnic. The texture of the meat, fat and skin is first changed by boiling, and then softened by pressing with a heavy weight, so both the fat and skin take on a silky texture. Don't think about trying to cut the fat out, it's the most important part of the dish.

This recipe is dead simple and only requires time. Sichuan Pickled Cucumbers are the perfect complement.

INGREDIENTS

- 1 kg (2 lb) boned pork shoulder
- 500 ml water
- 4 teaspoons sea salt
- 250 g (4 oz) Sichuan Pickled Cucumbers (page 49)

Dipping Sauce

- 4 tablespoons Chinese black-rice vinegar
- 2 teaspoons finely minced ginger

METHOD

Cut the meat lengthwise into three strips and rub with salt. Place in the fridge. Turn the meat every 8 hours to marinate in the brine that should be forming in the bottom of the container. Leave for 2 days.

Place a pot on the stove that will fit the pork snugly. Remove all the moisture and any undissolved salt from the pork with a paper towel. Place the pork in the pot, skin-side down, and pour over the 500 ml water and salt. Bring to the boil, and simmer for 1 hour with the lid on turning the meat halfway during cooking. Remove the lid and check that the water has evaporated. If not, boil vigorously with the lid off for a few minutes to remove the water and concentrate the salt.

Remove the meat from the pot and place in a container that is slightly smaller than the cuts of meat. Put a lid on top and a 5 kg (11 lb) weight on the meat. Press for 3 hours at room temperature. Remove the weight and refrigerate overnight.

To make the Dipping Sauce, mix together the vinegar and ginger, and allow to stand for 1 hour.

To serve, turn the container upside-down onto a cutting board and, with a very sharp knife, cut the pork into very thin strips. Place on a plate with some Sichuan Pickled Cucumbers and the dipping sauce.

FRYING

Frying is a technique little used in many European kitchens. In Asia and much of the subcontinent, it is one of the main cooking techniques. When you see the versatility of the wok as a frying implement, it's not hard to understand the Chinese's love of frying.

Woks purchased from Chinatown generally have a heavy coating of grease to stop them from rusting, so wash them very well with detergent. To season the wok, place over heat to evaporate the water and open the pores of the steel. When the wok starts to smoke pour in 2 cups of light oil and, with a cloth, wipe down the sides of the wok. Turn the heat down to very low, and leave for 10 minutes. Remove from the heat. Wipe down the sides of the wok and pour off the oil. Wipe off any excess and put away until ready to use. After each use, rinse and wipe the wok with oil. There should be no need to wash the wok with detergent again.

STIR-FRYING

Stir-frying is probably the most popular of all Chinese cooking methods. Stir-fried food has a crisp texture and taste, and the ingredients used should therefore be lip-smackingly fresh. At Wockpool we have some huge wok stalls and my tip is, be organised when you're stir-frying, or you'll end up burning something. The ingredients for stir-frying are usually cut finely and in some cases partly cooked. Your sauces must be at hand and you must be ready to handle a high heat.

I vividly remember the first time I cooked for service at Wockpool. A noodle bar order came in for Hokkien noodles, and I went to work Greg Frazer was talking to me about a problem while I cooked. I turned up the heat, tipped in the oil, added the garlic and ginger, swirled them around. Then I added the prawns, pork, vegetables, stirred, added the noodles, kept stirring, Greg's talking, I'm listening, not concentrating, things started to scorch, I got the stock in, some sauce ... and the whole thing turned black, the kitchen all smoked out. That wasn't the last time either.

Good Chinese cooks can make a wok sing but there is no reason for you not to get very good results at home. There are some rules. Woks are the best tools, but don't despair if you have electricity, as a pot or sauté pan will work as well. I don't recommend a flat-bottomed wok as the base is not touched by anywhere near as much heat as a pot on an electric stove top, and if there's one thing that's essential to stir-frying it's large quantities of heat. Wok-cooking is white heat so keep thinking hot. Another handy tool to have on hand when stir-frying is a curved wok spoon.

STIR-FRIED SQUID, ASPARAGUS AND MUSHROOMS

SERVES SIX AS A SHARED STARTER OR FOUR AS A MAIN COURSE

The fragrance of the coriander roots and white peppercorns in this dish is mouth-watering.

INGREDIENTS
- 4 cloves garlic
- 4 coriander (cilantro) roots
- 20 white peppercorns
- 1 teaspoon sea salt
- 80 ml (3 fl oz) peanut oil
- 250 g (8 oz) cleaned squid, cut into thin strips
- 8 asparagus spears, each sliced at an angle into sixths
- ½ punnet small fresh shiitake mushrooms, stems trimmed and halved if large
- ½ punnet oyster mushrooms, stems trimmed and halved if large
- ½ punnet enoki mushrooms, stems trimmed
- 12 English spinach leaves, with 5 cm (2 in) of stem attached
- 1 teaspoon castor sugar
- 2 tablespoons light soy sauce
- 100 ml (3.5 fl oz) Chicken Stock (page 122)

METHOD
In a mortar and pestle crush the garlic, coriander roots, white peppercorns and salt together to a fine paste.

Place a wok on the stove over high heat and add half the peanut oil. As soon as it starts to smoke add half the paste and the squid. With a wok spoon keep the ingredients moving and stir-fry for about 1½ to 2 minutes. Transfer the squid to a plate and keep warm.

Wipe out the wok with paper towels and return to the heat. Pour in the remaining oil and allow to smoke again. Add the rest of the paste, asparagus and mushrooms, and stir for 1 minute. Add the spinach and stir for 30 seconds. Add the sugar, soy sauce, and chicken stock, and cook for a further minute.

Return the squid to the pan and toss for 10 seconds. Remove from the heat, place in the middle of a large plate, and serve immediately.

STIR-FRIED HOKKIEN NOODLES WITH ROAST PORK

SERVES SIX AS A SHARED DISH

I loved the way Sydneysiders took to the front noodle bar at Rockpool, and used it as I had imagined — as a place to eat (not dine), and a place where hunger could be easily sated. The food was delicious and cheap, and it was a great feeling for the staff to turn around 70 happy punters out of 20 seats. These noodles are a great meal-in-a-bowl, and were really popular in the noodle bar. They hit the spot, are quick and delicious, and you can get in and out in 15 minutes. That's convenience food.

With this dish make sure the oil is smoking and move quickly, it's not that attractive black. The Hokkien noodles are readily available from Chinatown (of course).

METHOD

Place a wok on the stove over high heat, add the peanut oil and heat until it is smoking. Add the ginger and garlic and fry for 30 seconds. Add the noodles, cabbage, long beans and black beans, and stir for a further 30 seconds. Add the mustard greens, pork and beansprouts, then add the sugar, soy sauce and chicken stock. Cook for a further 30 seconds. Add the oyster sauce and cook for 1 minute.

Pour the noodles into a large bowl and sprinkle over the snowpea sprouts. Serve immediately.

INGREDIENTS

- 60 ml (2 fl oz) peanut oil
- 1 tablespoon chopped ginger
- 1 tablespoon crushed garlic
- 200 g (7 oz) fresh Hokkien noodles
- 3 leaves Chinese cabbage, sliced
- 6 long beans, cut into 7 cm (3 in) lengths
- 2 tablespoons black beans
- 60 g (2 oz) pickled mustard greens, thinly sliced
- 100 g (3 oz) Chinese barbecued pork (char slew),
- thinly sliced
- 30 g (1 oz) beans prouts
- 2 tablespoons palm sugar
- 3 tablespoons light soy sauce
- 80 ml (3 fl oz) Chicken Stock (page 122)
- 4 tablespoons oyster sauce
- 30 g (1 oz) snowpea sprouts

STIR-FRIED SPANNER CRAB OMELETTE

SERVES SIX AS PART OF A SHARED MEAL

This is a Rockpool classic and is usually made in a single serve as an entrée. I have given a recipe for a larger omelette that works well on a shared table. The texture of the crab, egg and beansprouts, and the perfume of the sesame oil make one of the greatest taste and texture treats imaginable. The crispy exterior, melting interior, and the crunchiness of the beansprouts all work so well together. Make sure the oil is very hot and smoking so that the eggs do not soak up the oil. This omelette can be cut into two or three little separate entrées if you like.

This is a classic example of an omelette that even the French would be pleased to eat. I grew up thinking that the French invented omelettes, now I know better. I would be more than happy to have a stir-fried crab omelette with rice for lunch, and a truffled omelette with a green salad and bread for dinner. That's the good thing about living in multicultural Australia — one is not bound by any tradition other than a love of good food.

INGREDIENTS
- 5 x 55 g (2 oz) eggs
- 1 tablespoon palm sugar
- 1 tablespoon fish sauce
- 200 g (7 oz) spanner crab meat
- 100 g (3 oz) beansprouts
- 50 g (1.5 oz) snowpea sprouts
- 15 Chinese yellow chives, washed and halved
- 150 ml (5 fl oz) peanut or vegetable oil
- 4 tablespoons oyster sauce

Broth
- 150 ml (5 fl oz) Chicken Stock (page 122)
- 3 tablespoons palm sugar
- 2 tablespoons fish sauce
- 1 teaspoon sesame oil

METHOD
To make the Broth, combine all the ingredients except the sesame oil in a pot. Bring to the boil, pour in the sesame oil, and keep warm.

Beat the eggs in a medium-sized bowl. In a small container dissolve the palm sugar in the fish sauce. Add to the eggs and whisk well.

Pick through the crabmeat for any cartilage and shell. Add the beansprouts, snowpea sprouts and chives, and mix well.

Place the oil in a wok and heat until it is smoking. Pour in the egg mixture (it should puff up). Cook for 3 minutes, then place the crab mixture in the middle. Cook for a further 3 minutes and remove from the heat.

Pour off the excess oil. Fold the omelette, and place it back in the wok for 1 minute. Turn off the heat and rest it near a heat source for a further 2 minutes.

Remove the omelette from the wok with a fish lifter and place on a board. Trim off the ends and place in a large bowl. Pour over the hot broth and top with oyster sauce.

DEEP-FRYING

Deep-frying is one of the most interesting cooking techniques at your disposal. Deep-fried food has a crisp exterior and moist interior, but unlike Western cooking, a deep-fried ingredient may have neither started in the fryer nor finished in it, but simply passed through to change its texture in some way. Dishes may be braised, steamed, dried, marinated and coated either before or after frying, or even double-fried. We use these methods in the restaurant, and recipes demonstrating these multiple cooking techniques follow.

In the home you will find the wok a very useful deep-fryer; it uses less oil than a pot and is more receptive to heat. I always use peanut oil and strain and re-use it as long as it remains fresh. If the ingredients start to brown and smoke quickly, it's time for an oil change. For wok-frying invest in a couple of large meshed spoons, they are indispensable for removing whole fish and larger pieces of meat and poultry. Chinese pastries and coated meats are quite often shallow-fried in a smaller amount of oil. Keep the temperature reasonably low so the bottom doesn't burn before the food's cooked.

s a combination of Eastern and Western techniques. The flavors are very Japanese, but the j
v Western. Apart from whole steamed fish I find the Chinese tend to overcook fish. Even in Jap
d fish too well done for my liking.

also one of those dishes that looks quite pretty on the plate, as the fillet is cut into rounds tha
ushi. The two fish fillets are stuffed with prawn stuffing, wrapped in a nori sheet, dipped in a

alia sand whiting and King George whiting work very well. In Europe or America I would sugge
flat fish. When wrapping the fish in nori don't wrap too tightly or the fish will split open as the stuf
r when cooking fish that it keeps on cooking on the way to the table, so err on the side of un
take the fish from the oven, grill, steamer or poacher. Most of the preparation for this dish ca
e, apart from the frying.

NTS
0 g (12 oz) whiting, left whole
ets nori
t or vegetable oil
(3 oz) salted ogo nori, rinsed to remove all
lt

ng
(7 oz) prawn meat
espoon chopped ginger
espoons fish sauce
espoons palm sugar
d shiitake mushrooms, soaked and
ed
espoon coriander leaves, chopped
l (3 fl oz) coconut cream

e
l (3 fl oz) mirin
(1 fl oz) rice-wine vinegar
(1 fl oz) light soy sauce
knob ginger, peeled and finely diced

Beer Batter
- 350 ml (12 fl oz) beer
- plain flour
- ice-cubes
- 250 g (8 oz) plain flour for dredging the

Vegetables
- 1 knob ginger, peeled and finely diced
- 2 cloves garlic, crushed
- 60 ml (2 fl oz) peanut oil
- 1 large yam, peeled and cut into 0.5 c
- 2 large carrots, peeled and cut into 0.
- 200 ml (7 fl oz) mirin
- 80 ml (2.5 fl oz) light soy sauce
- 80 ml (2.5 fl oz) rice-wine vinegar
- 100 g (3 oz) fresh black wood fungus, cut into julienne
- 100 g (3 oz) enoki mushrooms, base c about 2 cm (1 in) from the bottom
- 100 g (3 oz) fresh shiitake mushrooms removed and thinly sliced

METHOD

Fillet the fish by holding the head tightly on a board, and with a very sharp thin knife, cut to the back bone up near the head. Turn the knife blade to face the tail, and with one swift movement push straight through to the tail. You should now have one fillet. Turn the fish over and repeat the action. Place the 2 fillets together and repeat with the others. Cut a vee at the front of each fillet to remove the side bones and place each pair of fillets back together.

To make the stuffing purée the prawn meat, ginger, fish sauce and palm sugar in a food processor. Place in a bowl and add the mushrooms and coriander, and, swirling the meat around with your hand in one direction, slowly add the coconut cream and continue to beat until well incorporated. This helps make the mixture mousse-like.

Divide the mousse between the 6 pairs of fillets, turning each top fillet so it meets the tail of the bottom one to form a cylinder. Wet each nori sheet slightly, and roll up each pair of fillets in it. Do not roll too tightly or they will split. Cut the overhangs off each end. Place the rolls on a plate and refrigerate.

To make the sauce, mix all the ingredients together and allow to stand for at least 2 hours.

To make the Beer Batter, add enough plain flour to the beer to make it the consistency of pouring cream. Allow to stand for at least 10 minutes before using.

To prepare the vegetables in a frying pan sauté the ginger and garlic in the peanut oil until soft. Add the yam and carrots, and cook for another 2 minutes. Add the mirin, soy sauce and rice-wine vinegar, and bring to the boil. Cook until the liquid has almost disappeared, add the mushrooms, toss for 1 minute, and set aside.

To serve, preheat an oven to 180°C (350°F). Heat enough oil in a pot that will fit at least two of the fish at a time to 180°C (350°F). Roll the fish in the extra plain flour and then in the beer batter. Place the fish carefully in the hot oil and fry for 5 minutes. Remove to a tray with absorbent paper, and repeat with the remaining fish.

Trim the ends off each roll and cut each into 5 rounds. Place on an oiled baking tray and in the oven for 1 minute, or a little longer if necessary.

Place a mound of vegetables in the middle of the serving plates. Place the fish around the outside, and drizzle the sauce over the fish. Divide the ogo nori between the 6 plates. Serve immediately.

WHOLE FRIED FISH WITH SWEET AND SOUR SAUCE

SERVES SIX AS PART OF A SHARED MEAL

This fish is crispy on the outside and soft and delicious on the inside, and the sauce is delicious on rice. The approach to the sauce is typically Chinese except that I try never to use cornflour as a thickener. I find that reduction or the addition of another ingredient often works better. When ketchup or tomato sauce is called for you'll get a much better result from making your own tomato jam or paste. That little extra effort will produce a sauce of a greater quality. The recipe yields 500 ml, and the extra paste will keep in a sterilized jar the refrigerator for up to 4 weeks.

INGREDIENTS
- 1 x 750 g to 1 kg (1.6–2 lb) ocean perch, snapper, bream or other reef fish
- peanut or vegetable oil
- coriander (cilantro) leaves, to taste
- spring onions, sliced, to taste

Tomato Paste
- 15 vine-ripened tomatoes, cored
- 500 ml (1 pint) peanut oil
- 1 Spanish onion, chopped
- 4 cloves garlic, crushed
- 2 knobs ginger, peeled and cut into julienne

Sauce
- 60 ml (2 fl oz) peanut oil
- 10 spring onions, shredded
- 200 g (7 oz) castor sugar
- 100 ml (3 fl oz) Chinese black rice vinegar
- 100 ml (3 fl oz) tomato paste
- 60 ml (2 fl oz) light soy sauce
- 8 long red chilies, split and seeded
- 50 g (1.8 oz) pickled ginger
- 100 g (3 oz) preserved cucumbers in syrup
- 500 ml (1 pint) Chicken Stock (page 122)

METHOD

Preheat the oven to 180°C (350°F).

To make the Tomato Paste, place the tomatoes in a baking tray and place in the preheated oven until they soften, about 30 minutes. Put the tomatoes through a food mill. In a large heavy-based saucepan over medium heat add half the oil. When hot, add the onion, garlic and ginger and fry until golden brown and fragrant. Add the rest of the oil to the pan, and add the tomato juice. Cook, allowing the mixture to simmer in the oil until it is very thick, about 1½ hours. Pour the paste out of the pan and into a sterilized jar. Seal with a film of oil.

To make the sauce, place a wok over high heat and add the peanut oil. Once it starts to smoke add the spring onions and fry until fragrant. Add the sugar and allow it to caramelize, then add the vinegar and cook for 2 minutes. Add the tomato paste, soy sauce, chilies, ginger, cucumber and stock, and cook for about 5 minutes until the sauce thickens. Set aside and keep warm while you fry the fish. This sauce can be made in advance and warmed up when needed.

Take the fish and put it on a cutting board. Starting just below the head put 4 deep cuts into the fish at a 45-degree angle. Do the same in the opposite direction to form diamonds. Repeat on the other side. This helps the fish cook more evenly, but more importantly it gives the fish more crisp surface area.

In a large wok or pot heat enough oil to submerge the fish to 180°C (350°F). Slide in the fish and fry for about 10 to 12 minutes, until golden brown and very crispy.

Remove the fish with a mesh spoon and drain on kitchen paper. Place on a large plate and pour the hot sauce over the top. Garnish with the coriander and spring onions.

CHILI SALT SQUID

SERVES FOUR AS AN ENTREE

This is a great starter to a Chinese-style meal and makes a great canapé. The texture of the squid and the heat of the chili sit well together. I have had this many times when the squid has been dipped in egg, dredged in spicy flour and stir-fried, and although this is very good, I prefer it tossed in flour and deep-fried, the result is a little crisper. Use the freshest squid you can lay your hands on, and make sure you get the tentacles as well, they are the best part.

INGREDIENTS
- 500 g (1 lb) whole squid
- 100 g (3 oz) plain flour
- 2 tablespoons sea salt
- 1 tablespoon freshly ground white pepper
- 2 tablespoons chili powder
- peanut or vegetable oil for frying
- 6 sprigs coriander (cilantro)
- 1 lemon, cut into sixths

METHOD
Place the squid on a chopping board and pull out the tentacles. Pull off the side flaps, and cut the squid down the centre so it opens out flat. With a knife push out the gut and ink sac and discard. Scrape the skin off the body and flaps, and cut off and discard the hard beak. Wash the squid thoroughly and cut into strips.

Combine the flour, salt, pepper and chili in a bowl and mix well. In a wok heat enough oil to fry the squid in two lots and to 180°C (350°F). Place the squid in the flour mixture and toss to coat well. Shake off any excess and place carefully into the wok. Fry for 2 minutes and remove and drain on kitchen paper. Repeat with the next lot of squid.

Put the coriander in the oil and cook for 1 minute. This has a tendency to spit so be careful. Remove. Place the squid in the middle of a large plate and top with the fried coriander. Place the lemon wedges on the side and serve.

MULTIPLE COOKING METHODS

One of the things that makes Chinese cooking so fascinating is the lengths that you can go to in order to change the texture and taste of food. Multiple cooking methods work very well with duck, pork, pigeon, chicken, and even fish.

CRISPY SICHUAN DUCK WITH MANDARIN PANCAKES

SERVES UP TO EIGHT AS A SHARED DISH OR TWO DUCK LOVERS

To the people of Sichuan this duck is not only as good as Peking Duck, but also as famous for its crispness, lack of fat and melt-in-the-mouth flesh. The duck is first marinated, then steamed for a long time until it is almost confit-like, and the fat rendered. It is then dried and fried until crisp, the meat shredded, and served with either steamed buns or Mandarin Pancakes.

When I opened Wockpool, I really wanted to roast ducks in the Chinese manner. Unlike Rockpool, where they are part of a dish and four are enough for a night's service, I knew duck would be a huge seller and the Western kitchen that we had adapted would not cope. Thankfully we inherited a rather large deep-fryer in the kitchen and that, I knew, could handle the Sichuan duck. It was the Wockpool house specialty and 200 portions were sold weekly, which meant making some 1,500 to 2,000 pancakes per week!

The Mandarin Pancakes are made with a boiling-water dough; the heat brings out the gluten in the flour and makes it more pliable and silky. You must concentrate on rolling the pancakes as thinly as possible. The Flower Drum restaurant in Melbourne set a standard that Wockpool aspired to; their hallmark pancakes are so thin they are almost transparent. They are rolled in pairs so the steam created in the centre makes them soft and pliable. The recipe makes 20 pancakes, or 10 pairs.

INGREDIENTS
- 1 x 2 kg (4 lb) Peking duck
- 1 tablespoon sea salt
- 1 teaspoon five-spice powder
- 1 large knob ginger, peeled and cut into 4 slices
- 4 spring onions
- 2 tablespoons light soy sauce
- plain flour
- peanut oil for frying
- 8 Mandarin Pancakes
- 8 small spring onions (scallions), white part, with a bit of green left on
- 1 continental cucumber, cut into 8 batons
- 6 tablespoons hoisin sauce, mixed with 2 tablespoons sesame oil

Mandarin pancakes
- 400 g (14 oz) plain flour
- 190 ml (6.7 fl oz) boiling water
- 65 ml (2 fl oz) cold water
- sesame oil for rolling

METHOD

Rinse the duck, pat it dry with kitchen paper, and remove the fat from the cavity. Place the duck on a board and place both your palms on the breastbone. Push down hard to snap the side bones so the duck flattens slightly.

In a mortar and pestle crush the sea salt and mix with the five-spice powder. Rub the salt mixture all over the duck. Cover and refrigerate overnight.

Put the duck on a plate that will fit in a steamer. Place the ginger and spring onions in the cavity and place the cluck in the steamer over rapid boiling water. Steam for 3 hours — don't be alarmed by the long cooking time, this allows the fat to render and the skin to crisp when you fry it. Check the water level in the steamer during the cooking and top up with boiling water from the kettle as necessary. After 3 hours drain the duck and remove the ginger and spring onions from the cavity. Allow the duck to cool.

To make the Mandarin Pancakes, mix the plain flour and boiling water together in a bowl. Add the cold water and continue to mix until the dough forms a ball. Rest for 30 minutes. Place the dough on a lightly oiled bench and knead for about 10 minutes until smooth and silky. Roll into a long sausage shape and trim off the ends to make an even cylinder. Cut the sausage in half and each half in half again, and each quarter into five pieces. Roll out each piece with a rolling pin to a circle of 10 cm (4 in) diameter, brush lightly with sesame oil and place the two oiled sides together. You should now have 10 pairs of pancakes. Roll each pair of pancakes out to a 15 cm (6 in) diameter. Repeat

with the others, and store on a plate with a damp cloth over them.

Heat a frying pan over medium heat. Place the pancake in the pan and dry-fry for 20 to 30 seconds or until faint brown spots start to appear. Flip the pancake and cook the other side. The pancakes should puff up and separate. Remove the pancakes from the heat, peel apart and repeat. Store the cooked pancakes on a plate covered with a damp cloth and food wrap. When reheating make sure they are nice and hot, or they will be hard and unpalatable.

Brush the duck with the soy sauce and dust it with flour, blowing off any excess. In a large wok heat enough oil to half submerge the duck to 180°C (350°F). Place the duck in the wok, breast-side down. Turn over after 3 minutes and cook for another 2 minutes. Cook the duck for a total of 12 minutes, turning from side to side to ensure even cooking. Remove and drain on kitchen paper.

To serve first cut off the legs and, with a fork, loosen the fibres of the leg meat. Do the same with the breast meat. Loosen the skin underneath the duck and shred. Steam the pancakes and fold them into quarters. On a plate place the spring onions, cucumbers, pancakes, a bowl of the hoisin sauce mix, the shredded duck and serve.

Your diners should be encouraged to eat with their hands. To eat, place a pancake on the plate, spoon over some sauce, place a piece of cucumber and spring onion with some duck and roll up the crêpe.

VO AS A MAIN COURSE OR SIX AS PART OF A SHARED MEAL

---

avorite dish that has been on the menu for some years at Rockpool. It goes through sever
s that change the texture in different ways. Normally it would be served as a shared dish, how
ery satisfying served Western-style. Usually it would be served with my version of sweet and s
m sugar is used with fish sauce, the juice, flesh and zest of mandarins, and ginger. The sweetr
fset by stir-fried spinach with lots of soy sauce. The duck is first marinated to impart flavor, ther
essed to alter the texture of the muscle and fat, coated in egg white and flour, steamed again
fried until very crisp on the outside and tender in the middle.

NTS

g (4 lb) Peking duck

(3 oz) palm sugar

om 2 mandarins, pith removed and cut
ry fine julienne

spoons finely julienned ginger

2 fl oz) fish sauce

2 fl oz) mandarin juice

darins, filleted

oil for frying

ade

(1 fl oz) light soy sauce

2 fl oz) shaohsing wine

ng onions (scallions), white part only, cut
unds

es dried orange peel

- 1 knob ginger, peeled and finely diced
- 1 star anise, crushed
- 1 tablespoon yellow rock sugar
- coating
- 2 egg whites
- 100 g (3 oz) cornflour
- 50 g (2 oz) rice flour

Stir-Fried Spinach

- 1 teaspoon peanut oil
- 1 teaspoon julienned ginger
- 1 teaspoon crushed garlic
- 1 bunch English spinach, roots off, ste
  attached
- 30 ml (1 fl oz) light soy sauce
- 30 ml (1 fl oz) Chicken Stock (page 12
- 2 teaspoon sesame oil

METHOD

Place the duck on a chopping board and remove the fat from the cavity. Cut off the winglets and the neck, and with a cleaver, split the duck in half.

To make the marinade boil all the ingredients together for 2 minutes. Allow to cool and rub the marinade all over the duck, and marinate for at least 3 hours, preferably overnight.

Bring a pot of water to the boil and steam the duck for 45 minutes. Remove from the stove and allow to cool to the point where you can handle it. Carefully remove the bones, taking care not to break the skin. Use a small knife to ease out the wing and leg bone. Deboning is easier when the duck is slightly warm as it presses together much better.

At the end of this step you should have two rectangles of duck. Place them on a board and fold all the skin under. Cover them loosely with food wrap (allow some slack so they can spread). Put them in a container and place another container that fits inside the first on top, then a 5 kg (11 lb) weight. Refrigerate overnight.

Take the ducks out of the container and unwrap. You should have 2 solid pieces of duck with flat, smooth-skinned sides. Place a steamer on the stove over some boiling water.

Whisk the egg whites in a bowl until they start to thicken, but before soft peaks form. Mix the flours together.

Dip the duck into the egg whites, skin-side down. Ensure there is an even covering of egg white over the skin. With a sieve dust the duck with the two flours, blow off any excess and place on a heatproof plate. Repeat. Place both in a steamer and cook for 20 to 25 minutes. The egg-white crust should be dry to the touch, if it is undercooked it will detach from the duck during the frying process, so ensure that it is cooked through.

To make the sauce, place the palm sugar with a little water in a pot and bring to the boil on the stove. Add the peel and ginger, and continue to cook until the palm sugar reaches a dark caramel color. Add the fish sauce and mandarin juice and stir. Add the mandarin fillets and keep warm.

Add enough peanut oil in a wok to submerge the ducks, and bring the oil to 180°C (350°F). Add the ducks, and fry for about 6 minutes, or until the coating is crisp and the duck warmed through. Remove and drain. Rest in a warm place while you stir-fry the spinach.

To cook the spinach, place a wok on the stove over high heat and add the peanut oil. When it starts to smoke add the ginger and garlic, stirring all the time, and fry for 1 minute. Add the spinach and stir for 1 minute, then add the soy sauce and cook for 20 seconds. Add the chicken stock and sesame oil, and cook for a further 30 seconds. Remove from the heat.

To serve, divide the spinach into 2 piles with a pair of tongs and place on 2 warm plates with a spoonful of the cooking liquid. Cut the ducks into finger-wide slices and place next to the spinach. Spoon over the mandarin sauce and serve immediately.

CHINESE ROAST PIGEON WITH YAM AND GINGER LASAGNE

SERVES FOUR

I have always loved pigeon and some of my favorite three-star French meals have included pigeon, dripping with blood, a meal fit for a vampire. On a visit to Hong Kong I discovered the Lai Ching Heen in the Regent, a restaurant that, to this day, is one of my favorite dining experiences in the world, along with Fredy Girardet. I have had master-stocked and fried pigeon before in Sydney's Chinatown, but they were never crisp enough, or too dry, certainly no earth-shattering experience. Adele and I flew into Hong Kong late in the day and, needing something nourishing and comforting, headed down to the restaurant. I ordered some steamed prawns and garlic, baby bok choy braised in oyster sauce, roast pigeon and rice. The prawns had a silky texture with an almost overwhelming taste of garlic that pulled back at the last minute for the buttery, nutty flavor of the prawns to take centre stage. It was heavenly. Then the pigeon arrived, mahogany in color, chopped up and reformed, with lemon and Sichuan salt at its side. It was a wonderful vision, but the taste of the succulent wings, crispy and satiny flesh from the legs made me feel there may be a higher plane. This dish was so good that we ate there over the next three days, with different dishes each day, except for the pigeon, which didn't disappoint on any of those visits, or any of the further five times I've been there.

This recipe produces a pigeon that is somewhere in-between, but it is definitely well cooked. This dish lies somewhere between the French and Chinese pigeons The bird is first cooked in a master stock, dried, and fried until crisp. I take it off the bone for a more Western presentation and serve it with yam and ginger lasagne and stir-fried mustard greens. I think the lemon juice and Sichuan salt are indispensable. The Yam and Ginger Lasagne yields enough for 6 serves, so you can snack on the last 2 or buy more pigeons and find 2 more friends.

INGREDIENTS
- 4 x 500 g (1 lb) baby pigeons (squab)
- 1 litre (2 pints) peanut oil
- 60 ml (2 fl oz) lemon juice
- 8 tablespoons sea salt
- 1 teaspoon Sichuan peppercorns

Master Stock
- 2 litres (4 pints) water
- 200 ml (7 fl oz) shaohsing wine
- 100 ml (3 fl oz) light soy sauce
- 50 ml (2 fl oz) dark soy sauce
- 100 g (3 oz) yellow rock sugar
- 2 strips dried orange peel
- 2 pieces cassia bark
- 5 star anise
- 1 large knob ginger, peeled and sliced
- 4 cloves garlic, sliced

- 3 spring onions (scallions)

Yam And Ginger Lasagne
- 2 large knobs ginger, peeled and chopped
- 350 g (12 oz) yam or sweet potato, peeled and chopped
- 100 g (3 oz) unsalted butter
- sea salt and freshly ground white pepper
- 300 g (10.5 oz) Basic Pasta (page 191)
- peanut oil for frying

Mustard Greens
- 60 ml (2 fl oz) peanut oil
- 1 teaspoon crushed garlic
- 1 tablespoon palm sugar
- 1 large or 2 small heads mustard greens, washed and sliced
- 60 ml (2fl oz) light soy sauce

METHOD

To make the Master Stock, put all the ingredients in a pot large enough to fit the 4 pigeons, and boil for 20 minutes. Switch off the heat and allow the stock to sit for 1 hour to let the flavors mingle.

Cut the feet off the pigeons. Leave the head and winglets on. Bring the master stock back to the boil and immerse the pigeons. Place a plate on top to hold them down and cook for exactly 3 minutes. Remove from the heat and allow the pigeons to cool in the stock.

After 1 hour remove the pigeons and drain. Tie four pieces of string of about 20 cm (8 in) in length into loops, place it around the pigeons' necks and hang the pigeon up in front of a fan. Allow the pigeons to dry for 2 to 3 hours. The skin should feel like parchment when it is completely dry.

To make the Yam and Ginger Lasagne, place the ginger and yam in a snug-fitting pot. Fill the pot with water but do not cover the yam completely. Add the butter and some sea salt, and simmer for about 20 minutes or until the yam is cooked. At this stage there should be no water left, and the butter should have formed a thick sauce. Puree the yam and ginger and add some freshly ground pepper.

Divide the pasta dough into three pieces and, working with one piece at a time, roll through a pasta machine through the thinnest setting. Cook and assemble the lasagne as explained in Smoked Salmon Lasagne (page 192), replacing the salmon with the yam and ginger purée.

Preheat an oven to 180°C (350°F).

Turn out the lasagne and cut out four serves. In a frying pan large enough to fit all of them at the same time add some peanut oil and put it on the stove over medium heat. When it is almost smoking add the lasagna and allow it to take on color, about 2 minutes. Turn over and place the lasagnes in the oven and cook for 5 minutes. Turn the oven down to 70°C (160°F) and leave the door slightly ajar.

Heat the 1 litre (2 pints) peanut oil in a wok to 180°C (350°F) and add the pigeons. Fry until deep golden brown, about 6 minutes. Drain and place on a plate in the oven to rest.

To cook the mustard greens, place another wok on the stove over high heat and heat the peanut oil. When it starts to smoke add the garlic and stir for 1 minute. Add the mustard greens and stir for another minute. Add the palm sugar and caramelize. Add the soy sauce and cook for 30 seconds, then add the stock and sesame oil, and cook for a further minute.

Place the lasagne at one end of the plate and some stir-fried mustard greens in a little pile at the other end. Carve the pigeon by first cutting off the head and the neck (this is a great part for eating). Cut off each leg, the breast bone, and take off each breast. Place the legs on the mustard greens and the breast on the lasagna with the neck tucked away underneath, reforming the bird in a two-dimensional sense. Sprinkle over some lemon juice and Sichuan salt. Repeat with the other birds. Serve immediately with side dishes of lemon juice and Sichuan salt. The Chinese consider the head is the best part but most of my customers have a bit of a thing about it, so you decide.

THAI COOKING

Thai food differs greatly from Chinese, although some of the cooking techniques are similar. This is not at all surprising, it is thought that the original Thais fled China as a minority group. At the very least trade with China and the vast number of Chinese immigrants have had an effect on the food. Unlike other South-east Asian countries Thailand has never been conquered by another foreign power, so Thai food is dominant and not overrun by foreign influences. The result is a very distinct cuisine that manages to grow stronger with the advent of new produce and ideas. China, India, Cambodia, Laos, Indonesia and Portugal have all played a part in the evolution.

Rice is at the centre of Thai food. The main dishes are generally served all at once and the aim is to enjoy the food and company equally. Dishes such as fish cakes and spring rolls are snack food and would usually be bought from street hawkers. Noodles are generally eaten for lunch, and this is one of the few times one would use chopsticks. The balance of a meal is important. One host may offer a curry, a fried fish, a salad of some sort, maybe an omelette, but most definitely a soup. All the dishes would be served with rice and, unlike a typical Western meal, the emphasis would not be on how much protein was served, but on the balance of vegetables, rice, fish and meat.

For me the great dishes of Thailand are their salads, soups and curries; these set the food very much apart from the Chinese, even though frying, poaching, and steaming are the main cooking methods. Fish sauce, shrimp paste, spices and copious quantities of fresh herbs are used. The fragrance of Thai cooking is captured in freshly crushed garlic, coriander roots and pepper. The four main Thai flavors are hot, salty, sweet and sour; good Thai cooking will have a balance of those flavors, as well as those of texture and color.

There is no word as 'curry' in Thai, the pastes that are made (and there are hundreds of them) are called *gang*. A simple gang maybe used for a soup, and an incredibly elaborate one for a rich curry. It is very important in Thai cooking to cook with your nose (and not the clock), as fragrance is an essential part of the cooking process. The more you cook a curry paste, roast a spice and grill the kapi, the more you'll be accustomed to using your nose. That is the gift Asian cooking gives to the Western cook; apart from breads

Western cooks tend to use their noses far too little.

Learn to harness the powers of fish sauce, chilies, souring agents and sugar.

I remember vividly the first time I went to Thailand with Sydney's very own champion of Thai food, David Thompson and my beautiful (then) wife-to-be Adele. Having lived in Thailand for three years learning the language and studying the food, David returned to Sydney in 1989. When he left Sydney he was already a Western cook of considerable talent. When he returned, however, he taught us all what real Thai food was about. David's Western roots are long since lost, and his memory of cooking a good coq-au-vin is fading, but he is setting the benchmark for quality Thai food throughout the world. We are very lucky in Sydney to have Darley Street Thai.

It was a great opportunity for me to wander around Thailand with a fellow cook who speaks Thai. The first lunch we had was down by the river in a large restaurant. It was hot, so hot, we threw ice into our beers. David ordered the food, and first to arrive was a salad of smoked oysters with black wood fungus, dressed in a nam jim of chili and lime and it was mind-blowing. The reason was not just because it was hot — it was numbingly so — but because it was so well-balanced: hot, sour, sweet, salty, smoky, creamy and crunchy all at once. Then came the stir-fried river prawns with sator beans and tamarind. Again, perfection: creamy prawns, nutty crunchy beans in a sour, sweet sauce, a hint of chili and beautifully seasoned. That day down by the river I finally understood what Thai food was about — balance. Since then my ability to cook has improved tenfold. If you seek balance in all things in life, not just cooking, your life will be richer for it.

Many of the same basic cooking techniques explained in the Chinese section hold true for Thai cooking. Indispensable in the kitchen is a large mortar and pestle and a sauté pan or shallow pot for curries. You'll also need a blender to process the gang pastes.

Use fresh lime juice when it is called for and never substitute processed juice. Never put olive oil into a traditional Thai dish; it has too strong and pervasive a flavor. Look after spices when you're roasting them, burnt spices will lead to a bitter dish. Refrigerate the fish sauce after opening.

CURRY PASTES

One of the first things you notice when you arrive in Thailand is the fragrance of the place, whether in a taxi perfumed with jasmine flowers, or walking through the market, permeated with all the smells of fresh produce. For me most wonderful were the smells from the food stalls that filled the air — fresh curries, spices, lemongrass, coconut milk, lime leaves and shrimp paste.

I was lucky enough to have David Thompson, the guru of spice, talk, show, and impress upon me the importance of balance, and how one should go about cooking a real Thai curry. In the end I went about making curries that suited my own needs, but that was only possible because of the insight afforded me by this man's passion for all things Thai that is only outstripped by his generosity to others.

A fresh Thai curry is a flavorsome blend and layering of one flavor on another so that none dominates but all contribute to the satisfying end result. There are many pastes that make what we call curries in Thailand, but most would fall into two categories: boiled or fried. Fried pastes are generally done in coconut oil, and the result is rich and most satisfying. The time spent cooking out the paste is well worth it, and the result is far superior.

To make a curry paste, chop up all the ingredients as finely as you can, then pound them in a mortar and pestle. If you have a mincer at home put all the ingredients through a mincer twice. Or, put the pounded ingredients in a blender and blend with a little water until smooth. Use as little water as possible — the wetter he paste, the more trouble you'll have frying it properly. The fragrance and lift in a curry paste will be lost if it sits around, so make up fresh paste and cook it out as it is needed.

For the curry I use two-thirds coconut cream to one-third vegetable oil. In a heavy-based saucepan crack the coconut cream by boiling the water out until the cream gives up its fragrant oil. (Coconut oil is a saturated fat and very hard to digest. Vegetable oil makes the dish healthier without sacrificing flavor.) Your nose will tell you when it's ready. Add the paste and some lime leaves. Keep the heat on high, as all the ingredients must be cooked or the curry will have a raw flavor. Keep stirring as the paste and coconut solids burn easily if they sink to the bottom of the pan. Smell the aromas as they cook out. First the shallots and garlic, then the aromatic lemongrass and galangal, and finally, the shrimp paste and spices. When all these aromas blend together, add the palm sugar and fish sauce. These last two ingredients will bring all the aromas into line, and I believe that they contribute more than just seasoning, they do affect aroma and the balance of fragrance of the end curry. At this stage add the coconut milk and taste for seasoning adjustments. I would add my fish or meat, and vegetables now, and cook them slowly until just cooked. At this point the curry can be Westernised. The juice in Thai cooking seems to be given more consideration than the actual protein, causing most of the ingredients to be overcooked for my liking. (I'm sure there is a good explanation for this, but I haven't heard of an acceptable one yet.) Serve the finished curry with steamed jasmine rice.

GREEN CURRY OF KING PRAWNS

SERVES FOUR TO SIX AS PART OF A SHARED MEAL

This deliciously fresh curry relies on the fragrance and freshness of lemongrass, galangal and the fierce bite of green chilies. I first had this dish cooked for me by David Thompson, and was bowled over by the wonderful flavors, freshness, the citrus and lime tastes, and the nuttiness and crunchiness of the prawns. With each mouthful of prawn, sauce and rice, I became more and more convinced that beautiful fresh king prawns and green curry have a natural affinity. To this day this is my favorite green curry. If fresh prawns are not available use fresh fish, mussels or crayfish.

INGREDIENTS
- 200 ml (7 fl oz) coconut cream
- 100 ml (3 fl oz) vegetable oil
- 6 kaffir lime leaves
- 4 tablespoons fish sauce
- 1 tablespoon palm sugar
- 500 ml (1 pint) coconut milk
- 600 g (1 lb 3 oz) fresh king prawns, peeled and deveined
- 4 wild green chilies, lightly crushed
- 3 long red chilies, split and seeded
- 50 g (2 oz) pea eggplants
- 5 apple eggplants, quartered
- a dozen fresh sweet basil leaves

Curry Paste
- 5 coriander (cilantro) seeds
- 5 cumin seeds
- 5 white peppercorns
- 6 small wild green chilies, chopped and pounded
- 3 long green chilies, seeded, chopped and pounded
- 2 stalks lemongrass, chopped and pounded
- 2 tablespoons chopped galangal, pounded
- 10 red shallots, chopped and pounded
- 5 cloves garlic, chopped and pounded
- 3 coriander (cilantro) roots, chopped and pounded
- 1 tablespoon fresh turmeric, chopped and pounded
- zest of 1 kaffir lime, chopped and pounded
- 1 teaspoon shrimp paste, wrapped in foil and grilled until fragrant

METHOD

To make the Curry Paste, roast the coriander, cumin and peppercorns lightly and grind in a coffee grinder or spice grinder to a powder. Pass all the pounded and ground ingredients through a mincer twice. Alternatively, process in a blender until smooth, adding a little water if necessary to facilitate blending.

In a heavy-based frying pan over high heat, bring the coconut cream and vegetable oil to the boil. Keep stirring so it doesn't stick and burn. When the coconut cream splits, add the paste. Crush the lime leaves in your hand and add to the pan and continue frying. Keep cooking until all the aromas come out of the paste and it is sizzling fiercely. This will take between 10 and 15 minutes, use your nose.

Add the fish sauce and cook for 1 minute, add the palm sugar and coconut milk, and bring to the boil. Add the prawns, chilies and eggplants, and gently simmer until the prawns have turned opaque, but still translucent in the middle. Stir the basil through and pour into a large bowl. Serve immediately with steamed jasmine rice.

RED CURRY OF BEEF AND PEANUTS

SERVES FOUR TO SIX AS PART OF A SHARED MEAL

There are two ways I like attacking this recipe. Both are equally as good but produce very different textures and flavors. One is to barbecue either the beef fillet or sirloin, slice it and fold it through the curry at the end. The other is to use beef brisket left over from making pho stock and poaching it for 3 hours in coconut milk. This curry, with its deep spicy flavor and rich sweetness, is very moreish. I have developed a similar paste for Rockpool that marries beautifully with blue-eye cod. I removed some of the chilies and added more spice and lemongrass. To compensate for the red color lost by the reduction in chilies, I added paprika. I wouldn't recommend pulling out a first-growth 1961 to accompany this dish, but a young pinot or shiraz will do fine.

INGREDIENTS

- 400 ml (14 fl oz) coconut cream
- 100 ml (3 fl oz) vegetable oil
- 6 kaffir lime leaves
- 6 tablespoons palm sugar
- 125g (4 oz) roasted peanuts
- 4 tablespoons fish sauce
- 250 ml (8 fl oz) coconut milk
- 300 g (7 oz) cooked beef brisket or barbecued sirloin, cut into strips
- 4 long green eggplants or Japanese eggplants, halved and barbecued
- 100 g (3 oz) pea eggplants
- 4 large red chilies, seeded
- 20 Thai sweet basil leaves

Curry Paste

- 1 teaspoon white peppercorns
- 2 teaspoons cumin seeds
- 1 teaspoon coriander (cilantro) seeds
- 6 star anise
- 3 sticks cinnamon
- 6 dried long red chilies, split, seeded and ground
- 12 cloves garlic, chopped and pounded
- 10 red shallots, chopped and pounded
- 3 stalks lemongrass, chopped and pounded
- 2 tablespoons galangal, chopped and pounded
- 4 coriander (cilantro) roots, chopped and pounded
- zest of 1 kaffir lime, chopped and pounded
- 3 tablespoons shrimp paste, wrapped in foil and grilled until fragrant
- 1 tablespoon ground paprika

METHOD

To make the Curry Paste, roast the peppercorns, cumin, coriander, star anise and cinnamon until very fragrant and dark, but not burnt. Grind in a spice grinder. Put all the pounded and ground ingredients through a mincer twice or blend until smooth in a blender, adding a little water if necessary to facilitate blending.

In a heavy-based frying pan over high heat bring the coconut cream and vegetable oil to the boil and cook until the oil and the coconut solids separate. Add the paste, crush the lime leaves and add to the pan. Continue to stir to stop it from sticking and burning, and fry until all the elements of the curry cook out and become fragrant. This will take between 15 and 20 minutes.

Add the palm sugar and cook until well caramelized. Add the peanuts and stir. Add the fish sauce and cook for a further minute, then add the coconut milk and bring to the boil. The curry should be very thick with a generous amount of oil floating on top. Put in the beef brisket or sirloin and simmer for 4 minutes. Add the eggplants and chilies, and fold through. Add the basil and spoon into a large bowl. The beef brisket should be meltingly soft and easy to eat with a spoon.

This dish is a great way of using up leftover oxtail from making the oxtail jus in Spanner Crab Ravioli with Oxtail and Rosemary Jus (page 205). If you don't have any on hand, simply roast the oxtail until golden brown and poach in chicken stock with a little salt. The broth makes a terrific soup and the oxtail will be light and purged of most of its fat. If the more gelatinous cuts of meat, especially those from the extremities of the animal, are gently poached for as long as it takes to cook them, they will be much lighter and easier to digest than when braised in their own stock and served with a rich sauce. I find that people who have an aversion to the really meaty parts of the animal, such as my wife Adele, who has been known to say, 'I don't eat anyone's feet, nose, tongue, ears or tails', will eat this dish because of its lightness, and less meaty flavor.

INGREDIENTS

- 4 cloves garlic
- 10 red shallots
- 4 coriander (cilantro) roots
- 10 white peppercorns
- 60 ml (2 fl oz) peanut oil
- 4 tablespoons palm sugar
- 4 tablespoons fish sauce
- 500 g (1 lb) poached oxtail (bone and meat)
- 1 large daikon, peeled and sliced into 1 cm rounds
- 1 teaspoon sea salt
- 500 ml (1 pint) coconut milk
- 125 g (4 oz) Thai sweet basil leaves
- 125 g (4 oz) mint leaves

METHOD

In a mortar and pestle crush the garlic cloves, half the shallots, the coriander roots and white peppercorns to a fine paste.

Slice the rest of the shallots finely and fry until crisp in oil. Drain on kitchen paper.

In a wok over a high flame heat up the peanut oil until almost smoking. Add the paste and stir for 1 minute. As it starts to turn golden add the palm sugar and allow to caramelize. Add the fish sauce and oxtail, and stir for 30 seconds. Add the daikon, salt and coconut milk. Simmer until the coconut milk has all but disappeared, and in the last minute of cooking add the herbs and stir through.

Put the oxtail in a large bowl, sprinkle with the fried shallots and serve immediately.

KING SHRIMP CAKE AND SCALLOPS WITH SPICY PRAWN SAUCE

MAKES SIX ENTRÉES

I guess you could call this dish a meeting of East and West. I have had great success with it, and have served it at many Rockpool functions. It is also Adele's favorite. The dish is a blend of Western mousse-making technique and Asian flavors. The coconut cream makes the mousse a little heavier than one would normally expect, and the resulting cake is somewhere between the softness of a French mousse, whose texture I sometimes find a little disconcerting, and the firmness of fish cakes, whose texture is worked to give resistance to the bite. I find this in-between texture very pleasant. The mousses can be made in advance and gently steamed again when needed. It is important to use that amount of oil with the sauce, as the flavor compounds in the shells dissolve in the oil, not the stock.

INGREDIENTS

- 400 ml (14 fl oz) Prawn Stock (page 187)
- 6 kaffir lime leaves, cut into fine julienne
- 1 large knob ginger, cut into fine julienne
- 10 fresh water chestnuts, peeled and sliced
- 6 slices fresh bamboo shoots, cut into julienne
- 100 ml (3 fl oz) coconut cream
- palm sugar, to taste
- fish sauce, to taste
- 18 sea scallops
- 10 Thai sweet basil leaves, cut into fine julienne
- 50 g (2 oz) roasted peanuts, crushed

Mousse
- 3 cloves garlic
- 2 red shallots
- 3 coriander (cilantro) roots
- 10 white peppercorns
- 2 teaspoons sea salt
- 300 ml (10 fl oz) cream (35 per cent butterfat)
- 250 ml (9 fl oz) coconut cream
- 750 g (1.7 lb) fresh king prawns, to give 375 g (13 oz) flesh (save the heads and shells)

- 2 egg whites
- 1 egg yolk

Prawn Sauce
- 8 cloves garlic
- 6 red shallots
- 2 stalks lemongrass, chopped
- 1 slice galangal, peeled and chopped
- 2 slices fresh turmeric, peeled and chopped
- 1 strip kaffir lime zest, chopped
- 8 wild green chilies, chopped
- 1 teaspoon white peppercorns, roasted and ground
- 1 teaspoon fennel seeds, roasted and ground
- 1 teaspoon coriander (cilantro) seeds, roasted and ground
- 120 ml (4 fl oz) peanut oil
- prawn shells
- 100 ml (3 fl oz) whisky
- 300 ml (10 fl oz) Chicken Stock (page 122)
- 2 tomatoes, blanched, peeled, seeded and chopped

METHOD
Preheat the oven to 150°C (300°F).

To make the Mousse, spray 6 dariole moulds with Pure and Simple or lightly grease with a vegetable oil.

In a mortar and pestle crush the garlic, shallots, coriander roots, white peppercorns and sea salt to a fine paste. Chill the bowl of a food processor in the freezer. Mix the cream and coconut cream in a jug and place it in the freezer as well. Make sure the prawns are very cold. This is all necessary so the mousse will not split.

Place the bowl on the food processor and add the prawns and paste. Turn on the motor and add the egg whites, one at a time, followed by the egg. Add the cream mixture in a thin stream, making sure the processor isn't running for more than 2 minutes in all. Spoon the mousse into the greased moulds and tap them on the bench to knock out the air bubbles. Fill a bain-marie with hot water and place the moulds inside (the water should reach halfway up the moulds). Place in the preheated oven for 25 minutes.

To make the Prawn Sauce, in a mortar and pestle crush the garlic, shallots, lemongrass, galangal, turmeric, lime zest and chilies to a fine paste. Add the roasted and ground spices to the paste.

In a pot heat the peanut oil until almost smoking.

Add the prawn shells and the paste and fry, stirring continuously, until the paste is fragrant, the shells red, and the oil takes on the color of the prawns. Add the whisky and cook until it evaporates, then add the stock and fold through the tomatoes. Once the chicken stock hits the shells the sauce must not boil or it will become slightly bitter. Turn down the heat and leave on the stove without boiling for 20 minutes. Remove and strain through a fine sieve, pressing on the shells to extract the flavor.

Bring the prawn stock to the boil in a stockpot. Lower the heat so that it is just simmering. Add the lime leaves, ginger, water chestnuts, bamboo shoots and coconut cream. Season with palm sugar and fish sauce to round out the flavor. Make sure the mixture doesn't boil again as the coconut cream splits easily.

In a heavy-based saucepan or on a grill cook the sea scallops until golden brown on both sides but still translucent and succulent in the middle. In 6 large white bowls turn out the mousses by running a paring knife around the rim and turning out gently onto the plate. A little shake should be enough to dislodge them.

Spoon the sauce over the top of the mousse, about 80 ml per person, making sure each person gets some of the solids. Top with the sweet basil and sprinkle over some peanuts. Place three scallops around each mousse, and serve immediately.

NAM JIM

MAKES ABOUT ¼ CUP

There are many variations to this Thai vinaigrette or salad dressing. Most recipes in Thai cookbooks would refer to the balance of flavors, and the difference that you like between the sour, hot, sweet and salty can be changed at your whim, as long as there is balance. So if you like it very hot don't just increase the chili. If you did the nam jim would probably be too harsh. Similarly if you want it saltier it's not just a matter of adding more salt or fish sauce. It is important to understand how all the elements in the dressing relate and react to each other. Once you understand what you wish to achieve it will be quite easy to keep the taste balanced, no matter which of the four elements you would like to be more dominant.

The basic ingredients in nam jim are chilies (hot), salt or fish sauce (salty), palm or white sugar (sweet), and lime juice, coconut vinegar or tamarind (sour). Supporting roles are played by shallots, chili paste, coriander roots, garlic and so on. Don't ever substitute lemon for lime juice and never use bottled lime juice. Following is a starting point for a basic nam jim.

INGREDIENTS
- 2 cloves garlic
- 2 coriander (cilantro) roots
- 1 teaspoon sea salt
- 6 wild green chilies
- 1 tablespoon palm sugar
- 2 tablespoon fish sauce
- 4 tablespoon fresh lime juice
- 3 red shallots, thinly sliced

METHOD
Place the garlic, coriander roots and sea salt in a mortar and pestle and pound until well crushed. Don't reduce to a paste. Put in the chilies and crush lightly. If you crush them too much the sauce will get hotter, so be careful. Mix in the palm sugar, fish sauce, lime juice and shallots. The longer the nam jim sits the more intense the flavor. Make the dressing close to the time as you need it so that it tastes fresh.

MUDCRAB AND SWEET PORK SALAD WITH GREEN MANGO

SERVES SIX AS AN ENTRÉE

This is another Rockpool classic. Pork and crab have a natural affinity and in this dish the pork is caramelized to add sweetness to the sourness of the green mango. In this salad all the elements play off each other to perfection. I also have a great fondness for blue swimmer and spanner crabs. They are all quite unique in taste and texture, and I generally have all three varieties on the menu when they are in season. But when pushed I would have to say that my favorite crustacean is the mudcrab; the flavor and texture are unsurpassed. When selecting mudcrabs feel their weight. If it seems light for its size then it is either just out of hibernation or changed its shell and hasn't fattened up yet. Definitely to be avoided.

INGREDIENTS

- 10 red shallots, sliced
- 2 x 1 kg to 1.5 kg (2.5–3 lb)mudcrabs
- 1 Red-braised Pork Hock (page 62)
- 10 tablespoons palm sugar
- 6 tablespoons fish sauce
- 3 small green mangoes, peeled and cut into fine julienne
- 3 cloves garlic, sliced and fried until crisp
- 500 g (1 lb) shredded coriander leaves
- 125 g (4 oz) shredded mint leaves
- 60 g (2 oz)peanuts, roasted and crushed
- 2 quantities Nam Jim (page 110)

METHOD

Fry half the shallots until crisp and drain. Place the mudcrabs upside-down on a board. Push in a chopstick where the flap comes to a vee and out between the eyes to kill the crab. This is by far the quickest and most humane way of killing crabs. You can put them into a freezer until they go to sleep if you can't deal with it.

Pull back the flap and the entire top of the crab. Remove the lungs and discard. Wash. Remove the claws and, with a cleaver, cut the body in half. Chop the halves into halves again so you have four leg parts and two claws. Crack the claws with the back of a cleaver.

Bring water to the boil in a steamer and steam the crabs for 8 minutes. Remove from the heat. When cool enough, peel the crabs, taking care to remove all the shell and cartilage. Preheat the oven to 200°C (400°F). Trim the ends off the pork hock and cut into six even rounds. Place in a baking tray and cook in the preheated oven for 8 minutes. Put a pot with a little water and the palm sugar on the stove. Cook until caramelized and pour in the fish sauce. Remove from the heat and when the pork comes out of the oven pour over the sauce.

In a bowl mix all the other ingredients together except the crab and pork. To serve place a round of pork in the centre of each large white plate. Make 6 neat parcels of the green mango mix and sit them on the pork. Tip the excess dressing over so it runs onto the plate like a sauce. Make 6 very neat piles of tightly packed crab and place on top of the green mango mix. You should have 6 pretty towers. Pour over any leftover caramel sauce and serve immediately.

GRILLED OCTOPUS WITH A GREEN PAWPAW SALAD

SERVES BETWEEN SIX AND FOUR AS A SHARED STARTER

Green pawpaw is available in Chinatown and lends texture and structure to many Thai salads. The octopus is best when barbecued, tossed through with the pawpaw and served hot. The heat from the chili in the dressing and from the warm octopus give an interesting mouth feel.

INGREDIENTS
- 250 g (8 oz) whole octopus
- peanut oil for cooking
- 150 g (5 oz) green pawpaw, shredded
- 1 pomelo, peeled and filleted into segments
- 6 red shallots, thinly sliced
- 2 tablespoons shredded coriander leaves
- 2 tablespoons shredded mint leaves
- 1 quantity Nam Jim (page 110)
- 3 tablespoons roasted and crushed peanuts

METHOD
Split the octopus down the back of the head and scrape out the gut and ink sac. Pull out the hard beak. Remove the head and cut the legs into pairs, and marinate in the peanut oil.

Heat up a barbecue or a grill to high and add the octopus. Turn after about 3 minutes and cook for another 3 minutes. You can also sauté the octopus in a wok over high heat. Remove the octopus and put in a bowl. Add all the other ingredients except the peanuts and toss well. Place on a large white plate and sprinkle over the peanuts. Serve immediately.

have had some reasonable Vietnamese food in Sydney, but nothing that really knocked my socks off. I didn't think of Vietnam as a place I'd particularly like to visit or that its food would inspire my cooking. All of that was to change after a visit to France in 1993. Chris and Margie, our great friends from the Paramount restaurant in Sydney, had told us of an arrondissement in Paris that had many Chinese and Vietnamese restaurants and shops. After three weeks of three-star eating in and around Paris, Adele and I were busting for a chili fix. As we went down the street we walked past a shop packed with people, mostly Vietnamese. The laminex table tops were covered with sauces, chopped and dried chilies, spoons, chopsticks and serviettes, and all the patrons appeared to be slurping on soups and noodles. We decided this was for us.

The menus were in French and Vietnamese, and I could see that half the fun was seeing if we got what we thought we'd ordered. First came a beef pho, a soup with rice noodles and lots of fresh herbs and beansprouts on the side, and the choice of bottled, dried and fresh chilies. Next was a crisp mung-bean crepe full of beansprouts, cold-cut meats and fresh herbs. A bowl of nuoc mam cham was used as the dipping sauce, which again smacked of freshness. We finished with pork balls wrapped in rice-paper that were served with vermicelli noodles and lettuce for wrapping. It came with a hoisin dipping sauce. The underlying flavors were so pure, and the elements of each dish so fresh, that I knew I'd have to pursue this food on arrival back in Sydney.

Since then I have sought out many good Vietnamese meals in Sydney. Many of the very best restaurants are in the outlying suburb of Cabramatta. To me, Vietnamese cuisine seems more feminine than Thai cuisine. It has certainly been influenced by both French and Chinese occupation. Here are a few basic recipes used at the Wockpool noodle bar, and a couple of variations that have inspired food at the Rockpool.

NUOC CHAM

MAKES ABOUT ¾ CUP

This is Vietnam's nam jim or vinaigrette, used in and as a side dish to many salads and fresh rice-paper preparations. Barbecued octopus or squid tossed in nuoc cham and served on a bed of lettuce makes a really lovely fresh salad.

INGREDIENTS
- 2 fresh red chilies
- 1 clove garlic
- 1 tablespoon palm sugar
- 2 teaspoon lime juice
- 60 ml (1 fl oz) water
- 60 ml (1 fl oz) fish sauce
- 2 teaspoon rice-wine vinegar

METHOD
Pound the chilies and garlic to a fine paste. Add the sugar and stir to blend. Stir in the other liquids slowly until completely incorporated.

TRIPE AND CHILI SALAD

SERVES SIX AS A SHARED MAIN COURSE

I really love tripe. It's great braised, fried, or, as in this dish, a combination of both. Some of my favorite ways with tripe are a la lyonnaise, cooked with lots of onions until meltingly tender, or braised with chickpeas and vinegar in the Turkish way, or poached, crumbed, fried, and served with tartare sauce. Tripe adds a great crunch to this fresh and light salad. It goes beautifully with steamed jasmine rice.

INGREDIENTS

- 250 g (8 oz) honeycomb tripe
- 2 tablespoons ground roast rice
- ¼ Chinese cabbage, very finely shredded
- 100 g (3 oz) beansprouts
- 6 red shallots, peeled and thinly sliced
- 2 long red chilies, seeded and cut into thin julienne
- 4 small dried chilies, fried until black in a little peanut oil
- 180 ml (6 fl oz) Nuoc Cham
- 60 ml (1 fl oz) peanut oil

METHOD

Roll up the tripe into a cylinder and tie it up with kitchen string. Put into a pot large enough to hold it snugly with enough boiling water to cover, and simmer for 1½ hours. Lift out from the liquid, untie, cool and thoroughly dry. Slice the tripe into strips.

To roast rice heat some jasmine rice in a frying pan over a low heat until it colors slightly. Crush in a mortar and pestle. You may wish to use a blender, but I find that renders the rice too fine and powdery.

Place the cabbage, beansprouts, shallots and chilies in a bowl, and dress with the nuoc cham. Toss and allow to marinate for 5 minutes.

Place a wok on the stove over high heat and heat the peanut oil until it is smoking. Add the tripe and stir-fry until crisp, about 3 minutes. Remove and drain.

Place the tripe in the bowl with the other ingredients and toss to distribute the flavors. Place the mixture in the middle of a large white plate and sprinkle with the ground roast rice.

FRAGRANT BROTH WITH KING SHRIMP DUMPLINGS

SERVES SIX

This soup was inspired by the phos of Vietnam, those delicious beef and chicken broths served with noodles. The flavor and fragrance of this soup, and the addition of fresh herbs, beansprouts, lime and chili work very well with seafood. We often serve it with prawn or scallop dumplings and a mixture of prawn and beef balls at Rockpool. Once you've made this simple broth, you'll be addicted forever. I moisten the brisket with chicken stock just to give it a more unctuous quality, and a little more richness.

INGREDIENTS
- Broth
- 3 kg (6 lb) brisket, sliced
- 3 litres (6 pints) Chicken Stock (page 122)
- 100 ml (3 fl oz) peanut oil
- 5 cloves garlic, sliced
- 1 large knob ginger, peeled and sliced
- 15 red shallots, sliced
- 2 sticks cinnamon
- 3 star anise
- 25 coriander (cilantro) seeds

Dumpling Dough
- 300 g (10 oz) plain flour
- ½ egg, beaten
- 60 ml (2 fl oz) water
- a pinch of sea salt

Prawn (Shrimp) Filling
- 150 g (5 oz) finely minced prawn meat
- 1 tablespoon chopped coriander roots
- 1 tablespoon chopped coriander leaves
- ½ tablespoon chopped ginger
- 1 tablespoon light soy sauce
- ½ tablespoon shaohsing wine
- ½ tablespoon sesame oil

Chili Sauce
- 6 long red chilies, sliced
- 1 tablespoon sea salt
- 60 ml (2 fl oz) rice-wine vinegar
- 125 g (4 oz) castor sugar
- peanut oil
- 2 cloves garlic, sliced
- ½ small brown onion, very thinly sliced
- 5 tablespoons lemon juice
- spring onions, white part only, sliced into rounds coriander (cilantro) leaves
- 6 teaspoons palm sugar
- 6 tablespoons fish sauce
- freshly ground white pepper beansprouts
- mint leaves
- Vietnamese mint (rau ram) leaves
- Thai sweet basil leaves 2 limes

METHOD

To make the Broth, put the brisket in a pot large enough to hold 5 litres of water and bring to the boil. Boil vigorously for 10 minutes. Skim off all the scum and fat that rises to the top. Pour away the boiling water and wash the brisket carefully, removing all the bits of stuck-on protein and muck. Wash out the pot and put the brisket back in. Pour over the chicken stock. Bring to a simmer and cook very gently for 30 minutes, skimming constantly.

Add the peanut oil in a hot wok over high heat and fry the garlic, ginger and shallots until golden brown. Remove and drain. Add these to the brisket stock after the first 30 minutes. Simmer the stock for another hour.

Place the cinnamon, star anise and coriander seeds in a dry pan, and roast in the oven until fragrant. Tip these on top of the stock and simmer for a further 1½ hours. The stock should be very clear and full-flavored. Remove from the stove and pass through a fine strainer, then again through muslin.

Keep half the brisket for the soup (the other half can go into a Red Curry of Beef, page 125). Slice the brisket lengthwise very thinly and keep moist with a little of the broth until needed.

To make the Dumpling Dough sift the flour into a small bowl. Make a well in the middle, add the egg, and water mixed with a pinch of salt. Mix with a fork until the mixture comes together. Knead for 5 minutes until the dough is silky and smooth and forms a ball. Wrap, and rest on the bench for 30 minutes.

To make the filling, place all the ingredients in a food processor and purée for 1 minute. Transfer to a bowl. Lift the mixture and throw it back into the bowl, pushing and pulling at it repeatedly to make it more elastic.

Divide the dough in half and roll through a pasta machine on the thinnest possible setting. Cut out circles of dough to the size you want the dumplings. At Rockpool we make them about twice the size of a 50-cent piece. Place a teaspoonful of the filling in the centre and fold it over itself. Rub a little water around the rim of the pasta to help it stick. The pasta should be blanched immediately. They are ready to go into the soup when they float to the surface of the poaching liquid.

To make the Chili Sauce, place the chilies in a mortar. Add the salt and crush as well as you can. Bring the vinegar and sugar to the boil until the syrup coats the back of a spoon. In a wok with a small amount of oil, fry the garlic until golden brown. Place with the red chilies and crush. When the syrup cools down add to the chilies and mix. Serve this with the pho.

Salt the onions for 30 minutes. Rinse, dry and marinate the onions in the lemon juice. Divide the spring onions, coriander leaves and marinated onions between the 6 bowls. Place the brisket and dumplings on top. Place 1 teaspoon palm sugar and 1 tablespoon fish sauce in each bowl. Pour over the hot broth and add a pinch of freshly ground white pepper. Take the bowls to the table. On a central serving platter place the fresh herbs, beansprouts, limes and chili sauce for diners to season their soup as they wish.

FRESH VEGETARIAN RICE-PAPER ROLLS

MAKES EIGHT

These rolls can be made a little way in advance, but not too long as they dry out very easily and harden.

INGREDIENTS

- 50 g (2 oz) thin vermicelli rice noodles
- 2 large carrots, shredded
- 1 tablespoon roasted peanuts, ground
- 1 large continental cucumber, peeled and shredded
- 250 g (8 oz) fresh beansprouts
- 125 g (4 oz) mint leaves
- 125 g (4 oz) coriander (cilantro) leaves
- 8 tablespoons Nuoc Cham (page 114)
- 8 x 26 cm rice-paper rounds
- 8 Chinese (1o in) chives
- 4 tablespoons hoisin sauce
- ½ teaspoon ground peanuts
- 1 tablespoon sesame oil
- red oak lettuce and cos lettuce, washed and dried
- 1 cucumber, peeled, seeded and shredded
- 1 small carrot, peeled and shredded

METHOD

Soak the vermicelli in warm water until soft. Place the shredded carrots in ice-water for half an hour.

In a bowl mix the vermicelli, peanuts, carrots cucumber, beansprouts, mint, coriander leaves and dress with the nuoc cham sauce.

Make sure you have a tea-towel in front of you and a basin of tepid water beside you to moisten the rice-papers. Work with one or two sheets at a time and keep the others covered with a damp cloth; once they dehydrate they tend to break up and tear very easily. Place each sheet in the warm water and as it softens remove and place on the towel. Spoon one-eighth of the rice-noodle mix on the bottom third of the rice-paper. Start rolling and as you reach the centre fold in the edges to make a parcel. Continue rolling and as you near the end place one chive lengthwise so it sticks out 3 cm (1 in) through the roll. Keep rolling until you have a complete cylinder, the chive protruding. Place the roll on a tray and cover with a damp cloth. Repeat until all the filling is used up.

Put a shallow bowl with the hoisin sauce on a large plate. Sprinkle the peanuts over the sauce and add the sesame oil. Place the lettuces, cucumber and carrot on the side. Lay the rice rolls over each other on the plate and serve immediately.

CRISP RICE PANCAKE WITH COMBINATION STUFFING

SERVES EIGHT AS A SHARED DISH

This dish makes a fresh and vibrant starter for any summer luncheon. The crispy crepe encloses a lovely fresh herb and vermicelli salad. The dish is usually served with nuoc cham and lettuce. If you like, you can wrap the crêpe in the lettuce and eat it like a roll. Barbecued pork is readily available from Chinese food shops.

INGREDIENTS
- Crêpe Batter
- 60 g (2 oz) dried mung beans
- 200 ml (7 fl oz) coconut cream
- 100 g (3 oz) rice flour
- a pinch of sugar
- a pinch of salt
- a pinch of turmeric
- 2 tablespoons peanut oil

Filling
- 100 g (3 oz) Chinese barbecued pork
- 6 king prawns (shrimp), poached, shelled, deveined and halved
- 1 clove garlic, crushed
- 250 g (8 oz) fresh beansprouts
- 1 onion, thinly sliced
- 125 g (4 oz) rice vermicelli, soaked in warm water until soft
- 60 g (2 oz) snowpea sprouts
- 125 g (4 oz) mint leaves
- 125 g (4 oz) coriander leaves
- 125 g (4 oz) Thai sweet basil leaves
- 1 tablespoon fish sauce
- 1 tablespoon palm sugar
- cos and red-oak lettuce leaves
- shredded cucumber
- shredded carrot
- 150 ml Nuoc Cham (page 114)

METHOD
To make the batter soak the mung beans in water for 40 minutes. Drain. Put the mung beans and coconut cream in a blender and purëe. Add the rice flour, sugar, salt and turmeric, and blend well. Sieve the mixture and allow to stand for 30 minutes in the fridge.

To make the filling, combine all the ingredients in a bowl and mix well.

In a non-stick crêpe pan heat up the peanut oil until almost smoking. Add a ladleful of crêpe batter and tilt the pan to spread the mixture thinly around the pan. As the crêpe starts to set spoon over some of the filling and turn the crêpe over on itself. Leave on the heat for 1 minute. Turn off the heat and allow the crêpe to warm through for another minute. Make another crêpe following the same procedure.

Place both crepes on a plate with the lettuce leaves, shredded cucumber, carrot and nuoc cham. The nuoc cham can either be poured over the whole crêpe or be used as a dipping sauce.

My first visit to France was in 1984. I remember with fondness many wonderful meals at three-star restaurants and drinking some fabulous old bottles of Grand and Premier Cru wines. Who could forget their first taste of foie gras, wild mushrooms, spring lamb and fraises des bois, and their first poulet de Bresse? On returning to Australia, like so many other chefs who had had the same experiences, I went about trying to get produce of such calibre grown here.

All three-star experiences are hard to forget, but one of my most memorable would have to be at L'Archestrate in Paris, under chef Alain Senderens. The meals I've had there have been stunning from start to finish: a salad of lobster, mango and duck confit served slightly warm, the flavors clean and luscious. Or a piece of foie gras wrapped in cabbage, steamed, and served with sea salt and cracked pepper, which was crunchy, earthy, creamy and rich all at once — perfection. Or roasted spring lamb married with little vegetables and no sauce, with just the pure flavors of the ingredients in complete harmony. This was cooking at its very best.

In Italy, I have enjoyed some real salt-of-the-earth food, a stark change to the rich dining in three-star restaurants. I'll never forget a starter I had en route from Milan to Florence, at a truckstop. It was an experience that added to my cooking wisdom, and like all simple things, it was something I couldn't see initially. We had stopped for a set lunch at this little truck stop. The meal started with melon and prosciutto, followed by a pasta and a grilled meat, and dessert was Parmesan and pear. The lunch was delicious as a whole, but it was the first course of melon and prosciutto that was a revelation in its simplicity. It arrived, accompanied by a jug of house red. Unthinkingly I cut a piece and put it in my mouth, not expecting anything much. Then it hit me. Could this be flavor? Not only flavor, but perfect texture between soft and firm, give and take. The perfectly ripe melon, and dry, thinly sliced prosciutto had made the classic combination work. You need more than melon for this dish; you need ripe, luscious fruit ready to give itself to strong, full-flavored prosciutto. It gets right back to choosing the best produce. If the ingredient can't stand up on its own merits, how can it improve when combined with other flavors?

SAUCE

Sauce is the cornerstone of French cooking. It is the interplay between the sauce and its main ingredient that determines the quality of a dish. A good sauce will very rarely save a bad dish, but it will contribute to the downfall of the dish if it's not right. Many a three-star restaurant's reputation is built on the quality of its sauces. In a restaurant the saucier's position is usually the last to be filled; often, the saucier is the sous chef of the entire brigade or the owner of the restaurant.

Sauce-making is about capturing the essence of food flavor, and requires care and patience. Many chefs tend to drive away the aromatic qualities that they wanted to capture in the first place by over-cooking or allowing the sauce to sit around in a bain-marie for hours. This does nothing but produce harsh flavors. The taste and aroma of a sauce also change as it sits.

There are basically two types of sauces: sauces made directly from the juices of roasts, sautés and braises, and sauces made outside of the dish and added at the end. Use good ingredients when preparing bases for sauces and the sauce will retain its full integrity.

The basis of a good sauce is good stock. A stock is the essence of the ingredient it has been made from, so what we want is quality, not quantity. It's quite pointless trying to get the most liquid out of a stock, then having to turn around and reduce it to get the right texture and flavors. All the time it cooks, the stock is losing its aromatic qualities, and the bad flavors are intensified. You can't make an ordinary stock good, so take time at the beginning. When I first started running the kitchen at Barrenjoey House, beurre blancs, demi-glaces, mayonnaise, and vinaigrettes would be lovingly made every day for fish, meat, game and fowl.

I learnt many good skills from that time, but the most important ones from trying to cook without sauce, and more importantly, without butter and cream. My understanding of Asian cooking also made me aware that aroma and the balance of flavors between the ingredients were paramount. When I finally returned to sauces and butter — having realised that moderation was the key, not abstinence — I took with me the things from Asian cooking. The result is balance between the two. This section of the book may not be for purists. The stocks, for instance, are not traditional, but try them and taste the difference.

CHICKEN STOCK

MAKES 3 LITRES (6 PINTS)

This is the most used stock at Rockpool, either as the main stock in a sauce, or as a base for a more complicated sauce. I also use it with fish and shellfish as I don't like the flavor of fish stock; it also ages too quickly — within hours — to my taste. The only way to use fish stock is to make it and serve it immediately, as in fish soup.

With this stock look for nothing but the clear taste of chicken. It has a texture that's richer than most chicken stocks as it is made from the whole chicken and not just the bones. The use of whole chickens is very important as the rich mouth feel will not be there without the chicken flesh, nor will the flavor have any great depth. At Rockpool we have made this stock with all the different chickens available, and the verdict is: the best chicken makes the best stock. We use neither the aromatic vegetables that would be used in a French stock, nor ginger and spring onions that would be used in a Chinese stock.

Skim the stock well to ensure clarity, and never boil it vigorously. Boiling causes the fats that float to the surface to be taken back into the stock and distributed throughout, thus making it cloudy and flatter tasting.

INGREDIENTS
- 1 x 1.6 kg (3.5 lb) corn-fed chicken
- 3 litres (6 pints) water

METHOD
Wash the chicken and remove the fat from the cavity. With a large cook's knife or Chinese cleaver on chopping board, cut off the legs at the point where the thigh and drumstick meet. Cut into the flesh with the knife. Cut the wings off where they meet the breast then cut down the side of the chicken so the back comes off the breast. Cut the back and breast in half and again cut into the flesh slightly.

Place the chicken in a pot large enough to hold the chicken and water, and bring to the boil. As it boils turn down to a slow simmer, skim the stock well and simmer for 25 minutes. By this time the scum should have stopped coming to the surface. Turn the stove down until the surface is just moving and simmer for another 2½ hours.

Remove the stock from the stove and strain through some muslin or cheesecloth in a fine strainer. Discard the chicken and strain the stock again. This stock will last for 3 to 4 days in the refrigerator, or can be frozen for future use.

VEAL STOCK

MAKES 2 LITRES (4 PINTS)

While this stock is essentially French, we flavor and color it with fried onions, garlic and carrots. It is important to never boil your stock, or the protein solids and fats will go back through the stock and make it cloudy. Always start off a stock in cold water so the meat proteins coagulate slowly, gather, and float to the surface to be skimmed off. If they form too quickly, they will cloud the stock. Always skim the stock regularly. Instead of water, chicken or another veal stock can be used to start off the stock. The result is double stock, and because it has more flavor and a gelatinous quality, it needs little reduction, so what you have goes further. Don't pull the stock ingredients out of the stock before straining; much of the protein will be hanging onto the bones and meat, and you run the risk of clouding it. Ladle out the stock carefully through a fine strainer and tip the pot ever so gently at the end. Don't ruin the stock for the last 50 ml, it's not worth it. Strain the stock a second time.

INGREDIENTS

- 5 kg (11 lb) veal shanks, cut into rounds
- 15 cloves garlic
- 2 small or 1 large Spanish onion, finely diced
- 1 carrot, peeled and finely diced
- 500 ml (1 pint) vegetable oil
- 3 sprigs thyme
- 3 bay leaves
- 6 vine-ripened tomatoes, blanched, peeled, seeded and diced

METHOD

Preheat the oven to 220°C (425°F). Place the bones in a roasting tray and roast in the preheated oven until golden brown, turning once during the cooking time. Transfer the bones to a pot large enough to fit them snugly. Pour a little water into the roasting tray and scrape off all the residue. Add to the pot. Add enough water to just cover the bones. Place the pot on the stove over high heat and bring to the boil. Turn down to a gentle simmer and skim regularly for 30 minutes.

Place the garlic and Spanish onion in a mortar a pestle, and crush until you have a rough paste. Add the carrots and pound for another 2 minutes.

Heat up the vegetable oil in a wok. Add the vegetable paste and fry, stirring from time to time to stop the paste from burning, until it's dark brown. Strain the oil into a container and add the vegetables to the stock. It is important that the vegetables are very dark with being burnt, or the stock will be bitter.

Put the herbs and tomato dice into the stock and simmer very slowly, skimming from time to time, 5 hours. I believe that the bones have given up all good flavors and aromas by then. Any longer, and you get a stale taste that must then be tricked up to give it life.

Remove the pot from the stove and allow to cool. More fat will come to the surface as it cools. Skim off before straining. Carefully ladle the stock out of the pot and through a strainer. Lift the pot and allow the stock to run out freely, don't squeeze or push against bones as the sediment to run into the stock. Strain a second time though muslin and cool. The stock will last 5 to 6 days in the refrigerator, or it may be frozen until required.

RED-WINE REDUCTION

MAKES ABOUT ¾ CUP

This is probably the first sauce that most chefs learn to make, along with beurre blanc. Each step of the sauce needs to be followed carefully, so that each ingredient layers its flavor into the sauce. You will find a huge difference in flavor in sauces that have been reduced slowly and those that have been added together and boiled down to the desired consistency.

Red-wine reduction should be made with a full-bodied wine of good structure and reasonable quality. If it's not drinkable, then the sauce will also have those unappealing flavors. By the same token it's not necessary to use a great wine, as many of the nuances that make a great wine will be driven off during cooking. Don't use light-bodied wines as the structure is too light for a full-flavored sauce.

Cook some meat scraps or bacon with the reduction. The proteins in the meat will help reduce the tannins in the wine and remove the bitter and sour flavors. Whisking butter into the sauce just before serving also helps to fill out a sharp sauce. A dash of red-wine vinegar can enliven a flat sauce, and sharp acidic tastes can be removed from a sauce by adding a squeeze of fresh lemon juice. This reduction can be used as a base for a red-wine butter sauce. Or add veal stock for a red-wine demi-glace, or a combination of stock and butter for a sauce similar to a bordelaise, which has great affinity with bone marrow.

INGREDIENTS

- olive oil
- 1 small carrot, peeled and finely diced
- half a Spanish onion, peeled and finely diced
- 2 field mushrooms, chopped
- 2 cloves garlic, crushed and chopped
- 150 g (7 oz) meat trimmings, chopped
- 100 ml (3 fl oz) balsamic vinegar
- 50 ml (2 fl oz) red-wine vinegar
- 150 ml (7 fl oz) port
- 500 ml (1 pint) full-bodied red wine
- 2 sprigs thyme

METHOD

In a small saucepan pour in a little olive oil and add the carrot, onion, mushrooms, garlic and meat trimmings. Cook until the vegetables are lightly colored and the meat is well sealed.

Add the two vinegars and reduce to barely 50 ml. Pour in the port and reduce to about 50 ml. Add the red wine and thyme, and reduce to about 150 to 200 ml. Strain and reserve for use.

I think of red-wine sauce I automatically
...e marrow. The richness of the two just slide
...ther to create a wonderfully silky mouth
...asparagus and sweetbreads are another
... is close in texture, but soft and creamy in
...erent areas. The different elements of the
...similarities that layer themselves into one
...aste that is both creamy and soft. Make
...he bone marrow is poached gently in hot,
..., water. Be sure that it is cooked properly,
...ly one thing worse than eating tiny little
...lted bone marrow from overcooking, and
...ng a lump of hard fat from undercooking.
...applies to white asparagus, which requires
...oking than the green. This dish is great
...n some toasted brioche.

...NTS

(7 oz) bone marrow
(14 oz) veal sweetbreads
lt and freshly ground pepper
te asparagus
l (3 fl oz) Red-wine Reduction (page 124)
l (12 fl oz) reduced Veal Stock (page 123)
3 oz) unsalted butter, cold and cubed
s Brioche (page 223), toasted

METHOD

Soak the bone marrow overnight in coo...
remove some of the blood. Slice into large r...

Soak the sweetbreads overnight to remove...
The next day cover them in a pot with cold...
sea salt, and bring to the boil. Remove the sv...
once they float to the surface and when coo...
handle, peel off all the outer membrane. Pre...
2 dinner plates.

Break the last 2 cm (1 in) off the base of the...
and peel from top to bottom. Cook in sa...
water for 15 to 20 minutes. When tender r...
keep warm while you cook the marrow an...
sauce.

In a small pot on the stove over high hea...
red-wine reduction to the veal stock and r...
third. Add the butter and start whisking. Re...
the heat— and continue stirring, making su...
sauce is not over direct heat, if it comes ne...
will split. When the butter is completely inc...
season with salt and pepper. If the sauce...
squeeze in a drop or two of lemon juice. Ke...

Season the sweetbreads with salt and p...
sautê in some olive oil until golden brown....
lightly simmering salted water cook the bo...
until soft, about 2 minutes. Remove from th...

ROASTED FRESHWATER SALMON WITH RED-WINE AND BONE-MARROW SAUCE

SERVES SIX AS A MAIN COURSE

Freshwater salmon, salmon trout, brook trout and large trout all have an affinity with red-wine sauce and bone marrow; the rich earthiness of the fish marries so well with those same flavors in the wine. I first had a dish like this in France in 1984. It was served with cabbage and bacon, and I have since had versions of the dish at each of my restaurants. When I first started cooking this dish it had a red-wine butter sauce with braised cabbage and bone marrow. Then the cabbage took on a sweet-and-sour edge to cut the richness of the butter. Then the *beurre rouge* was turned into a red-wine sauce made from veal stock and red-wine reduction and the butter removed altogether. Eventually I realised that I needed a small quantity of butter to finish the sauce. The cabbage finally ended up with a palm sugar and rice-wine vinegar dressing. This dish has travelled a long way, changing all the time, I think, for the better. It is still rich, but now has a fresher edge due to the influences from other cultures.

INGREDIENTS

- 300 g (10.5 oz) bone marrow
- 1 x 1.8 kg (4 lb) freshwater salmon
- 150 ml (5 fl oz) Red-wine Reduction (page 124)
- 600 ml (1 pint 3 fl oz) Veal Stock (page 123)
- sea salt and freshly ground pepper
- olive oil
- 6 rashers bacon
- 30 g (1 oz) unsalted butter, cold and cubed

Braised Cabbage

- ½ Chinese cabbage
- 2 tablespoons sea salt
- 30 g (1 oz) unsalted butter
- 30 ml (1 fl oz) olive oil
- 1 small onion, very finely sliced
- 2 cloves garlic, crushed
- 1 knob ginger, peeled and cut into fine julienne
- 4 tablespoons palm sugar
- 6 tablespoons rice-wine vinegar
- 200 ml (7 fl oz) dry white wine

Soak the bone marrow overnight in cold water to remove some of the blood. Slice into thick round discs.

To make the Braised Cabbage, wash and dry the cabbage, sprinkle with salt and leave for 1 hour. Squeeze the excess water out of the cabbage, but don't wash. On the stove place a small pot and melt the butter in the oil. When it starts to foam add the onion, garlic and ginger, and cook until soft. Add the cabbage and stir for 3 minutes, then add the palm sugar. Once the sugar caramelizes, add the vinegar and cook for 2 more minutes. Add the white wine and turn down to a slow simmer and cook for 20 minutes.

Scale and fillet the fish as described in Tea-smoked Ocean Trout (page 64). Skin the fish. Cut the skin to fit the length of the fish and cover the two seams with the skin. Tie the fish at 2 cm intervals with kitchen string and trim the ends to form a square. Cut the fish in half, each half into 3, and set aside.

In a medium pot bring the red-wine reduction and veal stock to the boil. Lower the heat and reduce by two-thirds. Keep the sauce warm while you cook the fish.

Preheat the oven to 200°C (400°F).

Season the fish with salt and pepper. Heat some olive oil until almost smoking in a heavy-based frying pan. Add the fish and turn on all sides to color. Transfer to a baking dish and place in the preheated oven for 6 minutes. Remove and put in a warm place while you finish the sauce. It is very important to rest fish just as you would meat to allow it to relax and warm through to the centre.

In the same pan used for browning the fish, lightly sauté the bacon and place with the fish. Heat up the cabbage.

Put the bone marrow in a pot of hot, but not boiling water. Warm the sauce a little more and mount with the butter, whisking until the sauce falls from the whisk in ribbons. Check and adjust the seasoning.

Spoon the cabbage and a little juice into the centre of 6 large white bowls. Cut the string from the fish and place it on the cabbage. Top with the bacon, and with a slotted spoon, remove the bone marrow and put it on top of the bacon. Pour over the sauce and serve. Or put the sauce in a sauce boat and allow diners to help themselves. This also stops the sauce and cabbage juices from running everywhere and mingling too early.

MAYONNAISE

MAKES 1½ CUPS

This is one of the simplest sauces you can make, but once mastered you will use it often. Mayonnaise is versatile and lives happily in its various permutations with meat, fish and vegetables. To me, no other sauce offers the flavor sensation or versatility of the French garlic mayonnaise, aïoli. It is basically a thick, creamy dressing made from an emulsion of egg yolks, oil and vinegar or lemon juice. The critical point when making a mayonnaise is at the beginning, as you add the first lot of oil. It must be drizzled in very slowly, until the emulsion starts to take.

To make good mayonnaise, use good-quality oil, vinegar, fresh eggs, and lemon juice. For a basic mayonnaise I use only lemon juice, salt and pepper, and a good pure olive oil. I recommend hand-whisking your mayonnaise, I find machine-made mayonnaise lacks softness, and results in a heavier texture. If you break a mayonnaise put a little of the mix with a new egg yolk and carefully pour the split mix back in. Make sure that all the ingredients are at room temperature.

There are many variations on mayonnaise. The one I use most often is aïoli. What would bouillabaisse be without rouille and aïoli? Aïoli is also wonderful with fish, barbecued or roast meats, and with boiled vegetables. The next time artichokes are in season, boil them up and serve with some freshly made aïoli. You'll see what I mean.

We make aïoli in two ways. One is by adding raw garlic at the start with the lemon juice to give the finished aïoli a fresh bite. The other way is to add roasted and puréed garlic, which gives a rich, mellow finish that lends itself to barbecued and roast meats. Put a few stands of saffron in a little hot water,

incorporate, then whisk into the mayonnaise. We serve this mainly with mussels, and it's very special.

Mayonnaise is terrific with a little whipped cream and some horseradish. This goes well with beef, and surprisingly well with crayfish. In winter make a mustardy mayonnaise with lots of parsley. Fold through some julienned and blanched celeriac and you have the perfect accompaniment for cold meats. There is no end to the types of sauces possible using the different oils such as walnut, hazelnut, almond, truffle and sesame.

INGREDIENTS
- 3 egg yolks
- sea salt and freshly ground pepper
- 2 tablespoons fresh lemon juice
- 300 ml (10.5 fl oz) olive oil

METHOD
Place a pot on a bench large enough to hold a stainless-steel bowl. Make sure all the implements are very clean. Place a tea-towel around the edge of the pot and place the bowl on top of the towel to hold it steady while you whisk.

Place the eggs in the bowl and whisk. Add the sea salt and lemon juice, and, while whisking, drizzle in the oil very slowly. As the emulsion starts to form add the oil in a steady stream. Don't let the oil sit on the surface as this can cause the mayonnaise to split. Grind over some pepper and check for salt and lemon juice.

VINAIGRETTE

Vinaigrette is a basic sauce that blends together vinegar and oil. In the Rockpool kitchen it covers almost every type of dressing, including nam jims and nuoc chams. The vinaigrettes I make are strictly a combination of souring agent and oil. I don't like binding them with egg yolk to make them look more incorporated; I like the look of the puddles of oil with vinegar or lemon juice moving through.

Generally the ratio for salad dressing should be one-quarter vinegar or lemon juice to three-quarters oil. This is ideal for soft lettuces. As the strength of flavor and bitterness of the leaves increase so should the proportion of vinegar. The strength of the dressing must be proportional to the strength of the salad leaves to be dressed. Use good-quality extra-virgin olive oil with good balsamic, red-wine or sherry vinegar, or lemon juice, and season with garlic and herbs if you like. Adjust the acidity to suit your palate.

The following recipe gives a vinaigrette that we use to dress the house salad at Rockpool. I really am a product of the road I've travelled, and everything comes together best in my much loved salad.

GREEN SALAD

SERVES SIX

There are some things that I'm particular about and have been from the moment Rockpool opened. Most important was a sense of generosity and care for my customers. To me that manifests itself in the house salad that I'm a complete perfectionist about. Most people think I'm mad to give the salad to each customer who walks through the door, but I drive the staff to prepare it better and better everyday. Preparation takes two hours in the morning and in the evening.

I think salad is a very important part of the meal, a perfect palate cleanser, and for soaking up that little bit of juice left over from your main course. I have waiters serve it on the diners' plates towards the end of the meal so that each patron can get a sense of what I would like them to get out of the restaurant. For me, it's simple. The petit four, appetiser or salad that you give away is a sign of your generosity and care for your customers. These are the things that must be of the highest standard, and for me, there is nothing worse than poor hospitality. If you try hard with these everything else will fall into line.

The beautiful little lettuces and herbs for the Rockpool house salad are organically grown at my partner's farm, and picked when still tiny. To these we add mâche, coriander, dill, chervil, chives, tarragon and watercress. This salad dressing will bring out the flavor in your leaves. It has a touch of sweetness that lifts the strong flavors of the herbs.

INGREDIENTS
- 3 heads mâche
- ½ bunch tarragon
- 1 bunch coriander
- ½ bunch dill
- ½ bunch chervil
- 6 chives, cut into 2.5 cm (1 in) lengths
- 8 sprigs watercress
- small hearts of lettuces such as red oak, endive, cos and radicchio

Palm-Sugar vinaigrette
- 2 coriander (cilantro) roots
- 1 clove garlic
- 1 teaspoon sea salt
- 3 tablespoons palm sugar
- 2 teaspoon sherry vinegar
- 2 tablespoon red-wine vinegar
- 80 ml (3 fl oz) best-quality virgin olive oil
- 2 tablespoons chopped coriander (cilantro) leaves
- freshly ground white pepper

METHOD
To prepare the salad, soak the leaves in water for 5 minutes. Gently move them around in the sink, and spin them dry in a lettuce spinner, a handful at a time. Place them on a flat tray and refrigerate. Don't pile them up in a bucket or bowl.

To make the Palm-sugar Vinaigrette, crush the coriander roots, garlic and sea salt to a fine paste in a mortar and pestle. Caramelize the palm sugar in a small pot and add the sherry vinegar. Cook for 2 minutes, and allow to cool. Add the red-wine vinegar and palm sugar mixture to the coriander paste, then whisk in the olive oil.

To serve, put the salad mix in a bowl. Pour over the dressing and toss gently with the coriander leaves. Season with freshly ground pepper and carefully put on a plate. Serve immediately.

COMPOUND BUTTERS

Compound butters can be used in two ways: served straight on top of grilled or roast foods, or incorporated into sauces. I find the flavor and texture of seasoned butter in beurre blancs and so on more satisfying than plain butter, and have never moved away from using them. They were a staple at the Bluewater Grill, until I decided to do away with butter altogether. Over the years, however, I started to see the value in finishing sauces with butter again, though nowhere near the quantities I had used in the past. At Rockpool, we use a little butter to impart flavor and add a silkiness to the sauce; it's not too rich or hard to digest at all. Nearly all the butter that is used in the Rockpool sauces, with the exception of the red-wine sauce, are compound butters.

ANCHOVY BUTTER

MAKES 250 G (8 OZ)

I love this butter to pieces, and it's the one that turns up at home most of the time. It's wonderful with barbecued meat, especially beef and lamb. We use either Australian anchovies from Western Australia, which aren't true anchovies, but delicious all the same, and the Ortiz anchovies that Simon Johnson imports from Spain. This butter keeps for 3 to 4 days in the refrigerator, and freezes well.

INGREDIENTS
- 125 g (4 oz) anchovies
- 250 g (8 oz) unsalted butter
- lemon juice
- freshly ground pepper

METHOD
Purée the anchovies and butter in a food processor until well incorporated. Add the lemon juice and pepper. Roll in foil into a sausage shape or put in a container and refrigerate.

SEA-URCHIN BUTTER

MAKES 300 G (10.5 OZ)

This butter works well with all fish, especially with roasted blue-eye cod. Sea-urchin roe is available from fish markets or Japanese shops. It comes on wooden boards of about 100 g. If you can get live ones still in the shell, cut around the bottom beak with a pair of scissors, empty out the contents and remove the roe that is attached to the inside of the shell. The flesh is creamy, with a sweet sea flavor. This keeps for 2 to 3 days in the refrigerator and doesn't freeze well at all.

INGREDIENTS
- 200 g (7 oz) unsalted butter
- 100 g (3 oz) sea-urchin roe
- a pinch of sea salt
- freshly ground pepper
- lemon juice

METHOD
Process the butter and add the roe. Don't overwork or allow the roe to get hot. Season with salt and pepper, add the lemon juice and roll in foil in a sausage shape, or place in a container and refrigerate.

SHRIMP BUTTER

MAKES 250 G (8 OZ)

I like the flavor combination of chicken and prawn, and this very versatile butter is often used at Rockpool for poaching yabbies and spring vegetables, and to finish off chicken sauces. It freezes well, and is the ideal thing to make when you have leftover prawn shells. Although we use about 7 kilos of king prawns a day cooks are always fighting for them as we use the shells to make spicy prawn sauce, prawn jelly, prawn oil and this butter. The most important thing to remember is not to add the prawn shells to the butter while they are still hot, or even warm, or the butter will split.

The color compounds in crustacean shells don't fully dissolve in water or stock-based sauces, therefore it is important to use the oils to lift all the possible flavor out of the shells. The butter keeps for 3 to 4 days, refrigerated, or in the freezer.

INGREDIENTS
- 100 ml (3 fl oz) olive oil
- 500 g (1 lb) prawn (shrimp) shells
- 250 g (8 oz) unsalted butter
- sea salt
- lemon juice

METHOD

Pour the olive oil into a heavy-based frying pan. When the oil is hot add the prawn shells, and saute until they are well colored and the oil is red. Remove the pan from the heat and allow the shells to cool completely.

Puree the shells in a food processor. Add the butter and continue to process until they are well incorporated. Add the salt and lemon juice, and push the butter through a drum sieve. Roll in foil into a sausage shape or store in a container in the fridge.

MUSSEL AND SAFFRON BUTTER

MAKES 300 G (10OZ)

This butter works well with scallops or pan-fried fish such as John Dory or sole. You can sieve the butter if you wish, but I find that pieces of mussel left in the butter as it melts reinforces the texture and flavor. Make sure the saffron is soaked in the mussel water before use as it is a water-based spice, and will not release all its aroma and color if placed directly in the butter. The butter keeps for 3 days in the refrigerator.

INGREDIENTS
- 500 g (1 lb) mussels, debearded
- water
- 1 teaspoon saffron
- 250 g (8oz) unsalted butter
- lemon juice

METHOD

Bring the mussels to a boil in a pot large enough to hold the mussels with a little water. Cover the pot, give it a shake, and when the mussels have opened remove from the heat. When cool enough to handle remove the mussels from the shell, and set side. Strain the cooking liquid into a small pot. Add the saffron, bring the liquid to a boil, and reduce the juices to 50 ml (2 fl oz). Allow to cool.

In a food processor puree the mussels, cooking liquid and butter. Add the lemon juice to taste and roll in foil into a sausage shape or place in a container and refrigerate.

YABBIES POACHED IN SHRIMP BUTTER WITH SPRING VEGETABLES

SERVES FOUR AS A STARTER

This dish is an example of how I use butter now. I prepare many dishes in this way, and they are lighter, but still full-flavored. The sauce is more broth-like and nowhere as thick as it used to be.

Yabbies are similar to American crawfish and European écrevisses, and either could be substituted. Fresh green soybeans provide a nice nutty character to the dish. Prepare them as you would broad beans, just blanch the beans and shell.

INGREDIENTS

- 24 live yabbies
- 8 baby turnips, peeled and washed
- 8 golfball carrots, peeled and washed
- 300 g (10 oz) fresh peas, shelled
- 300 ml (10 fl oz) Chicken Stock (page 122)
- 300 g (10 oz) fresh soybeans, blanched and shelled
- 100 g (3 oz) Shrimp Butter (page 134), cold and cubed
- 10 Thai sweet basil leaves
- lemon juice
- sea salt and freshly ground pepper

METHOD

Bring some salted water to a boil in a pot large enough to hold the yabbies. When it's boiling plunge in the yabbies for 3 minutes. Remove and allow to cool. Peel the yabbies, crack the claws, and remove the intestinal tract. The shells can be used to make a flavored oil or butter if you wish.

In a little pot of boiling salted water cook the turnips for 3 minutes. Refresh in ice-water. Tip out the used water and boil up some water again to cook the carrots. Tip out the used water, top up the pot again and add some salt, a little sugar and some butter. Boil the peas for 1½ minutes. Refresh and drain.

In a pot bring the chicken stock to the boil. Add the soybeans and yabbies. Allow the ingredients to heat through, but don't boil or the yabbies will shrink. After a moment or two add the cubed butter, piece by piece, and whisk gently until it falls from the whisk in ribbons. Add the basil and remove from the heat while you incorporate the rest of the butter. Squeeze over some lemon juice, add some salt and pepper to taste.

To serve, divide the ingredients between the 4 warm bowls and pour over the broth. Serve immediately.

JERUSALEM ARTICHOKE AND MARRON SALAD

SERVES SIX AS A STARTER

This simple salad uses one of my favorite autumn vegetables, Jerusalem artichokes. These tubers are related to sunflowers, but have a flavor that is incredibly similar to artichokes. As the much loved fruits of summer give way to the vegetables of autumn and winter it is a terrific time to make salads from produce other than lettuce. The array is never-ending: fennel, artichoke, broad beans, celeriac and baby leeks — it just keeps on coming.

One year Damien Pignolet, then owner of Claude's, asked Tim Pak Poy to prepare a birthday dinner for me. The first thing to arrive at the table was a slow-roasted Jerusalem artichoke, served with a little crème fraîche and topped with fresh Black Pearl Osietra caviar. The flavor combination was wonderful, and what a treat it was.

For this salad, I have braised the artichokes and served them at room temperature. If marrons prove too difficult to find, use prawns or freshwater crayfish.

INGREDIENTS

- 6 x 250 g (8 oz) live marron
- 6 Jerusalem artichokes
- 60 ml (2fl oz) olive oil
- 12 red shallots, peeled
- 12 cloves garlic, blanched once in boiling water and peeled
- sea salt and freshly ground pepper
- 400 ml (14 fl oz) chicken stock (page 122)
- 100 ml (3 fl oz) balsamic vinegar
- 125 g (4 oz) flat-leaf parsley, cut into julienne
- 125 g (4 oz) mitzuna, cut into julienne
- 200 ml (5 fl oz) Marron Oil (page 138)
- 50 ml (2 fl oz) lemon juice
- 250 g (8 oz) twice-peeled broad beans, blanched quickly

METHOD

Bring a pot of salted water to the boil and plunge in the marrons. Cook for 4 minutes and remove. Allow to cool to room temperature, this will make sure the fish are not overcooked. Pull out the intestinal tract and peel the claws, leaving the body whole.

Peel the Jerusalem artichokes and cut them to the same size as the shallots. In a small pot add the olive oil and when it heats up add the shallots, garlic and diced artichokes. Salt well and stir for a minute or two. Add the chicken stock and simmer gently until all the stock has disappeared. Add the balsamic vinegar and cook until it is almost gone. Remove from the stove and spoon into a bowl and allow to cool. When it is at room temperature stir in the parsley and mitzuna, and season with pepper.

Mix the marron oil and lemon juice. To serve, divide the artichoke mixture evenly between 6 large white plates. Place a marron on top of each, then the peeled claws and the broad beans, and drizzle the oil over the top. Grind over some pepper and serve immediately.

MARRON OIL

MAKES 500 ML

This oil can be made with the shells of any crustacean and makes a wonderful vinaigrette. You can use a flavorless base oil such as vegetable oil to allow the full flavor of the shells to come to the fore. You'll get a far-superior tasting oil by using a good extra-virgin olive oil with the addition of some aromatics and cumin; the finished oil will have more complexity and a depth of flavor.

Marrons are a type of Australian freshwater crayfish, and are generally black in color. There is a blue variety with red claws, but is the black-shelled variety that is superior. Their delicate flavor and crunchy texture, make them ideal for salads.

The shells for this oil have to be crushed. You can do that by placing small amounts of shell in a food processor or bamix, but by far the easiest way is to wrap them up in a tea-towel and crush them with a rolling pin or the back of a cleaver. The oil keeps for a week in the refrigerator.

INGREDIENTS

- 60 ml (2 fl oz) olive oil
- 1 small onion, peeled and finely diced
- 1 small carrot, peeled and finely diced
- 2 cloves garlic, crushed
- 2 tablespoons cumin seeds, roasted and ground
- 1 kg (2lb) marron shells, cleaned and crushed
- 400 ml (14 fl oz) extra-virgin olive oil

METHOD
Heat up the olive oil in a large pot. Add the onion, carrot and garlic, and fry until golden brown, about 20 minutes. Add the cumin and cook for a further 5 minutes, stirring all the time so it doesn't burn. Add the shells and stir for 3 minutes. Add the extra-virgin olive oil and remove from the direct heat to a part of the stove that is warm. Leave to infuse for 1 hour, and strain through a fine sieve.

ROASTING

The roasting of meats and birds used to be done over fires on a spit. These days we normally roast in dry heat in an oven. Decide which temperature you want to roast in, as the meat will cook in quite a different way, producing slight differences in flavor and texture. Whichever way you choose to cook, use a method that maintains the integrity of the produce, and works best for you. Both are as good.

High-temperature roasting leaves a delicious crust on the outside, and sends the juices to the centre. When the meat is rested those juices will flow through the flesh, giving it a pink-to-red tinge and moistness. High-temperature roasting works well with prime cuts that are low in sinew, such as fillet and sirloin.

Slow-roasting involves cooking the meat in very low heat for a long time. Because the meat cooks very slowly it will be very pink throughout, and you'll get a beautiful rosiness. This way of cooking produces meltingly tender flesh, and works very well with some of the more sinewy and fatty cuts of meat like the shoulder, rump and round. While you won't get the lovely crust, you will have much less shrinkage.

For me, little is more delicious than a slow-roasted rack of lamb on the bone in a very low oven (less than 100°C/210°F). After 1 hour, take out the rack and allow to rest. Pull out all the fat and bones, and sear the lamb loin. This way, you'll get a beautiful crust with a melting finish.

I find slow-cooking works best for veal and any of the leg cuts. Wrap the meat in caul fat beforehand to stop it from drying out. Always season your meat before roasting and again as it rests to really bring out the flavor. Brush the meat with olive oil or roast it in a combination of butter and olive oil. If you're cooking over high heat seal the meat really well to give it a good hard, crisp coating. Put it in the oven and allow a third of its cooking time to be at 200°C (400°F), then lower to about 180°C (350°F) for the rest of the cooking time. It's very important to rest the meat before slicing and serving. Resting allows all the blood that's rushed to the centre of the meat to come out as the meat cools down, and really changes the tenderness dramatically. The juices caught in the roasting pan make a delicious sauce.

There is nothing as satisfying as a well-roasted chicken. A free-range chicken weighing about 2 kg will feed a family of four. Take the time to rest the chicken after it comes out of the oven. The juices can be mixed with some good olive oil, seasoned with salt and pepper, and finished off with either lemon juice or good red-wine vinegar. I like to serve this with a Green Salad (page 131), Potato Gratin (page 149) and garlic that the chicken has been roasted with.

INGREDIENTS

- 1 x 2 kg (4 lb) free-range chicken
- 2 tablespoons unsalted butter
- sea salt and freshly ground pepper
- 6 sprigs thyme
- 3 heads garlic, in cloves, blanched in salted boiling water and drained
- 2 tablespoons extra-virgin olive oil
- lemon juice
- extra-virgin olive oil

METHOD

Preheat the oven to 200°C (400°F).

Remove the chicken fat from the cavity and cut off the neck and ends of the wing. Reserve. Pull back the skin slightly over the breast and remove the wishbone with a sharp knife (this will make carving easier). Smear the butter over the chicken and season well with salt.

Place the chicken in a heavy-based roasting pan and add the neck, wing end, thyme and garlic. Pour olive oil over the chicken and garlic. Put the chicken in the preheated oven front-side towards the back and cook for 20 minutes. Baste and turn the oven down to 150°C (300°F) and cook for a further 50 minutes. Remove from the oven and cover with foil. Allow to rest for 20 minutes.

Tip the chicken juices from the cavity into the roasting pan. Add the lemon juice and extra-virgin olive oil. Scrape the bottom of the pan to remove all the stuck solids, season with salt and pepper, and spoon the dressing and garlic cloves over the chicken.

To serve, cut off the legs and breasts, joint the legs, and cut the breasts in half. On 4 warm plates put down a piece of leg, some breast on top, and a piece of potato gratin. Serve immediately with crusty bread and green salad.

ROAST SADDLE OF VENISON WITH CELERIAC AND HERB SALAD

SERVES TWELVE

I have cooked this dish for 100 in New Zealand, and also at a Krug dinner for the Australian Chamber Orchestra in 1995 to much success. Venison is one of the only game meats that doesn't suffer too much from being farmed. It cooks far better on the bone than off, and is ideal if you're planning a party of twelve to fourteen people. Be careful not to overcook the venison; it is very lean and dries out easily.

It was amazing to work in the kitchen in New Zealand, watching five people pick herbs for the salad, which took over four hours. When I did the same for the Krug dinner, and enlisted the help of all the waiters, someone yelled out 'Good idea, chef' (I think not). A saddle of deer will serve around eight people, and red deer, around twelve.

INGREDIENTS
- 1 x about 4 kg (8 lb) saddle venison
- sea salt and freshly ground pepper
- 100 ml (3 fl oz) olive oil
- 100 ml (3 fl oz) extra-virgin olive oil

Celeriac Purée
- 600 g (1 lb 3 oz) celeriac, peeled
- 400 g (14 oz) pink-eye potatoes, peeled
- 2 Granny Smiths, peeled
- 100 ml (3 fl oz) extra-virgin olive oil
- lemon juice
- sea salt and freshly ground pepper

Herb Salad
- 2 heads mâche
- 1 bunch mint
- 2 bunches chervil
- 1 bunch tarragon
- 2 bunches coriander
- 1 bunch dill
- 100 ml (3 fl oz) Palm-sugar Vinaigrette (page 131)

METHOD
Preheat the oven to 220°C (425°F).

With a sharp knife cut the silver sinew of the venison loin to expose the red-colored meat. Season well with sea salt and drizzle with olive oil. Put in a baking tray large enough to hold the saddle and place in the preheated oven. Roast for 20 minutes, then remove. Place some foil loosely over the roasting tray, and allow to rest for 15 minutes. To make the dressing for the venison, add the extra-virgin olive oil to the roasting juices. Taste and season.

To make the Celeriac Purée, place the celeriac and potatoes in a steamer over simmering water and steam for 20 minutes. Add the apples and steam for a further 10 minutes. Remove when they are soft. Pass the celeriac, potato and apples through a food mill. Place in a bowl and slowly incorporate the extra-virgin olive oil, lemon juice, salt and pepper. Keep warm in a bain-marie or in a slow steamer.

To prepare the Salad, pick and wash all the leaves from the mâche and herbs. Combine and refrigerate.

To serve, place a spoonful of celeriac purée to the side of each plate. Toss the herb salad with the palm-sugar vinaigrette in a bowl, and place next to the celeriac purée. Remove the loin from the saddle and slice. Place the meat in the centre of the plates, and pour the venison dressing over the meat. Serve immediately.

ROAST ILLABO LAMB WITH TOMATO, OLIVES AND AÏOLI

SERVES SIX AS A MAIN COURSE

The availability of Illabo lamb on the Australian market is due to Tony Lehmann's efforts. He is one of the few Australian producers who understands what the market wants, and delivers, in no uncertain terms, a quality product that is markedly better than the bland, generic produce grown for the large corporations. It is because of suppliers like Tony that the quality and variety of fine produce we have available in Australia is maintained. This is the driving force behind fabulous multicultural cooking.

This dish is flavorsome, tender and has a wonderful clean taste that is unmatched. The accompanying sauce rich, flavorsome and has no Asian ingredients, except for little ginger, for good luck. The only necessary addition is green salad à la Rockpool. The recipe for Tomato Jam yields 750 ml (1 pint 8 fl oz). It is also very good with raw fish, and will keep for up to a month in the refrigerator.

INGREDIENTS
- 2 x 1 kg (2 lb) Illabo or other milk-fed lamb legs
- sea salt and freshly ground pepper
- olive oil
- 1 kg (2 lb) pink-eye potatoes, boiled in their skins in salted water for 20 minutes, peeled and quartered
- 18 large green olives
- 18 large black olives

Tomato Jam
- 15 vine-ripened tomatoes, cored
- 1 Spanish onion, peeled and finely diced
- 10 cloves garlic, crushed
- 2 large knobs ginger, peeled and chopped
- 400 ml (14 fl oz) olive oil
- 1 tablespoon fennel seeds, roasted and ground
- 1 tablespoon coriander seeds, roasted and ground
- 1 teaspoon cumin, roasted and ground
- 6 tablespoons palm sugar
- 4 tablespoons fish sauce
- 6 tablespoons red-wine vinegar

Aïoli
- 125 ml (4 fl oz) extra-virgin olive oil

- 125 ml (4 fl oz) olive oil
- 3 cloves garlic
- 1 teaspoon sea salt
- 3 egg yolks
- juice of half a lemon
- freshly ground pepper

Braised Vegetables
- 1 large eggplant
- olive oil
- 10 basil leaves
- 15 flat-leaf parsley leaves
- 100 ml (3 fl oz) extra-virgin olive oil
- 1 small onion, peeled and cut into small dice
- 3 cloves garlic, crushed
- sea salt and freshly ground pepper
- 2 red capsicums, seeded and cut into small dice
- 3 anchovies, minced
- 2 vine-ripened tomatoes, blanched, peeled, seeded and cut into small dice
- 25 small capers, rinsed
- lemon juice

METHOD

Preheat the oven to 180°C (350°F).

To make the Tomato Jam, place the tomatoes in the preheated oven for 20 to 30 minutes. Put the tomatoes through a food mill. In a food processor or bamix purée the onion, garlic and ginger with 100 ml of the olive oil. Add the ground fennel, coriander and cumin to the onion mix.

Place a heavy-based pot on the stove and pour in the remaining olive oil. Add the paste, and cook for 30 minutes over low heat or until the paste caramelizes. Put in the palm sugar and allow to caramelize. Add the fish sauce and reduce slightly. Add the vinegar and cook for 1 minute, then the tomato juice. Stir, and cook slowly for 2 hours. You should be left with a thick, spicy and sweet jam with no liquid. To store, place in a sterilized jar, cover with a film of oil and refrigerate.

To make the Aïoli, first combine the olive oils. Crush the garlic and salt together in a mortar and pestle. Whisk in the egg yolks, add the lemon juice and continue whisking while adding the olive oils in a thin stream until the emulsion thickens. Taste and adjust the seasoning if necessary.

To make the Braised Vegetables, peel the eggplant and cut the skins into small cubes (reserve the flesh for another use). Pour the olive oil into a heavy-based saucepan. Add the eggplant skins and fry until golden brown. Remove, and add the basil and parsley. Fry until dark green and crisp. Remove and strain the oil, reserving it for another use. Pour the extra-virgin olive oil into the pan and heat. Put in the onion, garlic and sea salt, and cook until soft. Add the capsicums and anchovies, and cook for a further 2 minutes. Add the tomatoes, herbs and capers, and return the eggplant to the pan. Add the lemon juice and taste for seasoning. Cook for 1 minute, then remove and set aside.

Preheat the oven to 200°C (400°F).

Trim any excess fat off the lamb legs, leaving the shank on. Rub all over with sea salt and olive oil, and place in the preheated oven for 10 minutes. Turn the lamb and add the potatoes. Cook for a further 15 minutes. Turn off the oven, remove the potatoes and cover the lamb loosely with foil. Leave the oven door open, and rest the lamb for 15 minutes.

In a pot combine the braised vegetables with the tomato jam in a 3:1 ratio. Add the olives and potatoes. Heat through, but don't boil.

Remove the lamb from the oven. Divide the vegetables and potatoes between 6 large white plates. Carve the lamb and place on top of the vegetables. Spoon over the aïoli, and grind over some pepper. Serve immediately.

SWORDFISH WITH SMOKED PORK CHEEK AND BLACK VINEGAR

SERVES SIX

Swordfish is ideal for roasting and grilling. Cooked this way, the fish retains a firm crust that slices into a rare, melt-in-the-mouth centre. I use a Chinese black rice vinegar to sharpen the sauce, and reduce the veal stock until it is quite syrupy. The combination of smoked pork cheek and fish works well together, and the creamy potato sets the dish off beautifully. Pork cheek is readily available whole or sliced from a good butcher, just like prosciutto.

INGREDIENTS
- 1 x 1 kg (2 lb) swordfish, in one piece, skin on
- sea salt and freshly ground pepper
- olive oil
- 1 bunch asparagus
- 12 slices smoked pork cheek

Mashed Potato
- 400 g (14 oz) bintje potatoes
- sea salt and freshly ground pepper

- 100 ml (3 fl oz) milk
- 150 g (5 oz) unsalted butter, cut into 2 cm (1 in) cubes
- lemon juice

Black Vinegar Jus
- 150 ml (5 fl oz) Chinese black rice vinegar
- 700 ml (1 pint 5 fl oz) Veal Stock (page 123)
- sea salt
- lemon juice

METHOD

To make the Mashed Potato, either steam the potatoes or boil them in their skins for about 20 minutes. When cool enough to handle peel and put through a food mill. In a saucepan over medium heat place the potatoes and season with sea salt. In another saucepan heat the milk, but don't boil. Add the milk to the potatoes in a thin stream while stirring with a wooden spoon. Add the butter, a cube at a time, stirring to incorporate. At this stage the mixture should be soft and creamy. Check for seasoning and add a little lemon juice to lift the potato flavor. Keep warm while cooking the fish. Try substituting extra-virgin olive oil instead of butter if you like, the result is quite wonderful.

To make the Black Vinegar Jus, in a stainless-steel saucepan add the vinegar and reduce by half. Add the veal stock and reduce to 180 ml (6 fl oz). Taste, and season with salt and lemon juice. Keep warm.

Preheat the oven to 220°C (425°F).

Cut the swordfish in half so that both pieces have some skin on. Cut each half into 3 for 6 thick chunks. Season with sea salt.

In two heavy-based frying pans heat up some olive oil until it's nearly smoking. Add 3 pieces of fish to each and brown on all sides. Place the pan with the fish in the preheated oven and cook for 5 minutes. Turn off the oven and open the door. Rest for 10 minutes.

Trim off the last 2 cm (1 in) of the asparagus and halve. Cut each half down the middle and then into julienne strips. Cook the asparagus in salted boiling water for 1 minute and remove.

Add the pork cheeks to the warm sauce, don't boil. Cut each piece of fish into three slices (it should be rare inside).

To serve, place a dollop of mashed potato in the middle of 6 large white plates. Place the fish on the potato and then some asparagus on the fish. Put slices of pork cheek on top of the asparagus and strain 30 ml of the jus over each plate. Grind over some pepper and serve immediately.

HERB-CRUSTED BLUE-EYE COD WITH SEA-URCHIN BUTTER

SERVES SIX AS A MAIN COURSE

Blue-eye cod is one of the best eating fishes in Australia. It has sweet, white flesh and is oily enough to be roasted and grilled. It's also lovely steamed, and flakes beautifully. The sauce is a delicious broth flavored with sea-urchin butter and chicken stock, which gives richness without being too heavy. The herb crust has a few Asian flavors thrown in for good measure. The crisp and caramelized potato gratin offers a lovely textural and flavor dimension to the dish.

INGREDIENTS

- 1 x 1 kg (2 lb) blue-eye cod, skinned
- 600 ml (1 pint 3 fl oz) Chicken Stock (page 122)
- 200 g (5 oz) Sea-urchin Butter (page 133), cold and cut into 1 cm (0.5 in) cubes
- sea salt and freshly ground pepper
- lemon juice
- 6 tablespoons flying-fish roe

Herb Crust

- 4 slices sourdough bread
- 2 tablespoons palm sugar
- 2 tablespoons fish sauce

- 250 g unsalted butter, softened
- leaves from ½ bunch coriander (cilantro)
- 5 coriander (cilantro) roots, crushed to a paste
- 1 large knob ginger, peeled and cut into fine julienne
- 6 red shallots, finely sliced
- 20 coriander (cilantro) seeds, toasted and ground

Potato Gratin

- 6 bintje potatoes, peeled
- 50 g (2 oz) unsalted butter
- 200 ml (7 fl oz) cream (35 per cent butterfat)
- sea salt and freshly ground pepper

METHOD

To make the Herb Crust, lightly toast the bread and process into breadcrumbs. Caramelize the palm sugar in a saucepan, add the fish sauce, and allow to cool. Place all the other ingredients in another bowl with the breadcrumbs and add the cooled palm sugar mixture. Mix until the crust sticks together. Refrigerate until needed.

Preheat the oven to 180°C (350°F).

To make the Potato Gratin, cut the potatoes into slices of 1 mm thickness. Butter a 30 cm x 20 cm (12 in x 8 in) baking tray, and place the sliced potatoes in a line down the tray, overlapping slightly. There should be enough for three layers. Pour over the cream and season with salt and pepper. Cook in the preheated oven for 30 minutes, or until the cream has been absorbed and the potatoes cooked. Keep warm.

Preheat the oven to 220°C (425°F).

Cut the blue-eye cod into 6 equal portions. Flatten the herb crust out on a bench and cut to fit the top of each piece of fish. Lift the herb crust off the bench with a fish lifter and place on top of the fish. Place the fish in a baking tray and pour over a little chicken stock to keep them moist during cooking. Place the fish in the preheated oven and cook for about 12 minutes. The crust should start to crisp up and color. Open the oven door and turn off the oven. Allow the fish to rest while you make the sauce.

In a saucepan bring the remaining chicken stock to the boil. Remove from the heat and whisk in the butter, a cube at a time, until all the butter is incorporated. Season with salt, freshly ground pepper and lemon juice, and keep warm.

To serve, cut the gratin into 6 pieces about the same size as the fish. Remove the fish from the oven, a place a piece of fish in the middle of each bowl. Place a gratin on top. Stir the flying-fish roe into the sauce and spoon around the fish. Serve immediately.

SAUTÉING

Sautéing is one of my favorite ways of cooking poultry and fish. It seals the meat, giving it a really lovely crust and seals in all the juices. Fish, shellfish and thin slices of meat should be seared very quickly on both sides and then allowed to rest a few moments before being served. Be careful not to put too much oil in the pan (that is shallow-frying), and allow the pan to heat up before using. Don't add too many ingredients to the pan when sautéing; this will result in a drop in temperature, causing the food to stew.

Sautéing can be done in oil or a combination of oil and butter. (The oil stops the butter from burning.) Sautéing also leaves behind pan juices that can be turned into a delicious dressing or sauce.

My favorite sauté dish is chicken with vinegar, a crisp-skinned chicken cooked on the bone. The flesh is meltingly soft, with lovely caramelized juices. This was something that we used to cook at Stephanie's for Friday lunch and I continued to cook it while at Barrenjoey House. It's also easy. Take a 1.8 kg corn-fed chicken. Cut out the drumsticks, thighs and breasts (leave the winglets on). Season the chicken well and sauté in olive oil and butter until a lovely crust forms. Lower the heat, add a little stock, and let it cook slowly on top of the stove for 20 minutes. As the stock disappears the juices from the chicken will be released. Deglaze the pan with a tablespoon of good red-wine vinegar, throw in a lump of butter and swirl round the pan. Grind over some pepper, sprinkle over some chopped parsley, and serve. This makes an absolutely fantastic Sunday lunch dish served with pasta or roast potatoes.

SAUTÉED SEA SCALLOPS WITH MUSSEL AND SAFFRON BUTTER AND ASPARAGUS SALAD

SERVES SIX

This dish is very easy to prepare, and a perfect starter to a dinner with a more complicated main course. When serving ensure that the asparagus and mâche are at room temperature. The sea scallops must be of the highest quality: round, very firm and dry, almost greasy. Make sure they have not been sitting in water — fish absorb fresh water very quickly, which dilutes their flavors and has an adverse effect on the texture. Soaked scallops will also shrink during cooking, and the water that leaches out will also stop them from caramelising properly. The asparagus should be smooth skinned, without dimples, be heavy for its size, and pliable.

INGREDIENTS

- 18 spears large asparagus
- 24 large sea scallops
- sea salt and freshly ground pepper
- 60 ml (2 fl oz) olive oil
- 30 ml (1 fl oz) water
- 180 g (6 oz) Mussel and Saffron Butter (page 135), diced and at room temperature
- lemon juice
- 100 ml (3 fl oz) extra-virgin olive oil
- leaves from 6 heads mâche, washed and dried

METHOD

Break off the last 2 cm (1 in) of the asparagus, and peel from tip to base very carefully. Bring a large pot of salted water to the boil and put in the asparagus. Cook for 4 minutes until tender. Take out with a slotted spoon and refresh in ice-water. Pat dry with kitchen paper, and cut the asparagus on an angle every 6 cm (3 in).

Season the scallops with a little salt. In a heavy-based frying pan put in 2 teaspoon of the olive oil and turn up the heat to high. Just before it smokes add 6 of the scallops, and cook until caramelized. Turn over and cook the other side. Remove with a fish lifter and place on a plate. Add a little more oil and sear the others, 6 at a time, until all the scallops are cooked. They should be brown and crispy on the outside and still rare in the middle.

Pour the water into the pan and add the butter, scraping the bottom of the pan to remove all the crusted flavors. Swirl the pan around, allow it to split a little, and add the lemon juice and the extra-virgin olive oil.

Divide the asparagus and mâche between the 6 plates. Make a little pile in the centre of each plate, place 4 scallops on top, and pour over the sauce. Grind over some pepper and serve immediately.

HERB AND SPICE CRUSTED TUNA WITH AUBERGINE SALAD

SERVES FOUR

This dish was on the menu from the day Rockpool opened. It has endured quite simply for one reason — it is perfect.

Tuna and chermoula are made for each other. To me chermoula is like the gang pastes of Thailand — there are many varieties, and it's up to you to decide what you wish to do with them. In most Moroccan dishes chermoula would figure in the initial marinade and be used during the cooking process. It is blackened to add another dimension of flavor and texture to this dish. Any leftovers will last for up to a week in the refrigerator.

My memories of those first few months at Rockpool are of running round the kitchen around lunchtime, setting up for service. We'd all be starving, but there would always be a container of freshly made eggplant salad. So in the interests of keeping the show on the road we would all grab a roll, throw on some salad and gulp it down just as the first of the punters walked in the door. I remember working lunch and dinner every day for 4 months, and good as they were, I got so sick of those eggplant rolls. I still have the odd eggplant sandwich for lunch these days; relieved that it's not every day. Instead of serving the eggplant salad with fiery harissa, I've used a luscious red pepper oil.

INGREDIENTS
- 4 x 200 g (7 oz) tuna steaks
- olive oil
- juice of 1 lemon

Red Pepper Oil
- 2 large red capsicums
- sea salt
- 150 ml (5 fl oz) extra-virgin olive oil
- juice of 1 lemon
-

Braised Aubergine Salad
- 3 eggplants (aubergine), sliced into 1 cm (0.5 in) rounds
- sea salt and freshly ground pepper
- olive oil
- 3 tablespoons flat-leaf parsley leaves

- 4 vine-ripened tomatoes, blanched, peeled, seeded and diced
- 1 tablespoon ground cumin
- lemon juice
-

Chermoula
- ½ bunch flat-leaf parsley
- ½ bunch coriander (cilantro)
- 1 large Spanish onion
- 4 cloves garlic
- 1 tablespoon ground cumin
- 1 tablespoon ground turmeric
- 1 tablespoon chili powder
- ½ tablespoon paprika
- 1 teaspoon sea salt
- 150 ml (5 fl oz) olive oil
- juice of 1 lemon

METHOD

To make Red Pepper Oil, roast a capsicum in the oven or over a barbecue. When blackened place in a bowl and cover with cling wrap. The steam makes the capsicum easier to peel. Slice the other capsicum and seed. Put through a juice extractor to obtain the juice and throw out the fibres. Peel the blackened capsicum and cut the flesh into julienne. Add the capsicum juice and a good pinch of sea salt. Place in a small pot and simmer on top of the stove for 10 minutes over medium heat. Add the olive oil, lower the heat, and allow to stew for 10 minutes. Add the lemon juice and allow to cool to room temperature.

To make the Braised Aubergine Salad, salt the eggplants and leave for 1 hour. Wash and dry with kitchen paper. In a large frying pan heat enough olive oil to shallow-fry the eggplants in two or three batches until dark brown on both sides. Transfer to a bowl. Put the parsley in the hot oil and fry until crisp (stand back, it will spit). Remove the parsley and place with the eggplant. Tip out most of the oil, leaving about a cup in the pan. Add the tomatoes and cumin, and stir for 3 minutes to cook out the spices. Return the eggplant and parsley to the pan, and stir for 1 minute. Add the lemon juice and check for salt and pepper. Keep warm.

To make the Chermoula, place everything except the olive oil and lemon juice in a food processor or bamix. Process for 1 minute and slowly pour in the olive oil until a thick paste forms. Stir through the lemon juice. If making ahead, refrigerate until ready to use.

Preheat the oven to 100°C (210°F).

Coat both sides of the tuna evenly with the chermoula. Heat 2 heavy-based frying pans that will each hold 2 serves of tuna and, in each, pour in 20 ml of olive oil. Heat until almost smoking. Add the tuna and sear. Don't jiggle or move the pans about as it will stop a firm crust from forming. Cook for 2 minutes and, with a fish lifter, gently turn the fish and cook for another 1½ minutes. Transfer to a plate and place the fish in a warm oven with the door slightly ajar for 5 minutes. The tuna will still be very rare in the centre, but warmed through.

To serve, on 4 large white plates place a spoonful of eggplant salad, and over that pour some red pepper oil. Place the tuna steak on top and finish with a squeeze of lemon. Serve immediately.

SAUTÉED GREEN-LIP ABALONE AND VEAL SWEETBREADS

SERVES FOUR TO SIX AS A STARTER

Abalone is one of the great taste sensations and, like a freshly shucked oyster, tastes at its best if cooked as soon as possible after it's been opened. You can shuck and slice them very finely, then stir-fry with ginger and beansprouts for a few seconds. Or, flatten it with a rolling pin and sauté it as a big steak with lemon and butter. After you shuck the abalone trim away the hard lip. Place it in a plastic freezer bag, and bash it with a rolling pin or the back of a cleaver until it is of 1 cm thickness. Be careful not to break it up.

INGREDIENTS

- 400 g (14 oz) veal sweetbreads, soaked in salted water
  overnight
- 1 x 600 g to 750 g (1.3 to 1.7 lb) live abalone
- olive oil
- 24 English spinach leaves, 4 cm (2 in) of stem left on
- 200 ml (7 fl oz) extra-virgin olive oil
- 50 ml (2 fl oz) lemon juice
- sea salt and freshly ground pepper
- 4 tablespoons chopped parsley

METHOD

Wash the sweetbreads and bring them to the boil in a pot of salted water. Simmer for 5 minutes and lift out of the water. When they are cool enough to handle, remove the membrane and veins, press between 2 plates and place a weight on top. Refrigerate for 1 hour.

To shuck the abalone, pull out the foot and place a sharp knife between the shell and muscle. Work the knife down until the whole muscle comes out. Remove the attached gut and cut away the tough lip. Discard. Place the abalone in a freezer bag and flatten to 1 cm thickness with a rolling pin.

Take the sweetbreads from the fridge and cut into 2 cm squares. Quarter the abalone. Place a large heavy-based pan on the stove and pour in a little olive oil. When it is almost smoking put in 2 pieces of abalone, cook for 1 minute on one side and then on the other. Remove and keep warm. Repeat with the others. Add more olive oil to the pan and, when smoking, add the sweetbreads. Cook for 1 minute, turn over, and keep cooking until golden brown. Remove from the heat.

Put the pan back on the stove. Add the spinach, and as soon as it starts to wilt add the extra-virgin olive oil, lemon juice, salt, parsley and pepper, and remove from the heat.

To serve, place a piece of abalone in the middle of each plate. Pile on the diced sweetbreads. Pour over the dressing and distribute the spinach leaves. Serve immediately.

JOHN DORY FILLETS SEARED IN INDIAN PASTRY WITH TOMATO CARDAMOM SAUCE

SERVES FOUR AS A MAIN COURSE

In this dish, the combination of pastry, fish, sauce, yogurt and spinach makes a complete dish. The cardamom and tomato are a perfect match, and the fish steams gently inside as the outside of the pastry crisps up. This dish also works beautifully with the flat fish of Europe and America. It is important that the vegetables are well-seasoned and cooked until they caramelize to impart their flavor to the sauce. The depth of flavor of aromatics is so often lost when they are not allowed to do their job properly.

The Tomato and Cardamom Sauce goes nicely with all seafood; its deep, rich flavor enlivens the tastebuds. The tomatoes are cut up, skin, seeds and all. Slice into thin rounds, then into julienne and chop the julienne to give a uniform dice. Don't chop them as if cutting for concassé, they lose too much juice that way.

INGREDIENTS

- 2 x 1.2 to 1.4 kg (2.6 to 3 lb) John Dory, bought whole and filleted
- 100 g (3 oz) baby spinach
- 60 ml (2 fl oz) clarified butter
- 4 tablespoons yogurt

Tomato And Cardamom Sauce
- 200 ml (7 fl oz) peanut oil
- 1 large onion, finely diced
- 2 large knobs ginger, peeled and finely diced
- 10 cloves garlic, finely diced
- 2 tablespoons sea salt

- 1 knob fresh turmeric, peeled and finely chopped
- 6 cloves, roasted and ground
- 8 cardamom pods, roasted and ground
- 8 vine-ripened tomatoes, diced

Indian Pastry
- 250 g (8 oz) plain flour
- 125 g (4 oz) wholemeal flour
- a pinch of sea salt
- 1 x 55 g (2 oz) egg
- 100 ml (3 fl oz) yogurt
- 2 teaspoons peanut oil
- 1 teaspoon water

METHOD

To make the Tomato and Cardamom Sauce, heat the oil until very hot in a heavy-based pot. Add the onion, ginger, garlic and salt. Lower the heat and cook over a moderate heat, stirring constantly to prevent burning. Cook until well caramelized, approximately 1 hour. Add the turmeric, cloves and cardamom, and cook for a further 5 minutes. Add the tomatoes and cook slowly for 20 minutes until a thickish sauce forms. Set aside.

To make the Indian Pastry, combine the two flours with the salt in a bowl. Make a well in the middle and add the egg, yogurt, oil and water. Mix with a fork until they form a sticky mass, then knead on a bench for 5 minutes until smooth and elastic. Allow the dough to rest for 30 minutes. Divide the dough into 4. Roll them out as thinly as possible on a lightly floured bench. Place them between sheets of greaseproof paper and stack them on top of each other and refrigerate until needed. Don't roll them out in advance of the time you need them, as they do not keep well when rolled out.

Lay out the pastry sheets on a chopping board and place a fillet at one end. Fold the other half of the sheet over to completely enclose the fish, and trim the pastry right to the edge of the fish. Brush both sides of the pastry with clarified butter and wrap in greaseproof paper. Refrigerate for 10 minutes. Repeat with the others.

Heat up the sauce and keep warm. Set up a steamer to cook the spinach. Place a heavy-based frying pan on the stove to cook the fish (do 2 at a time). Put the clarified butter in the pan and heat to almost smoking. Add the fish and cook for about 3 minutes. Turn the fish over with a fish slice, and cook for a further 2 minutes. Remove and drain on kitchen paper. Wipe out the pan and repeat the process. Steam the spinach.

To serve, spoon about 100 to 120 ml (3 to 3.5 fl oz) of the Tomato and Cardamom Sauce into the middle of 4 white plates. Place the yogurt on top and the spinach on the yogurt. Cut each piece of fish in half and place on top. Serve immediately.

EAMING

ng is one of the most terrific ways of bringing out the fresh flavors in seafood and vegetables. T
he in exactly the same way as Chinese steaming, and many of the same rules apply. Ensure t
s simmering and you're getting good steam.

Rockpool we also steam-cook in an oven bag, in the old French way of cooking en vessie (in
r), and in paper. Both these methods hermetically seal the ingredient and allow it to steam in
This is a particularly unctuous way of cooking fish and chicken. There is a recipe in the sec
for chicken cooked in a bag (page 172).

STEAMED SNAPPER FILLET WITH RED PEPPER AND LEEK COULIS

SERVES SIX

Snapper is a flaky, white-fleshed fish that retains its wonderful texture and delicate flavor when properly cooked. It is a very lean fish, and the best way of cooking is to steam it in a little stock. This delicious vegetable sauce is rich but the subtle flavors work well with the snapper's reserve. I would serve this dish with potato puree and a green salad. It also works well with zucchini (courgette) braised in olive oil.

INGREDIENTS

- 100 ml (3 fl oz) olive oil
- 2 leeks, white part only, cut into 2 cm (1 in) cubes
- 4 large red capsicums (red pepper), seeded and cut into 2 cm (1 in) cubes
- 3 cloves garlic, peeled and lightly crushed
- sea salt and freshly ground pepper
- 150 ml (5 fl oz) dry white wine
- 150 ml (5 fl oz) Chicken Stock (page 122)
- 6 x 180 g (7 oz) snapper, cut from a fillet, skin left on
- 60 ml (2 fl oz) extra-virgin olive oil

METHOD

Preheat the oven to 140°C (290°F).

In a small roasting tray pour in the 100 ml (3 fl oz) olive oil and add the leek, capsicum and garlic. Season well with salt, and cook in the preheated oven for 30 minutes. Add the wine and stir. Cook for a further 30 minutes until the wine has reduced. Add the stock and cook for a further 30 minutes. Remove from the oven and pass through a food mill (don't purée or you will end up with a much thicker and less delicate sauce). Keep warm while you steam the fish.

You will need two steamers for the fish. Place a bowl in each steamer, place 3 pieces of fish in each, and pour a little chicken stock halfway up the fish to cover. Place the steamer over boiling water and steam for between 8 and 10 minutes. The fish should start to feel firm to the touch. Take the steamer off the stove, lift the lid to release the excess steam, and put it back on the steamer baskets. Leave on the bench for 2 minutes for the fish to rest.

To serve pour equal amounts of sauce in the centre of each plate. Place a piece of fish, skin-side up, on each plate, drizzle each with 2 teaspoon of extra-virgin olive oil and grind over some pepper. Serve immediately.

GRILLING OR BARBECUING

The most important thing about grilling or barbecuing is to have a good heavy grill either over an open fire or jets of gas. The wood-burning or fire oven or grill is by far the best. Remember when barbecuing or grilling that you want a good, high heat so you can seal the piece of meat, fish or the vegetables properly, and allow the juices to remain inside. Don't turn the meat constantly: it should cook on one side and then the other. Don't cut into the meat while cooking or turn it with a fork, this allows the precious juices to escape. Rest the meat for 10 to 15 minutes to allow the juices to flow back into the flesh. All grilled foods should be lightly brushed with olive oil and seasoned before going on the grill.

AGED BEEF WITH GRILLED VEGETABLE SALAD AND ANCHOVY BUTTER

SERVES SIX

The beef for this dish has been aged on the bone for 20 days. At Rockpool we age rumps and loins, including the fillet, but you could get the butcher to age a standing rib for you, which would serve about six to eight people. Fillet is more tender, but for flavor, I prefer rump. At Rockpool we cut the meat into very large steaks and grill two serves at a time. This allows us to keep it on the grill longer to achieve a really crisp, smoky crust (it is so thick it will still be melting and rare in the middle). The flavors of the anchovy butter, beef and charred vegetables are meant for each other. Remember to turn the meat only once during cooking.

INGREDIENTS
- 2 x 600 g (1.3 lb) slices rump
- olive oil
- sea salt and freshly ground pepper
- 300 g (7 oz) Anchovy Butter (page 133), cut into 6 pieces and at room temperature

Salad
- 100 ml (3 fl oz) olive oil
- 2 bunches asparagus, cut off at 2 cm (1 in) from the base
- 1 large Spanish onion, peeled and cut into 1 cm (0.5 in) rings
- 3 cloves garlic, minced
- 6 large field mushrooms, cut into 1 cm slices
- 5 pink-eye potatoes, cooked for 20 minutes in boiling salted water, then peeled
- 80 ml (3 fl oz) extra-virgin olive oil
- juice of 2 lemons
- sea salt and freshly ground pepper

METHOD
Make a fire or turn on the gas barbecue. If using a wood fire wait until the fire has burnt down to very hot embers.

Brush the steaks with olive oil and season well with sea salt. Place on the heated grill. Cook on one side for about 10 minutes, flip, and cook for a further 8 minutes on the other side. Transfer to a plate, and allow the meat to rest in a warm place for 15 minutes.

Rub the grill with an oily rag or cloth with some olive oil. Oil the asparagus and place on the grill. Cook for 3 minutes, turn, and cook for a further 2 minutes. Remove from the grill. Place the Spanish onions on the grill with some oil and put the minced garlic on top. Oil the field mushrooms and put over the heat. Turn after a few minutes and when they have softened, transfer to a bowl. Cut the asparagus in half on an angle and place in the bowl with the onions, garlic and mushrooms. Cut the potatoes (they should still be warm) and add to the mix. Add the extra-virgin olive oil, lemon juice, sea salt and pepper.

Divide the asparagus salad into neat piles between 6 large white plates. Cut the beef into thin slices and place over the salad. Pour the juices from the meat plate over the beef, place a slice of butter on top of the meat and grind over some pepper. Serve immediately.

DEEP FRYING

The most important thing when deep-frying Western-style is to keep the temperature of the oil between 170°C (340°F) and 180°C (350°F) for the food to brown properly. This allows the heat to penetrate to the centre without absorbing too much oil. It's very important not to overload the fryer; the sudden drop in temperature will cause the food to absorb the oil and become soggy. Be very careful when frying. Use a thermometer to ensure that your oil doesn't get too hot, and ensure that the oil is fresh.

FRIED FLATHEAD FILLETS WITH TURMERIC POTATOES AND TZATZIKI

SERVES FOUR

This dish was very popular with the lunchtime crowd at the MCA cafe when we ran it. The potatoes are served warm and the tzatziki gives the fish a real Mediterranean flavor. These potatoes are delicious with salad, and the tzatziki, paired with hummus and flat bread, make a great starter at picnics.

INGREDIENTS
- vegetable oil
- 4 x 180 g (6 oz) flathead fillets, or 2 small fillets per person
- 1 quantity Beer Batter (page 85)
- plain flour for dusting

Tzatziki
- 1 cucumber, peeled, seeded and finely shredded 200 ml (5 fl oz) fresh farm yogurt
- 2 cloves garlic, crushed
- 1 bunch mint leaves, shredded
- lemon juice
- sea salt and freshly ground pepper

Turmeric Potatoes
- 2 small onions, finely diced
- 3 cloves garlic, crushed
- 60 ml (2 fl oz) olive oil
- sea salt and freshly ground pepper
- 2 tablespoons ground turmeric
- 1 kg (2 lb) desirée potatoes, peeled and sliced
- 200 ml (5 fl oz) cream (35 per cent butterfat)

METHOD
To make the Tzatziki, salt the cucumber for 1 hour. Drain and add the yogurt. Add the garlic and mint to the yogurt mix. Season with lemon juice, salt and pepper, and refrigerate until needed

To make the Turmeric Potatoes, first preheat the oven to 180°C (350°F). In a large frying pan cook the onions and garlic in the olive oil until soft but not colored. Add the salt and turmeric, and cook for 3 minutes. Add the potatoes, cream and pepper, and toss for 1 minute. Transfer to a baking tray and place in the preheated oven for 30 minutes or until the crust is golden brown.

Heat up the vegetable oil to 180°C (350°F) in a large pot. Lower the heat if necessary; don't let the oil get hotter as it will burn and darken the fish too much.

Dust the fillets with flour and dip in the batter (fry 2 at a time so the oil temperature doesn't drop too much). Carefully put them into the oil, and cook for about 5 minutes until the batter is golden brown. Remove with a slotted spoon and drain on kitchen paper while you cook the rest.

To serve, place a spoonful of potatoes in the centre of the plates, pour over the tzatziki and top with a fish fillet. Serve immediately.

FRIED ARTICHOKES WITH PARMESAN

SERVES SIX

This works well for the small artichokes that appear in the markets towards the end of spring. They make an ideal starter when served with lemons, and complement roasted meats or even pan-fried fish. I love them with a drizzle of extra-virgin olive oil and a little aioli.

INGREDIENTS
- 12 small artichokes
- plain flour for dusting
- sea salt and freshly ground pepper
- freshly grated Parmesan
- lemon wedges
- Aïoli (page 144)

METHOD

Cut the first 1.5 cm (0.8 in) off the top of the artichoke. Pull off the tough outer leaves, peel the stalk and base, and rub with lemon juice to stop it from discoloring. Push the artichoke down on a bench and fan out the leaves so they look like little flowers. Prepare the others in the same way.

Combine the flour and salt. Heat up a pot of vegetable oil to 180°C (350°F). Dust the artichokes with the flour. Place 2 or 3 artichokes at a time in the heated oil and fry until crisp. Drain on kitchen paper. Repeat with the rest. Toss the fried artichokes in the Parmesan and freshly ground pepper. Place 2 on each plate and serve with lemon and aïoli.

POACHING

Poaching can be carried out in rapidly boiling water, as in blanching, and in gently simmering water of anywhere between 80°C (175°F) and 90°C (195°F). Both these methods are used for different things. Green vegetables should be blanched in rapidly boiling salted water. Make sure you have lots of ice-water on hand to refresh the vegetables, and don't leave them too long or they will get water-logged.

I prefer to poach fish slowly, over a period of time, in a bouillon. The slower the cooking, the more tender and smaller the chance of the fish drying out.

Braising is a way of cooking vegetables, meat and fish in a sauce of stock. Again I find slow-cooking the best way of retaining the integrity of the ingredient.

STUFFED ARTICHOKES

SERVES SIX

This simple dish makes an ideal starter. The braising juices are served in a bowl with the artichokes and should be mopped up with lots of crispy bread. It keeps well, so if you make it earlier, make sure the artichokes are at room temperature before serving.

INGREDIENTS
- 6 large globe artichokes
- lemon juice
- 60 ml (2 fl oz) olive oil
- 50 g (2 oz) unsalted butter
- 1 large onion, peeled and finely diced
- 2 cloves garlic, minced
- sea salt and freshly ground pepper
- 6 leaves sage, chopped
- 125 g (4 oz) flat-leaf parsley leaves, sliced
- 2 slices sourdough bread, oven-dried and processed into crumbs
- 6 slices prosciutto

Braising Liquid
- 150 ml (5 fl oz) olive oil
- 1 small onion, peeled and thinly sliced
- 1 small leek, cut into julienne
- 1 carrot, peeled and cut into julienne
- 2 cloves garlic, chopped
- sea salt
- 3 sprigs thyme
- 4 sprigs flat-leaf parsley
- 10 white peppercorns
- zest of ½ lemon
- 100 ml (3 fl oz) dry white wine
- Chicken Stock (page 122)
- juice of 2 lemons

METHOD

Clean the artichoke by pulling off the tough outer leaves. Cut off the first 2 cm (1 in) from the top and peel the base and stalk. Rub the artichoke with lemon juice. Push a teaspoon into the centre of the artichoke and twist it around to remove the choke from the centre. Drip in some lemon juice, and repeat with the others.

To make the stuffing place the olive oil and butter in a small frying pan and heat until the butter starts to bubble. Add the onion, garlic, a good pinch of sea salt, and cook until softened. Add the herbs and remove from the heat. Mix in the breadcrumbs and season with pepper.

Place a tablespoon of stuffing in each artichoke and push it down. Keep filling until the artichoke is completely full. Place a slice of prosciutto over the artichoke and tie it on with kitchen string to secure. Repeat with the others.

In a pot or braising pan large enough to hold the artichokes side by side quite snugly, pour in 50 ml of the olive oil and heat. Add the onion, leek, carrot, garlic and a good pinch of sea salt. Cook until soft but not colored. Add the artichokes, herbs, peppercorns, lemon zest and white wine and cook for 3 minutes. Add the remaining olive oil and pour in enough chicken stock to half cover the artichokes. Bring to the boil and reduce to a simmer. Cover and leave for 20 minutes. Remove the lid and carefully turn the artichokes over, replace the lid and cook for a further 10 minutes. Check to see that they are cooked by inserting a paring knife into the base, it should slip in easily. Remove from the heat, add the lemon juice and check the seasoning.

Remove the string from the artichokes. Place the artichokes in the middle of 6 white bowls and ladle over some stock and vegetables. Serve immediately with good crusty bread.

RED EMPEROR FILLETS POACHED IN COCONUT MILK WITH GARAM MASALA

SERVES SIX

This long-time performer is so delicious that many regulars are addicted to it. We cook the fish in a copper pot, which we take to the table. I do not want the customers to miss the glorious perfume of the garam masala and Thai sweet basil when the lid is lifted. Cook the fish properly so it flakes and remains moist. Snapper and other reef fish are excellent substitutes.

Garam masala is a house spice mix. There is no value in making a lot of this at a time, fresh is best as the spices lose their aroma when stored. Roast each spice separately, then combine and grind.

For maximum flavor intensity caramelize the onions properly before adding the tomatoes when making the Tomato and Chili Base.

INGREDIENTS

- 1 litre coconut milk
- 6 kaffir lime leaves, cut into fine julienne
- 1 knob ginger, cut into fine julienne
- 30 ml (1 fl oz) fish sauce
- 4 tablespoons palm sugar
- 1 x 1 kg (2 lb) red emperor, boned and skinned, and cut into 6 portions
- 50 ml (2 fl oz) coconut cream
- leaves from 2 bunches Thai sweet basil

Tomato And Chili Base
- 1 large brown onion, peeled and finely diced
- 3 cloves garlic, minced

- 1 x 2 cm (1 in) piece fresh turmeric, minced
- 5 wild green chilies, finely chopped
- 1 large knob ginger, peeled and minced
- 250 ml (8 fl oz) vegetable oil
- sea salt
- 6 vine-ripened tomatoes, cored

Garam Masala
- 60g (2 oz) green cardamom pods, roasted
- 1 teaspoon cloves, roasted
- 1 teaspoon white peppercorns, roasted
- 2 sticks cinnamon, roasted
- 4 star anise, roasted

METHOD

To make the Tomato and Chili Base, cook the onions, garlic, turmeric, chilies and ginger in the vegetable oil in a heavy-based pot. Season with salt and cook slowly until caramelized (this can take up to 1 hour). Slice the tomatoes finely, cut into julienne, and into 5 mm dice. When the onion mixture has caramelized, add the tomatoes and cook for 10 minutes. Remove and set aside until ready to use.

To make the Garam Masala, crack the roasted cardamom pods in a mortar and pestle and remove the black seeds. Combine with the rest of the spices and grind finely. Store in an air-tight container.

In a pot with a tight-fitting lid large enough to hold the fish snugly, add the coconut milk, tomato and chili base, lime leaves, ginger, garam masala, fish sauce and palm sugar. Bring to the boil. Add the fish, presentation side up, and lower the heat to just under a boil. Put a lid on and cook very, very slowly for 8 minutes, making sure that the mixture never boils.

Remove from the heat and rest for 5 minutes. Add the coconut cream and the basil and replace the lid. You can either serve the fish in the dining room or plate it in the kitchen. At Rockpool we serve the fish with noodles and snowpeas. Prepare and cook some noodles and blanch some snowpeas. Place the cooked noodles and snowpeas in 6 bowls and put the fish on top. Spoon lots of broth over the fish, and serve.

TRUFFLES, CAVIAR & OYSTERS

THE TRUFFLE STORY

Truffles are a subterranean fungi known to grow near oak trees in Europe. There are many varieties, but the most prized are the white truffles from Alba, Italy and the black truffles from Perigord, France. Although very expensive, you only need a little of it to make a big impact, so they are worth their asking price. They have a rich, earthy perfume and an almost petroleum flavor (in a good sense) that awakens and warms the senses. Truffles are elusive — expect a huge aroma but a fine, subtle flavor. They will bring out extra dimensions of flavor in produce such as chicken, eggs and potatoes. The flavor compounds in truffles dissolve best in fats, so eggs, butter and oil are the best carriers.

Truffles are at their best when used as close to the time they are out of the ground, and if possible, use within ten days. There is a point during cooking when their aroma and flavor are at their height; beyond that they'll start to dissipate. With experience you'll learn to recognise those qualities. I've found that salt and garlic bring out the best flavors in black truffles. Most sauces benefit from truffles being added during the last 10 minutes of cooking, and a lid put on to hold in the aroma.

Black truffles are in season from December to the end of February in Europe. They are sublime and unbeatable when used fresh, and should be firm, in whole pieces, and free from bore marks. Store them in Arborio rice or eggs. Both will absorb the truffle aromas, and the eggs especially make the most splendid omelettes. Truffles are also available preserved. Buy first-cooked preserved truffles (premiere cuisson) that have been stored in a little water that becomes their juice. These are terrific when quickly warmed through in salads.

I was very sceptical of truffles early on in my cooking career and thought them an expensive oddity. The turning point came in 1993 after sampling a truffle dégustation menu in France. Adele, Trish and Lyn and I were in France in January, and met up with Simon Johnson, a very good friend of ours, in Paris. He was with gourmand extraordinaire, Ken Horn, and his partner Daniel Taurines. We all agreed to meet up at Robuchon's for a truffle dégustation lunch one day, which was sublime and enlightening. More good things were to follow.

We were also fortunate enough to be invited down to Cahors, in the south-west of Paris, to meet Jacques Pébeyre, the merchant for nearly half the truffles grown in France, and the ones most revered by the three-star chefs. We were met at the train station by the Pébeyres, and the next day, went truffle-hunting with Pierre-Jean, Jacques's son. For lunch, we were taken to not so much a restaurant as a door that led through a kitchen and into a small room, much like a worker's canteen (if only Sydney canteens served food like this). We were greeted by a wonderful woman with a beaming smile and big, swollen, workers' hands. A myriad of pots bubbled away on the stove. As we walked through the kitchen Monsieur Pébeyre discreetly passed her a very large handful of truffles from his pocket. She smiled and winked in reply. We went into a large dining room with bench-like tables, where many men were sitting around having their lunch. The menu was set at 50 francs, and for that we had a beautiful terrine and salad, followed by braised veal head. Two very large chickens (from Madame's backyard), completely blackened under the skin with truffles, with large hunks floating in the braising sauce were next. That's one of the things you can be sure of enjoying in France — chickens that taste wonderful, with a beautiful silky texture. The meal finished with a simple cheese and coffee, and we then headed for Pébeyre factory.

Walking into that factory was like being a kid in a candy store. I couldn't believe my eyes or my nose: truffles were being sorted, washed and lovingly brushed, preserved, cooled, and packed in delicate tissue within woven wooden boxes for restaurants the likes of Robuchon and Bocuse. The aroma was so intense that within three minutes my sense of smell was dissipated and exhausted.

We were then invited to dinner at Pébeyre's home, the only time in France that I've enjoyed the hospitality of a household. Monsieur and Madame were incredibly generous and I was allowed into the kitchen to watch Madame Pébeyre cook. Huge chunks of truffles sat in two bowls with about fifteen eggs in each, unwhisked. When she was ready to use them, Madame whisked them gently with a fork and poured them into simmering butter to give them a nice crust, turned them over and presented us with two beautiful omelettes. We ate these omelettes in record time, washed down with a 1970 magnum of Cos-de'Estournel. This wine complemented the truffles with its marvellous aromas of leather, barnyard and earth.

Next course was a wonderful saucisson that Monsieur Pébeyre had made by the best sausage-maker in Lyons, a friend of the family. The sausages were poached, sliced and served with a warm lentil salad. To finish we had a simple cheese from the area, a perfectly ripe cabacou wrapped in a chestnut leaf. Afterwards Jacques pulled out his collection of eau-de-vies and we drank happily until the wee hours of the morning. I think we were drunkenly unaware of how late it was, and what a merry mood we were all in, as we all sang and skipped down the street late that night, setting the local dogs barking and waking the sleeping villagers who had to call for quiet from their windows!

It was after that Cahors trip that Simon Johnson decided to import fresh French truffles to Australia (we'd only seen Italian ones so far). He asked me to prepare a dinner that showcased these fresh truffles. The day before, Simon presented me with four kilos of fresh truffles not four days out of the ground. I ran around the kitchen with joy when I saw these little black gems.

We started off with garlic toast topped with sliced truffles, and a salad with a thin veil of truffles over the top. The main course was Glenloth chickens stuffed with butter, salt and slices of truffle until completely black under the skin (the French call these 'chickens in half-mourning'). We put them in oven bags, added more butter, salt, stock and aromatic vegetables, and sealed them up. The chickens were steamed for 1½ hours for the truffle flavor to permeate the breasts and through the whole chicken. When the bag was cut, the room filled with those delicious aromas. We sliced and carved the chickens, poured over the truffle-flavored butter and juices, and served them with basmati rice cooked in stock with at least $1000 worth of truffles. Greg Frazer took this into the dining room and served each person separately.

We served the dinner with a red wine that Joe Grilli had made for Rockpool in 1991. The beautiful aromas, earthiness, Chianti-like truffle smells and fine dusty tannins in the wine worked beautifully with the dinner from start to finish. We finished with Gabrielle Kervella's matured goats cheese, wrapped in a fig leaf, and a few bottles of eau-de-vie made from prunes from the truffles' native Cahors. I think everyone left as happily as we did the night we had dinner with the Pébeyres.

TRUFFLE OMELETTE

SERVES FOUR TO SIX

This is one of the purest ways to enjoy the taste and mystique of truffles. Eggshells, being semi-permeable, allow truffle aromas into the egg and saturate the fat, thereby boosting the truffle flavor. The only way to have truffles is with enormous generosity, so enjoy them fresh during the season as often as you can afford to. I would say to any restaurant chef that it is paramount to use a decent amount per dish, and this should be reflected in the price. If patrons are unwilling to pay the price perhaps you should not persist with using them, or name your dishes accurately.

That truffles are available fresh during the festive season only adds to one's desire to be a good host. One year I had a truly wonderful Christmas Eve dinner with just my immediate family. The meal was a simple truffle omelette and salad, served with a glass of good red. The eggs I used had been sitting with 600 g of truffles for three days and we had 100 g between the four of us, certainly a luxury. For four people I would suggest about 50 g truffles. Don't add salt to the raw eggs as it toughens the protein and will affect the texture of the omelette.

INGREDIENTS

- 12 x 55 g (2 oz) eggs
- water
- 50 g (2 oz) fresh black truffles
- 4 x ½ eggshells
- 50 g (2oz) unsalted butter
- sea salt and freshly ground pepper
- 50 g (2 oz) freshly grated Parmesan
- 30 ml (1 fl oz) extra-virgin olive oil

METHOD

Three days before, store the eggs in a jar with the truffles. When ready to use, break the eggs into a ceramic bowl.

Peel the hard skin off the truffles and place the peelings in a jar that you can use to make mayonnaise. Slice the truffle thinly (a potato peeler works well) and place on top of the eggs. Fold them through gently without breaking the eggs and place a plate over the bowl to trap the aroma. Allow to stand for a couple of hours.

Gently whisk the eggs with a fork and add the water (this lightens the omelette). In a large omelette pan over high heat add the butter and as it starts to foam add the eggs. Once a bottom crust starts to form pull the back away from the side of the pan and allow the raw egg mixture to run onto the bottom of the pan. Repeat this several times. Cook until the base is set, and the inside still moist. Sprinkle with salt and pepper and add the cheese. With a palette knife or fish lifter turn half the omelette back on itself, and turn it out onto a big serving plate. Drizzle with the olive oil and serve in the middle of the table with salad, crusty sourdough bread and a glass of red wine.

TRUFFLE AND POTATO SALAD

SERVES FOUR

Fresh truffles have always been the highlight of my meals at Robuchon, and this salad was inspired by one I had on my last visit. Robuchon makes a wonderful tart covered in thick round slices of truffles with onions and smoked bacon. There is no denying that this is a truly beautiful dish, not only to eat, but to look at, but once I had the truffle, potato and Parmesan salad with garlic toast I was hooked. It's terrific with preserved truffles, but mind-blowing with fresh.

INGREDIENTS

- 350 g (12 oz) pink-eye or other full-flavored potato
- 50 g (2 oz) fresh black truffles
- 250 ml (8 fl oz) extra-virgin olive oil
- sea salt and freshly ground pepper
- 3 vine-ripened tomatoes, skinned, seeded and quartered, centre ribs removed
- juice of 1 lemon
- 100 g (3 oz) finely shaved Reggiano

Garlic Toast
- 2 cloves garlic
- sea salt
- 60 ml (2 fl oz) extra-virgin olive oil
- 4 slices sourdough bread

METHOD

Cook the potatoes with their skins on for 20 minutes in a pot of boiling salted water until they are soft. Allow to cool and peel. Slice into thick rounds.

To make the Garlic Toast, crush the garlic with some salt in a mortar and pestle. Add the olive oil, mix well and brush the garlic oil over the bread. Grill the bread until it is golden brown.

If you are using preserved truffles, slice. If you are using fresh truffles, peel carefully and slice them finely, reserving the peelings for mayonnaise.

In a heavy-based frying pan with a close-fitting lid, heat up the olive oil. Add the potatoes, and season with a generous amount of sea salt. Cook over very low heat for 3 minutes, then add the truffles and tomatoes. Put the lid on and leave over a low heat for a further 2 minutes. Remove from the heat and keep covered for another 5 minutes. Season with pepper and lemon juice.

To serve, spoon the potatoes, tomatoes and truffles into large bowls. Put the cheese shavings over the top, place a piece of bread on the side, and serve. Or, take the pot to the table and open the lid for the guests to savour the aroma. Serve the toast and cheese in separate bowls, and spoon the warm salad over.

TRUFFLED CHICKEN COOKED IN A BAG

SERVES TWO

I cooked this dish for a truffle dinner at Simon Johnson's. An oven bag allows the truffles to mingle within the aromas and flavors of the chicken, and to permeate the flesh. Seek out the best chickens available — I recommend those from Glenloth or Kangaroo Island chickens. You'll also need a pot that fits a 30 cm (12 in) Chinese steamer. I find an inverted wok makes an ideal lid, as it allows the steam to move around the chicken. The first time we had it on the menu a small wedding party of eight came in for lunch. The bride and groom were the first people to order it. I often think of them when I cook this dish, and hope the rest of their lives together will be as special as their first lunch together as man and wife.

INGREDIENTS

- 1 x 1.8 kg (4 lb) corn-fed chicken
- 125 g (4 oz) unsalted butter
- 1 small leek, cut into julienne
- ½ small onion, finely sliced
- 2 cloves garlic
- 1 small carrot, peeled and cut into julienne
- sea salt and freshly ground pepper
- 50 to 100 g (2 to 3 oz) fresh truffles, depending on how far your love goes
- 60 ml (2 fl oz) Chicken Stock (page 122)

Basmati Rice

- 250 g (8 oz) basmati rice
- 3 tablespoons olive oil
- ½ onion, diced
- sea salt
- 350 ml (12 fl oz) Chicken Stock (page 122)
- truffle peelings or peelings and 10 g (0.3 oz) truffles, cut into julienne

METHOD

Place the chicken on a board and remove the winglets. Cut off the neck and remove the wishbone — it makes carving much easier. Take the fatty glands out of the cavity and rinse the chicken. Pat dry with kitchen paper.

Melt 60 g (2 oz) of the butter in a heavy-based saucepan and gently stew the leek, onion, garlic and carrot with a pinch of sea salt until soft. Remove from the heat. Stuff the chicken with the vegetables. Peel the truffles, and reserve the skin for mayonnaise. Slice into fine rounds.

Bring some water to boil in a steamer. Put your finger up under the skin at the start of the breast to loosen the skin from the flesh, and gently work your way up to the thighs and drumsticks. Carefully slide slice after slice of truffle up under the skin, stuffing the drumsticks and working your way back to the breast. The chicken should look black, with bits of white flesh in-between. Rub the rest of the butter over the chicken, season with salt and pepper, and place in a large oven bag. Pour over the stock and seal the bag with a twist. Place in the steamer and steam for 1½ hours. Remove from the steamer and allow to sit for 10 minutes.

To prepare the Basmati Rice, sauté the rice in the oil in a little pot with a tight-fitting lid. Add the onion and fry until it is coated. Add the sea salt, stock, truffles and bring to the boil. Put a lid on and cook on a low heat for 15 minutes. Place a pastry ring or wok ring under the pot, and turn the heat down as low as it will go. Heat through for a further 10 minutes. Take to the table and serve with the truffled chicken.

It is best to cut open the bag at the table so that your guests can savour the aroma. Remove the chicken from the bag. Cut off the leg and remove the breast. Place a leg and breast on each plate. Take the aromatic vegetables out of the cavity and place on the plate. Spoon the cooking juices over the chicken, and serve with the truffled basmati rice and a salad.

POACHED VEAL SHANK WITH TRUFFLE MAYONNAISE

SERVES FOUR

Truffle mayonnaise is a delicious way of using fresh truffle peelings. The skin is quite hard but has loads of flavor. The process of crushing it softens the texture, and if you like, more truffles can be added to make the sauce even more luxurious. It is delicious with roasted and boiled meats. This dish is very light as the shanks are poached in a light chicken broth, and not braised in a heavy meat stock until quite sticky, as with many other shank dishes. The broth itself is not used in the dish, but it makes a great soup with the addition of beans or pasta, and a drizzling of truffle oil. Any leftover truffles make a great toasted garlic sandwich to float in the broth with white beans.

INGREDIENTS

- 4 veal shanks, left whole
- 2 litres (4 pints) Chicken Stock (page 122)
- sea salt and freshly ground pepper
- 60 ml (2 fl oz) olive oil
- 1 brown onion, cut into 1 cm (0.5 in) dice
- 1 carrot, cut into 1 cm (0.5 in) dice
- 1 leek, cut into 1 cm (0.5 in) dice
- 2 cloves garlic, chopped
- 2 sprigs thyme
- 2 bay leaves
- 4 sprigs flat-leaf parsley
- 4 sprigs tarragon
- 6 vine-ripened tomatoes, blanched, peeled, seeded and roughly chopped
- 300 g (10 oz) pink-eye potatoes, peeled and thickly sliced
- extra-virgin olive oil

Truffle Mayonnaise
- fresh truffle peelings or fresh truffle julienne
- 3 egg yolks
- sea salt
- juice of ½ lemon
- 250 ml (8 oz) olive oil, half pure and half extra-virgin

METHOD

Place the veal shanks in a large pot with the chicken stock and sea salt. Bring to the boil, lower to a very gentle simmer and skim for the first 15 minutes.

In a heavy-based saucepan add the olive oil and heat until just smoking. Add the onion, carrot, leek and garlic and sweat until it colors slightly. Put the vegetables in with the shanks and add the thyme and bay leaves. Simmer for another hour and add the parsley, tarragon and tomatoes. Cook for another 1 to 1½ hours, or until tender.

To make the Truffle Mayonnaise, crush the truffle shavings in a mortar and pestle. Add the egg yolks, salt, and lemon juice and whisk together. Add the oil in a thin stream, whisking constantly, to form an emulsion with the egg mixture. Check the seasoning and add more lemon juice or salt if necessary. The consistency should be a little firmer than cream but not thick.

Steam the potatoes until tender, and toss in some extra-virgin olive oil. Season with salt and pepper. Place the potatoes in the middle of 4 large plates. Carefully remove the veal from the stock, place on top of the potatoes and pour the truffle mayonnaise over the meat. Serve with a green salad.

CAVIAR

Caviar is the glistening black pearl of the sea, and the sexiest food I know. The word is used to refer to the roe of the sturgeon, and should not be used for anything else; it is incorrect to call salmon or lumpfish roe caviar. Until the nineteenth century it was mainly eaten by fishermen, the fish being sold as the main product of the harvest.

Fortunately for us, Babak Hadi chose to finish his PhD in aquaculture in Australia. Born of an Iranian father and German mother, and growing up in Iran, Babak had a very interesting diet as a child, which included caviar on toast for breakfast. When he came to Australia Babak's father suggested he import some caviar to support himself. This was how the Australian chapter of Black Pearl caviar began. I believe that caviar bearing the Black Pearl label has a guarantee of quality in Australia that is unsurpassed. Every can that comes into the country is checked and repacked, as the quality varies from fish to fish.

Sturgeons were once prolific in the seas of the northern hemisphere, and a source of cheap food in America and Europe. They were fished to the point of near-extinction, except for the land-locked area around the Caspian Sea. Iran and the former USSR formally agreed to protect the site to ensure a perfectly clean aquaculture site for the restocking and fishing of the sturgeon. Since the Russians were the only ones with the technology to turn the roe into caviar, they helped the Iranians develop their own industry in the 1950s, and levied a tax on each harvest right up until the mid-1980s. This was why some Iranian caviar was labelled and sold by the Russians as Russian caviar. A tight government-controlled industry meant that it should have had a long and bright future, but the fall of the USSR has spelled a possible end to this perfect situation, since five states, not two, now border the sea. The Russians have ceased restocking, and quality and supplies can no longer be guaranteed. The discovery of large quantities of oil in Azerbaijan is also threatening the environment.

Three species of sturgeon are harvested for caviar Sevruga, Osietra and Beluga. These fish all reach sexual maturity and start producing eggs at different ages: Sevruga between three and five years, Osietra five to eight years, and Beluga, fifteen years and over. The roe is removed from the belly by an incision down the stomach (this is done immediately after the demise of the fish, as the adrenalin from a fish dead longer than five minutes spoils the roe.) The roe is then sieved, drained and salted to season and preserve them, and tinned. Caviar comes either fresh or pasteurised. Pasteurisation is carried out to improve shelf life. During pasteurisation the caviar is heated, which cooks the shell of the eggs slightly. You also tend to lose some of the characteristics of the flavor.

Sevruga eggs come from the smallest sturgeon. The black, soft-shelled eggs are the smallest, with a long and salty taste of good fish oils. They are the strongest-tasting caviar, with a creamy texture. Osietra eggs are larger than Sevruga, and range in color from golden to black. It is usual for Osietra to have a brown tinge to it. The texture is firmer than that of Sevruga, and the flavor very nutty, buttery and clean, with a wonderful complexity and is, to that end, my favorite. Beluga eggs are the largest and black to dark grey with no secondary colors. This fish is very rare, and amounts to only 2 per cent of the entire harvest. (This has led to the practice of substituting black large-grained Osietra for Beluga.) The texture of the eggs is very soft, and the taste, clean and complete. Being very delicate it rarely arrives in good order. For my money I believe that Osietra is better-tasting and better value.

Caviar should never be served with a silver spoon as it will react and blacken the spoon, thereby affecting the taste. To my mind the best way to eat caviar is to eat lots of it, off a spoon, and really savour the flavor completely unadorned. Crush the eggs against the roof of your mouth for the explosion of flavors. Close your eyes and feel the taste and texture — this is three-dimensional food. If you must, a piece of toast. Caviar also goes well with potatoes and creamed eggs.

FRESH IRANIAN SEVRUGA CAVIAR WITH SCRAMBLED EGG TARTLET

SERVES SIX

This was on the menu at Rockpool for a very long time. The extra saltiness and more direct flavor of Sevruga works well with the creaminess of the eggs and earthy flavors of the spinach. You'll need 6 x 10 cm tartlet tins with loose bases for this recipe.

INGREDIENTS
- 10 x 55 g (2 oz) eggs
- 100 ml (3 fl oz) cream (35 per cent butterfat)
- 350 g (11 oz) Puff Pastry (page 220)
- 1 bunch English spinach
- 100 g (3 oz) unsalted butter
- sea salt and freshly ground pepper
- 180 g (6 oz) fresh Sevruga caviar (as a starting point)

METHOD
Preheat the oven to 180°C (350°C).

Break the eggs into a bowl and whisk. Whisk in the cream until completely incorporated. Set aside.

Lightly flour a cool bench and roll out the puff pastry to a square of 1 mm thickness. Cut out 6 circles that are large enough to fill the tartlet cases with some overhang. Spray the moulds with Pure and Simple or lightly oil, and drape over a sheet of pastry. Push in the sides gently and allow some of the pastry to hang over. Rest in the refrigerator for 30 minutes. Line the inside of the pastry with foil and fill with rice. Bake in the oven for 20 minutes. Remove the foil and rice, and brush the insides of the tartlet cases with the egg and cream mixture. Return to the oven for another 10 minutes to brown. Keep warm.

Pick the spinach leaves from the stem and steam over simmering water for 5 minutes. Squeeze out any excess water. Place in a container with 50 g of butter and sea salt and purée. Keep warm.

In a heavy-based frying pan put in the remaining butter and when it starts to bubble pour in the egg mixture. Lower the heat to medium and cook, stirring from time to time. Continue stirring as it starts to set. Add some sea salt and freshly ground pepper and remove from the heat. Keep stirring as it starts to set. It is ready to serve as soon as it starts to hold together and is creamy.

Place the 6 tartlet cases on 6 large white plates. Place a spoonful of spinach purée in each case and spoon the eggs over the top. On top of each tart place 30 g of fresh caviar, and serve immediately.

FRESH IRANIAN OSIETRA CAVIAR WITH PRAWN CUSTARD

SERVES SIX

I first tasted the combination of caviar and cauliflower at Robuchon's. The creaminess of the custard and earthiness of the cauliflower work very well with the more complex flavors of Osietra. At Rockpool we start by making a prawn stock and cook it with eggs the way the Japanese make steamed custards chawan – mushi. It can be eaten either warm or cold, but I prefer it cold.

INGREDIENTS

- 180 g (6 oz) fresh Osietra caviar

Spinach Oil
- 1 bunch English spinach, stems removed
- sea salt and freshly ground pepper
- 180 ml (6 fl oz) extra-virgin olive oil

Prawn Stock
- 100 ml (3 fl oz) olive oil
- 1 kg (2 lb) green prawn shells
- ½ small onion, finely diced
- 1 small carrot, finely diced
- 2 cloves garlic, minced
- ½ small leek, washed and finely diced
- 125 ml (4 fl oz) brandy
- 125ml (4 fl oz) port
- 250 ml (8 fl oz) dry white wine
- 250 ml (8 fl oz) Chicken Stock (page 122)

- 4 vine-ripened tomatoes, blanched, peeled, seeded and finely chopped
- leaves from ½ bunch thyme
- leaves from ½ bunch tarragon
- cauliflower puree
- 50 ml (2 fl oz) olive oil
- 50 g (2 oz) unsalted butter
- ½ small onion
- 1 clove garlic minced
- sea salt and freshly ground pepper
- ¼ cauliflower, chopped into small pieces
- 200 ml (5 fl oz) Chicken Stock (page 122)
- juice of 1 lemon
- 125 ml (4 fl oz) extra-virgin olive oil

Prawn Custard
- 250 ml (8 fl oz) eggs (about 4 x 55 g/2 oz), whisked
- 250 ml (8 fl oz) prawn stock (page 183)
- 1 teaspoon fish sauce
- 1 teaspoon palm sugar

METHOD

To make the Spinach Oil steam the spinach leaves for 5 minutes over rapid boiling water. Squeeze out any excess water, place in a container and purée. Add the salt, pepper and olive oil, and purée until very smooth. Leave to infuse for 1 hour and pour through a few layers of muslin. Squeeze out all the oil and discard the solids. Strain the oil through a fine sieve and store at room temperature until ready to use.

To make the Prawn Stock, place a heavy-based pot on the stove and heat the olive oil until very hot. Add the shells and stir for 5 minutes until colored. Add the onion, carrot, garlic and leek, and cook for a further 5 minutes. Add the brandy and reduce until it almost disappears. Add the port and reduce, then the white wine and reduce until almost gone. Pour in the chicken stock and add the tomatoes and herbs. Lower the heat and don't allow the stock to boil again. Cook for 20 minutes. Put through a food mill and then through a fine strainer.

To make the Cauliflower Purée, put the olive oil and butter in a heavy-based saucepan and heat until the butter foams. Add the onion, garlic, a little salt and cook until soft but not colored. Add the cauliflower and stir. Add the chicken stock and cook for about 15 minutes over a slow heat. Don't burn the sides or bottom or the cauliflower will discolor. Keep stirring, especially towards the end as the liquid cooks away. When all the liquid is gone, purée. Add the lemon juice and extra-virgin olive oil slowly to lighten the texture of the purée. Season with pepper and cool to room temperature.

Preheat the oven to 130°C (275°F).

To make the Prawn Custard whisk the eggs and pour in the prawn stock. Keep whisking until completely incorporated. Season with the fish sauce and palm sugar, and skim the foam off the surface. Spray 6 small dariole moulds with Pure and Simple (or lightly oil). Pour the mix into the moulds and place in a bain-marie with hot water. Cover the top loosely with foil and place in the preheated oven. Cook for 30 to 40 minutes. The custard will appear to set on the outside but will still be runny in the middle Remove before it sets too firmly. Allow to cool, and refrigerate until required.

In the middle of 6 large white plates spread out a spoonful of cauliflower purée. Run a knife around the edge of the dariole mould and turn out the custard onto the centre of each plate. Drizzle spinach oil around the outside and place 30 g (1 oz) of caviar on each. Serve immediately.

OYSTERS

Oysters are the perfect fresh food, living until the moment they are consumed, remaining fresh until the last minute as they await their demise. They are certainly one of the sexy foods along with caviar.

Some 300 steps down from our backyard was a boathouse, and the beautiful rocks running into the river used to be laden with oysters. I spent half my time running up to Mum, screaming, because I'd slipped on the rocks and cut my feet to pieces. My father and brothers used to go down to the rocks regularly and knock these beautiful oysters off the rocks and shuck them fresh for all of us. If one did that today on the Georges River it would probably bring about their demise! Those oysters were, however, delicious, silky and salty, with a perfect balance of flavor and a self-saucing mechanism.

After that time I never really got into oysters in restaurants, perhaps because those beautiful fresh oysters of my youth were a different beast from the ones available, which have been opened, killed, washed in fresh water and packed under paper for god knows how many days. While at the Bluewater Grill John Susman and I decided to bring up fresh Pacifics from Tasmania. These would arrive unopened, full of their beautiful brine and still squirming as they slithered down our throats. Real oysters, not the lifeless, pretend type. In Paris, London and New York to serve pre-opened dead oysters without their brine would be unthinkable. One could sit up at oyster bars watching the dexterous waiters shucking oysters and setting them in front of you. And the varieties available, each with their own subtle nuances of flavor and texture. This was what I endeavoured to repeat when I returned to Sydney.

There was no question that oysters would be opened fresh on demand at Rockpool. John Susman was employed as our seafood supplier and the Flying Squid Brothers was born the very same day Rockpool opened its doors. We offered the choice of Sydney Rock, Pacific, and Belons from Tasmania, and the lids are not taken off until the orders come in. They're then put on ice with their juices — so integral to the taste of an oyster — and delivered to the table. This is the only way to eat oysters.

In my mind the smaller varieties are the tastiest. The best is the Sydney Rock oyster, with its iodine and rich seafood flavor, which is creamy and salty all at once. There is incredible complexity that you don't often see in any other oyster. The Pacifics display a wonderful saltiness, it's like a dump in the surf, and a flinty–firm texture. The Belons are subtle and meaty, with a sublime texture.

It would be wonderful if all consumers said 'No, stop. Enough of this rubbish, no more dead oysters. Take the lid off and serve them to me fresh.' To me, this is the way we've got to go, not in the other direction. There is a recipe for steamed oysters in the section on Eastern cooking (page 42). Pacifics are perfect for cooking; it would be an absolute sacrilege for the small oyster to be eaten any way other than fresh off the shell To shuck an oyster have ready an oyster knife and a tea-towel. Wrap the tea-towel around one hand and hold the oyster firmly on a wooden board with the hinge part of the oyster protruding. Take your knife and gently wedge it into the hinge, and jiggle it until it finds its way in. Don't force or push, you could easily slip and cut your hand. Once you've wedged the knife in, turn it sideways. The hinge will twist and cut through the muscle, and you're in. It's as simple as that.

PASTA, RISOTTO AND PIZZA

PASTA

Pasta, risotto and pizza are three foods that would bring a smile to the faces of almost all the world's population. I've yet to meet anyone who didn't have a soft spot for at least two of them. These foods are, or form part of, the staples in Italy. The pasta eaters of the south and the rice eaters of the north have slightly different views as to which is the more important, but in a country such as Australia, that isn't an issue at all. Hand in hand with the noodle and rice dishes of Asia, pasta and risotto would have to make up the staples for most of us on the planet. And so they should — they are delicious, good for us, and so convenient.

We make many types of pasta at Rockpool. One apprentice makes them in the morning from 8 a.m. until around 12.30 p.m. for the lunch service. Another young pasta maker works from 3 p.m. until dinner service at 6.30 p.m. They usually hold the position for 6 months, after which they'll have great skills and are ready to move on to the next station. A usual morning includes making tortellini, tortelli, ravioli, plain and colored lasagne sheets, fine noodles, semolina noodles, spring onion cakes, wonton wrappers, prawn dumplings and murtabak sheets.

Skill with pasta takes a long time to master because the gluten content in the flour varies with the weather and humidity — one must therefore master the feel rather than the recipe. You'll find the basic recipe a little dry one day or too wet on another, so make adjustments as necessary. All this may sound daunting, but it all comes down to experience.

Pasta-making is very satisfying; there is nothing quite like flicking the flour off a sheet of pasta, rolling it, cutting it into the desired shape, and then cooking with it. The experience of making pasta puts you in touch with the craft of cooking, and with the joy that good work and skill brings.

Most of our pastas are rolled through a pasta machine, which has two opposing stainless-steel rollers on a gear that allows them to be adjusted inwards or outwards as you work the dough. The numbers usually go from 1 (thinnest) to 9 (thickest). Some machines go to half-settings as well.

The real challenge is to produce a noodle with a silky texture and taste while retaining a firm bite. The Italians call this al dente, meaning the noodle should give way under, the bite, offering a sweet resistance, not a struggle.

The simplest pasta is made of flour, eggs and salt, and this suits most of our requirements. All our doughs are handmade; I find pasta made in a food-processor of inferior quality, and no-one has managed to convince me otherwise yet. The dough must not be overworked and it is imperative that it is rested for at least half an hour before continuing with the recipe. Allow 100 g (3 oz) of pasta per person.

INGREDIENTS

- 100 g (3 oz) plain flour
- sea salt
- 1 x 55 g (2 oz) egg

METHOD

Place the flour and salt on a bench and make a well the middle. Break the egg into the well and whisk with a fork. Start incorporating the flour as you whisk bringing the flour from bottom to top and over on itself to form a rough dough.

With your hands start to bring the dough together, incorporating the flour with a metal pastry scraper. The dough will start to form a rough ball. Push it together with your hands and knead for 1 or 2 minutes, no longer. At this point the dough will feel quite hard, but as it rests the moisture will soften the flour. Wrap the dough in plastic and rest it on the bench for at least 30 minutes before using. At this point it can refrigerated, but I believe it is best used fresh.

Flatten the dough and roll out with a rolling pin to the width of the pasta machine. Working in small lots (usually about 200 g (5 oz) at a time for a domestic machine), roll the dough through with the machine on the widest setting. Feed it through in one motion to prevent stop marks on the pasta.

Lightly flour one side of the rolled pasta and fold the sheet into three by folding one side a third of the way up, and folding the top third over. Press the seam of the dough together and roll the pasta through the machine 4 to 5 times, lowering the setting each time you pass the pasta through. Feed the seam side into the rollers first, and flour the sheet lightly between each roll. The pasta should be smooth and elastic. Allow the pasta sheets to dry slightly before cutting. Don't leave them for too long or they will become too dry and brittle.

SMOKED SALMON LASAGNE WITH EGGPLANT CAVIAR

SERVES SIX

This dish was inspired by my good friend Steve Manfredi. It was the high standard that both Steve and his mother, Franca, set that has inspired me to work harder on our pasta dishes. I've developed and refined this dish over many years. It works very well even with numbers of 500 or more — we can be confident of the taste, texture and style of each plate, and that's usually not easy when dealing with such large numbers. I have stylised the dish more and more over the years. From layers of smoked salmon, eggplant, sorrel and pasta served with a tomato vinaigrette, it is now layers of pasta and smoked salmon with the rest of the previous filling a salad that sits on top, drizzled with a little red pepper oil. I like the interplay between all the ingredients more now. The eggplant salad is a rustic version of eggplant caviar. I recommend Mohr's salmon in Australia, I believe it is among the finest in the world. You'll also need a 26 cm x 19 cm plastic lunch box or food storage container that has a capacity of 3 litres.

INGREDIENTS

Lasagne
- 2 x Basic Pasta (page 191), cut into 5 sheets 500 g (1 lb) Mohr smoked salmon, sliced
- 180 ml (6 fl oz) Red Pepper Oil (page 153)

Eggplant Caviar
- 2 medium eggplants
- juice of 2 lemons

- 150 ml (5 fl oz) extra-virgin olive oil
- 1 onion, peeled and finely diced
- 2 cloves garlic, crushed and chopped
- sea salt and freshly ground pepper
- 2 tomatoes, blanched, peeled, seeded and roughly chopped
- leaves from 3 sprigs French tarragon

heets of pasta into 1 on the pasta machine.
' are twice as long as they are wide, making
are slightly larger than the mould. As you
heet flour and place it on the next. Cook
alted water with a little added olive oil for
inutes. Remove and refresh in ice-water.
en brush with olive oil. The sheets may
on top of each other with a plastic sheet
ach layer.

bottom of the lunch box with olive oil. Lay
plastic along the bottom and up the sides
e used to pull the lasagne out. Make sure
s very smooth on the bottom, any wrinkles
p on the pasta. Place a sheet of pasta on
d put the lunch box over it. Trim around the
scard the extra. Repeat with all the other
ts.

heet of pasta on the bottom of the box
n it out. The only pasta layer that must be
he bottom one, patch any broken sheets
r the other layers. Add a layer of smoked
aking sure no pasta is showing, but without
g the salmon too much, or the overall affect
chunky. Add another layer of pasta and
of salmon, and so one until there are five

pasta and four salmon layers. After the lasa
together place a flat piece of cardboard
the mould and place a 1 kg (2 lb) weigh
Refrigerate for at least an hour.

To make the Eggplant Caviar, peel off the
the eggplants, and cut into large dice of al
(1 in) square. Toss the cubes in the juice c
and a cup of water. Set up a steamer on
and steam the eggplants for 20 minute
tender. Heat the olive oil in a frying pan ar
onion and garlic. Season with sea salt and
soft. Squeeze the excess water out of the
and add to the onions. Add the tomatoe
Remove from the heat and add the remair
juice, tarragon and freshly ground pepper.
is best served at room temperature.

To serve, turn the lasagne out onto a cut
and remove the plastic sheet. Trim all the
neaten. Cut the lasagne down the middle le
then cut each half into 3. Take 6 large wh
and place a lasagne in the middle of each
ml of red pepper oil with some pepper jul
each lasagne. Place a large tablespoon o
caviar on each lasagne. Season each wi
and serve.

KING SHRIMP AND GOAT'S CHEESE TORTELLINI

SERVES SIX

One chef at Rockpool, Michael McEnearney, came in during the second year of his apprenticeship. He had spent time in each section of the kitchen and was the sous chef, running the Rockpool team when he was twenty-three. I watched him grow up as a person, and along the way develop into a very fine cook with great pride.

When Michael was in the middle of his stint in the pasta section he went on a holiday to Spain and Italy. The year before Annie Feolde from the Restaurant Enoteca Pinchorri in Florence had done a promotion in the Regent in Sydney. Serge Dansereau, the executive chef at the Regent, who's also a good friend, brought her in for dinner. Annie enjoyed herself immensely and said that if any of my staff or I were in Italy we were more than welcome in her kitchen for a day or two. (I have since had a terrific meal in her restaurant and not only is the food great, but she has the best wine list in Europe, at a third of the price of French three-stars.) I took her up on her offer, and she was more than happy to look after Michael in the kitchen. This is the kind of generosity that makes new cooks aspire to a higher plane. I don't agree with the practice of charging people for the privilege, it changes a gift into something grubby.

Michael had told Annie that he was doing pasta at the restaurant, so she put him to work with the chef on that section for two days. He enjoyed himself, learnt heaps and saw how hard the crew worked in a European restaurant. After his stint in the kitchen he had lunch there, and observed from the other side how the service staff weaved their magic, and realised the effort required to make a great restaurant, and the attention to detail necessary.

On his return to the kitchen, Michael spoke about a potato gnocchi dough filled with pesto and rolled into a tortellini shape that he had been very impressed with. He made some for us to look at. It had a great texture, almost as resilient as normal pasta, but at least three times silkier. We had to do something with this, but what? That very week a good friend, Gabrielle Kervella, who makes the best goat's cheese in Australia, sent us a fresh soft curd that she called goat's ricotta. I thought we might stuff the potato dough with it and have a taste. It was bliss, they were meant for each other. The silkiness of the dough and the slight sourness of the cheese needed something firm, however, and it just so happened that we had some large Yamba king prawns that weren't being used. The firm crunch and buttery taste of the prawns almost finished the dish, but it needed one more thing. Then I remembered the wonderful Sicilian pastas with raisins and pinenuts. That added the dimension I was looking for, the bit of sweetness that I would normally use to balance Asian dishes. I added burnt butter to intensify the nuttiness. So many good dishes start this way, from one inspiration and the riches of the season, the way it should be.

INGREDIENTS

- 12 large Yamba king prawns (shrimps), or any large wild king prawn, peeled and deveined
- 125 g (4 oz) raisins, soaked in hot English Breakfast tea
- 60 g (2 oz) pinenuts, roasted until golden brown
- 125 g (4 oz) freshly grated Parmesan
- 200 g (7 oz) unsalted butter

- tortellini
- 350 g (12 oz) potatoes, unpeeled (kipflers, bintjes, pink-eye and King Edwards are best)
- 150 g (5 oz) fresh goat's ricotta
- lemon juice
- sea salt and freshly ground pepper
- 150 g (5 oz) hard (baker's) flour

METHOD

To make the Tortellini, boil the potatoes in salted water for about 20 minutes or until cooked. Season the goats cheese with lemon juice, salt and pepper. Spoon the mixture into a piping bag.

When the potatoes are cooked, drain and leave until cool enough to handle (the dough works through the pasta machine much better when warm). Peel the potatoes and push through a potato ricer or a food mill. Add the sea salt and flour, and mix into a cohesive mass.

Take half the dough and cover with a tea-towel to keep warm. Put the other half through the pasta machine. Dust the dough with a little flour each time you put it through if it's sticking, but it shouldn't be necessary. After about the third time through, the dough will start to come together, but don't expect it to look as smooth as normal pasta dough. Lower the machine to the fifth setting, fold the dough into 3 and with a rolling pin roll out the seam end evenly. Make sure that the width of the dough is the width of the pasta machine. Open the machine out to 10 again and roll the dough through. It should become silkier and smoother with each passing. Continue down the scale again until you reach 3. This dough is not as thin as a normal

ravioli, but it does have a sexy mouth feel.

Lay the pasta sheet on the bench and trim the edges with a pizza cutter. Cut the sheet in half lengthwise, then cut the halves into perfect squares of about 3 cm square. It is very important that you work in squares, as the sides fold over to make a triangle. This dough doesn't need water to stick together, however you must be very careful not to use too much flour on the bench or in the last winding through, as the flour stops the tortellini from sticking together. The dough also deteriorates as it gets cold so try to work with it while hot.

With the dough directly in front of you, pipe a bit of goat's cheese towards the top left-hand corner of each square. Fold the bottom right-hand corner to the top to form a triangle enveloping the goat's cheese. You should have triangles on the bias with the point facing away from you to the top left. Fold the base of the triangle lengthwise so it is level with, and covers, the top point. You will have a long skinny piece of pasta with a bump in the middle. Pick up the pasta and wrap it around your index finger, with the top point of the triangle facing away from you. Squeeze the two ends together where they overlap and remove your finger. Place on a floured tray and repeat with the

Place a heavy-based frying pan on high heat and add a little olive oil. When it starts to smoke add half the prawns. Cook for 1 to 1½ minutes on each side. Be careful not to overcook, they should still be opaque in the middle. Repeat with the other half of the prawns.

Bring a large pot of water to the boil. Salt the water and add 2 tablespoons of olive oil. Place the tortellini in the boiling water, and as soon as they float back to the surface remove with a slotted spoon.

To serve place 4 tortellini around the outside of each bowl and 2 king prawns in the middle. Sprinkle the prawns with the raisins and pinenuts, and sprinkle the pasta with Parmesan.

In the same pan that you cooked the prawns add the butter and burn it until it's nut brown. I don't worry about removing the milk solids from the butter as they have a nice flavor. If they are burnt then so is the butter, so throw it out and start again. Black butter will spoil the dish. Don't think I'm doubting your common sense by saying that. If I had a dollar for every time I've pulled an apprentice or even an experienced cook up and told them to start again, I could probably comfortably retire. Put a spoonful of hot butter over the tortellini and serve immediately.

SALTCOD TORTELLI WITH BURNT BUTTER AND YOGURT

This dish is a collaboration with a chef who worked with me for six years, Kahn Dennis. Kahn came to me just after Rockpool opened for an apprenticeship, having dropped out of art school and was driving taxis for extra money. He was about twenty-four and knew he really wanted to cook, and that meant working in a good restaurant and starting at the bottom, in the larder. However, he spent his last eighteen months at Rockpool as head chef. He has turned out a caring cook, with great sensitivity to balancing Asian and Mediterranean flavors. It is with Kahn's native Turkey that this dish has part of its inspiration; the rest comes from the other side of the Mediterranean, Italy.

Kahn used to talk of the beautiful handmade dishes that his mother would make, of the baklava with her own filo, and of mantis, the lamb ravioli of Turkey that she would finish with burnt butter, little crunchy croutons and garlic-flavored yogurt. It sounds far too heavy when you think about it, but to taste Kahn's mother's mantis (as I have) is to taste one of those dishes that never leave the memory. It's something you must eat again, a treasure. I have enjoyed working with Kahn and hope that one day we might cook in a kitchen together again, if fate were to be that kind. As one door closes, another opens; I now have another fine young chef running the Rockpool kitchen — Ross Lusted, and with Michael McEnearney, they form a dynamic duo.

I can't even remember when we thought of using saltcod, but as we were more seafood-oriented at that stage, I guess we thought lamb was out of the question. I choose tortelli as the shape of the pasta because it has such a fine join down each side. You get very little overlapping of pasta and the result is more delicate than a lot of ravioli.

This recipe is here to see if you're starting to think for yourself. There are ideas and enough information here for a good cook to produce a terrific dish.

INGREDIENTS
Saltcod Purée
- saltcod
- court-bouillon
- olive oil
- garlic
- Mashed Potato (page 146)
- milk
- lemon juice
- freshly ground pepper

- Basic Pasta (page 191)
- olive oil
- freshly grated Parmesan
- butter for burning
- day-old sourdough bread, cut into little tiny croutons and cooked in butter until golden brown yogurt, seasoned with garlic,
- lemon juice, salt and pepper

METHOD

To make the Saltcod Purée soak the saltcod in fresh water for 24 to 48 hours, changing the water every few hours, depending on how salty you like it. Personally I like a distinct salty flavor. Poach the fish in a court-bouillon for 25 minutes and remove. When it is cool enough to handle, remove all the bones and skin. Gently fry the fish in olive oil with garlic, and when it flakes add the mashed potato and a little milk. Continue to stir until you have a purée. Add some good olive oil, lemon juice and a grind of pepper. When it cools it is ready for use in the ravioli.

Roll the pasta through the machine. Take it through on the lowest setting twice, to get the sheets as fine as possible. Lay the pasta sheet on the bench and cut in half lengthwise, then cut the halves into squares. Place a spoonful of saltcod towards the bottom right-hand corner of the square. Carefully brush the other three sides of the pasta with a damp pastry brush so the pasta will stick to itself. Roll the bottom right-hand corner over and into the middle of the square of pasta, continue to roll it over flat, then press the sides down with the sides of your hands or with each index finger You should have a lovely little parcel reminiscent of a Minties lolly. Repeat with the other squares. Lightly flour and place on a board, turning occasionally to allow them to dry properly. This type of ravioli or tortelli is never the same when pre-blanched and reheated, so make it on the day you wish to serve it.

Place a pot of boiling salted water with a little olive oil on the stove. Add the tortelli and cook for 5 minutes, longer if they have dried out. Place a frying pan on the stove and burn the butter until it is nut brown. Drain the pasta and place in the middle of a bowl. Sprinkle with Parmesan and spoon over the burnt butter. Sprinkle with croutons and add a spoonful of garlic-flavored yogurt. Serve immediately.

TAGLIATELLE WITH ZUCCHINI SAUCE

SERVES TWO

My wife Adele usually prepares the meals at home — simple, wonderful pastas, risottos and, sometimes, a laksa. This is one of her favorite sauces, and comes from those Italian sauces that feature vegetables and olive oil as the dressing. In Italy it would be served as a second course after the antipasto, just before the main course. Adele not only cooks zucchinis in this manner, but all types of vegetables. The basis of the dish is a good olive oil, in which you stew some finely sliced garlic, onion, chili flakes and salt until they soften. Add the grated vegetable to the oil and cook until the vegetable is as firm or soft as you like. Finish with some freshly grated Parmesan. Adele uses broccoli, asparagus, peppers, cauliflower and other vegetables, either singularly or in combination. She uses extra-virgin olive oil, and I don't believe that all the flavors are driven off during cooking, and the sauce tastes better at the end. Treat yourself one day and deep-fry with it, and see the difference. Dry pasta works as well as fresh. Adele feels that it's vital you cook more pasta than you need. I'm not sure exactly why, but we always manage to eat what's left anyway.

INGREDIENTS
- 250 ml (8 fl oz) good-quality extra-virgin olive oil
- ½ small onion, finely diced
- 2 cloves garlic
- a sprinkle of chili flakes (we use the ones from Thailand)
- sea salt and freshly ground pepper
- 2 large zucchinis, grated through the largest holes in the grater
- 200 g (5 oz) Basic Pasta (page 191), cut into tagliatelle or dry spaghetti or penne
- juice of 1 lemon freshly grated Parmesan

METHOD
Heat up the olive oil in a frying pan and sauté onion, garlic and chili flakes. Season with sea salt and cook until soft. Add the grated zucchini and cook for further 5 minutes, stirring from time to time. Squeeze lemon juice into the pan and season with freshly ground pepper.

Cook the pasta in salted boiling water until it is al dente. Strain through a colander and run hot water over the pasta for 1 minute to remove the excess starch and to stop the pasta from sticking together. Place the pasta in a bowl and top with the zucchini sauce, making sure you add lots of the olive oil. Serve with grated Parmesan.

A SIMPLE TOMATO SAUCE

SERVES TWO PEOPLE WHO LOVE EACH OTHER (THERE IS A LOT OF GARLIC USED, DON'T CONTEMPLATE USING LESS, IT'S NOT THE SAME).

Nothing is more satisfying, or as simple and wholesome, than a good tomato sauce and pasta. The only fresh tomatoes worth using are the vine-ripened varieties that are prolific during summer. When good, ripe, fresh tomatoes are unavailable canned ones are a very good substitute. Unfortunately for Australia's balance of payments, the best-quality canned tomatoes seem to be Italian plum tomatoes.

I was on one of my buy Australian drives when I noticed Adele making pasta sauce with a tin of Italian tomatoes. I made a jibe about the tomatoes, and asked why she hadn't heeded my edict on household purchases. I copped an earful back — it was explained to me that while I was the boss at Rockpool at home I was merely Adele's helper. Besides, Australian tomatoes were really awful. I took all this back into my box and wondered why. You'd think it would be possible to take a beautifully ripe tomato and put it in a can, but in Australia, most canned tomatoes are green, not a rich red. Please, Australian growers and producers, grow tomatoes for flavor, not shelf-life, and can the properly ripe ones. Is flavor and quality too much to ask for? It is my desire to one day see a tin of Australian tomatoes reach the heights of Italian ones.

INGREDIENTS

- 150 ml (3 fl oz) extra-virgin olive oil
- 8 cloves garlic, thinly sliced
- a good pinch of chili flakes (optional)
- a good pinch of sea salt
- a good pinch of sugar

METHOD

In a heavy-based saucepan heat the oil and add the garlic, chili flakes, salt and sugar. Cook until soft but not colored.

If using canned tomatoes, put a knife into the open can and cut the tomatoes roughly. If using fresh tomatoes blanch, peel and chop them. Add the tomatoes to the pan and simmer slowly for 20 minutes. Serve with spaghetti and grate over some Reggiano Parmigano.

HARBOR SHRIMP LASAGNE WITH WHITE ASPARAGUS AND SAFFRON DRESSING

SERVES SIX

This is a free-form lasagne that's like a pasta salad. Not only is it not really a lasagne, but the dressing has Indian influences. Its blend of texture and flavor works well and the dish is representative of the way I cook, and a direct result of my multicultural surroundings. The two main ingredients of this dish are available in Sydney over summer. Harbour prawns are small king prawns that spawn in the bays and harbours of Sydney and swim up the coast; the season starts at the beginning of November and runs through to the end of February. White asparagus, which has only been available recently, comes in a couple of weeks before and runs a week or two less. They are a different beast to the green, and require longer cooking to be palatable.

I use Iranian saffron in this dish, which are all stamens, with none of the straw on the bottom, unlike most Spanish varieties. Remember that saffron is a water-based spice, and must be infused in hot water before going into dish. If it comes into direct contact with oil before, the true flavor will be lost.

INGREDIENTS
- 700 g (1.5 lb) fresh harbour or school prawns
- 24 spears white asparagus
- 1 avocado, cut into 0.5 cm cubes
- 1 bunch rocket, sliced

Pasta
- 300 g (1o oz) plain flour
- sea salt
- 2 x 55 g (2 oz) eggs
- a large pinch of saffron, dissolved in 20 ml hot water
- olive oil

Dressing
- 300 ml (10 oz) extra-virgin olive oil
- 1 small onion, finely diced
- 4 cloves garlic, crushed and finely diced
- 1 knob ginger, finely diced
- ½ tablespoon sea salt
- 4 tomatoes, blanched,
- peeled, seeded and finely chopped
- 20 white peppercorns, roasted and ground
- 15 cumin seeds, roasted and ground
- 15 coriander (cilantro) seeds, roasted and ground
- 6 cardamom seeds, roasted and ground
- 3 good pinches saffron,
- dissolved in 30 ml (1 fl oz) hot water
- 100 ml (3 fl oz) yogurt

PASTA

METHOD

To make the Pasta, mix the flour and salt together in a bowl and make a well in the centre. Beat the eggs and saffron water together with a fork, mix it into the well of the flour and knead briefly to make a dough. Wrap in plastic and rest for 30 minutes. Roll through the pasta machine, finishing on the lowest setting. Cut the pasta into 7 cm (2.8 in) squares and cook in boiling, salted water with some olive oil. Refresh in ice-water. Pat the squares dry and brush with olive oil. Store with plastic between each layer.

To make the Dressing, in a heavy-based frying pan place 100 ml (3 fl oz) of the olive oil, the onion, garlic, ginger and sea salt, and cook over medium heat until the mixture has caramelized, about 20 minutes. Add the diced tomato and cook for 10 minutes. Add the spices and saffron water and cook for a further 5 minutes. Add the yogurt and cook for another 5 minutes. Remove from the heat. When the mixture has cooled stir through the remaining 200 ml of olive oil.

Cook the prawns in boiling salted water for 4 minutes. Refresh in ice-water and drain. Peel and devein.

Peel the asparagus from tip to base. Break off the last 3 cm of the base and repeat with the others. Bring a pot of salted water to the boil and add the asparagus. Place a plate wrapped in a cloth over the top to keep the asparagus from floating to the surface. Simmer for 15 to 20 minutes, depending on the thickness of the stems. The asparagus should not be crunchy. Refresh in ice-water and pat dry. Cut into 0.5 cm dice.

Place the asparagus, avocado and rocket in a bowl. Add the harbour prawns. Place 100 ml (3 fl oz) of dressing in the bowl and toss to coat. Place a square of pasta on each plate, add one-twelfth of the salad mix on each piece of pasta and top with another sheet of pasta, at a slightly different angle. Put another twelfth of the salad on top of each pasta square and top with another sheet of pasta, placed at the same angle as the bottom sheet. Spoon over the remaining dressing. Serve immediately.

SPANNER CRAB RAVIOLI WITH OXTAIL AND ROSEMARY JUS

SERVES SIX

This dish represents the harmony of flavors from Eastern and Western cooking that make up Rockpool. The layers of flavor and texture in the dish come together to form an extraordinary harmony of taste, and the lightness of the broth carries the delicate texture of the crab beautifully. The broth starts out with a very Asian purpose and direction, but is subtly changed with the addition of olive oil and rosemary. The crabmeat ravioli has preserved lemon and coriander mixed through, which adds to the dish's perfume and lifts the flavor. The addition of skordalia with its rich garlicky taste and scent, and the crunch of radish really round out the dish. Most of the various parts of this dish can be made in advance. The skordalia is by no means traditional, but it's a nice variation, and I use it often as a sauce with roast lamb.

INGREDIENTS

- 10 cloves garlic
- 10 red shallots
- 5 coriander (cilantro) roots
- sea salt and freshly ground pepper
- 15 white peppercorns, roasted and ground
- 10 coriander seeds, roasted and ground
- 2 kg (4 lb) oxtail, cut and trimmed
- 50 ml (2 fl oz) peanut oil
- 100 ml (3 fl oz) whisky
- 8 tablespoons palm sugar
- 4 tablespoons fish sauce
- 2 litres Chicken Stock (page 122)
- 2 cloves garlic
- 3 red shallots
- 2 coriander roots
- 6 white peppercorns
- 50 ml (2 fl oz) peanut oil
- meat from 6 pieces cooked oxtail
- 3 tablespoons palm sugar
- 2 tablespoons fish sauce

- 150 ml (5 fl oz) coconut milk
- 15 mint leaves
- 15 coriander (cilantro) leaves
- 4 sprigs rosemary
- 90 ml (3 fl oz) extra-virgin olive oil
- 6 red radishes, sliced into rounds

Ravioli

- 400 g (14 oz) cooked spanner crab meat
- ½ preserved lemon
- 2 tablespoons chopped coriander (cilantro) leaves 2 coriander roots, ground to a paste
- with 1 teaspoon sea salt
- 200 g (7 oz) Basic Pasta (page 191)

Skordalia

- 4 heads garlic, left whole
- 2 large pink-eye potatoes
- sea salt and freshly ground pepper
- juice of 1 to 2 lemons
- 50 ml (2 fl oz) extra-virgin olive oil

METHOD

Preheat the oven to 220°C (425°F).

In a mortar and pestle place the garlic, shallots and coriander roots with a teaspoon of sea salt and crush to a paste. Add the ground peppercorns and coriander to the paste. In a heavy-based pan that will fit into the preheated oven roast the oxtail bones in some olive oil for 30 minutes, or until golden brown. Place the bones in a pot and tip the excess oil out of the pan. Place the pot over high heat on top of the stove. Add the peanut oil and paste, and stir continuously with a wooden spoon until it goes dark brown (but not black). Add the whisky, reduce until it's gone, then add the palm sugar. Caramelize until it is dark brown (again make sure it's not black). Add the fish sauce and stir for 2 minutes. Place in the pot with the oxtail, scraping the bottom of the pan to remove all the solids. Cover with the chicken stock and bring to the boil. Turn down to a very gentle simmer and skim the stock regularly. Simmer gently for 3 hours or until the oxtail is tender.

Remove from the heat and allow the oxtail to stand for 20 minutes. Skim off any remaining fat that floats to the top to ensure the overall clarity of the stock.

Carefully ladle the stock out of the pot and strain into a container. Gently lift up the pot and allow the stock to run off the bones. Don't try to press out more juice or you'll spoil the stock. Strain a second time through muslin. Reserve the oxtail for use in the dish (the extra makes a great stir-fry). Reserve the stock to cook the ravioli. This stock does not retain its true flavor for more than 2 days, so if you make it in advance, freeze it. It's not quite the same, though.

To make the Ravioli, place the crabmeat in a bowl and remove any bits of shell and cartilage. Rinse and cut out the pulp of the preserved lemon. Discard the pulp and finely dice the peel. Add the lemon, coriander leaves and roots, and ground pepper to the crabmeat and mix thoroughly. Divide into 12 balls.

Put half the pasta through the machine twice on the lowest setting. Lay the pasta down on the bench and cut out 12 circles of 7 cm (3 in) in diameter. Place a crab ball on 6 circles and, with a pastry brush dipped in water, moisten the edge of the circle. Top with the other sheet of pastry and squeeze the two edges together to seal the ravioli. Continue with the rest, and repeat with the leftover pasta. You should have 12 pieces of ravioli in all. At this stage the ravioli can be lightly floured and left on the bench, or placed in the refrigerator on a wooden board until needed, or blanched and refreshed, brushed with oil and refrigerated. While they keep well, they are at their best when cooked and served immediately.

Preheat the oven to 130°C (275°F).

To make the Skordalia, place the garlic in a roasting pan and put in the preheated oven for about 1 hour, or until soft. This process renders a lot of the volatile oils that give garlic its strong taste and smell; by doing this you'll end up with a rich, mellow flavor that is wonderful on roasts. Remove the garlic from the oven and when cool enough to handle cut in half and squeeze out the garlic. Peel, slice and steam the potatoes for 15 minutes or until soft. Push through a ricer or food mill, and place in a bowl. Add the garlic, salt and juice of 1 lemon. Add the olive oil in a thin stream and grind over some pepper. Check the seasoning, adding more lemon juice as necessary. The flavor should be garlicky and tangy. The olive oil and potato should blend together to give a rich creamy flavor and texture. Each flavor should follow the other, none should dominate. Keep the mixture in a warm place, but don't overheat or it will split.

Place the garlic, shallots, coriander roots and white peppercorns in a mortar and pestle, and pound to a paste. Put a wok on the stove and pour in the peanut oil. Add the paste and fry until golden brown. Add the oxtail and, while stirring, add the palm sugar. Once caramelized, add the fish sauce and stir. Add the coconut milk and herbs, and cook until the liquid is almost gone. Remove from the stove and gently take the meat off the bone with a pair of tongs. It should just fall off the bone.

Place the stock used to cook the oxtail in a pot. Add the rosemary, and bring to a simmer. Place a pot of boiling salted water with a little olive oil on the stove to cook or reheat the ravioli.

To serve, place 2 pieces of pasta in each bowl. Strain over the oxtail broth, making sure there is at least 100 ml per person. Add a spoonful of skordalia on top and a large piece of oxtail. Place some radish on top and drizzle 15 ml extra-virgin olive oil over the top. Grind over some pepper and serve.

risotto is like the warmth and love of a family, it nourishes not only the body, but the soul as well. I always have an incredible feeling of well-being when I eat a good risotto; you can almost feel the goodness from the creamy stew of rice and its flavoring partners.

Although most Italians would eat risotto as a second course after the appetiser and before the main, I much prefer it as a course on its own, with good bread, olive oil and a glass of sound wine, followed by a salad. Risotto is one dish you can serve your friends at home, knowing that it's better than 99 per cent of those served in restaurants.

I don't believe there's any substitute for adding the stock bit by bit and faithfully stirring the rice out. This is the very process that develops the creaminess in the rice. There are cooks who will tell you to pour warm broth over the rice, put a lid on and walk away while it cooks — to me this is not risotto, it's a rice pilaf, and nothing more.

Risotto has three major elements: rice, broth, and ingredients that are added at the end of the cooking time. These ingredients are usually pre-cooked and only need heating through. I always add butter and Parmesan at the end, and have yet to meet a risotto they didn't improve. Many people would say that cheese and fish don't go well together; to my taste, however, they do. Use good-quality Arborio rice and the freshest finishing ingredients you can find. While it seems quite obvious, many cooks pay too little attention to the quality of the stock, which is the main flavoring ingredient. Please use a fresh full-flavored stock every time you cook a risotto.

softened. The rice is added and fried until it starts to stick together. As the starch starts to come out, a little wine is added, and cooked until it evaporates. Boiling stock is then added to cover the rice, which must neither be drowned nor be too dry. Stir so that the rice will not sink to the bottom and catch. Continue stirring for the duration of the cooking, and add the final ingredients with the last of the stock. I always stir in the last of the ingredients, put a lid on and remove the pot from the stove for 4 minutes. To get to this point takes between 15 and 18 minutes. After you have added the last ingredients and prepared to serve, the dish would have taken somewhere between 20 to 24 minutes. The risotto should have the consistency of wet porridge and at no time must it be dry.

Risotto should be served the moment it is ready, it will not wait — nor should it if you have put in all that effort.

The combinations of ingredients in risotto are endless. Vegetables work well, as do roasted or barbecued game meats. Just make sure that all the ingredients are at room temperature.

Adele makes a beautiful East-meets-West risotto after a trip to Chinatown. She slices up some barbecued pork, debones and slices some roast duck, and chops up some spring onions, fried shallots, coriander leaves and fried tofu. She uses chicken stock and two sauce containers of roast duck sauce from the barbecue shop as the base. Fry the rice in peanut oil with lots of ginger and garlic and proceed with the stock as for normal risotto. Then add in all the other ingredients. We usually have it with chili sauce from the same shop, and it's great with a light shiraz or bigger pinot-style wine.

MUSHROOM RISOTTO

SERVES SIX AS AN ENTREE AND FOUR AS A MAIN COURSE

The mushrooms used in this dish can vary depending on the season. We don't have a great wild mushroom season in Australia, and those available tend to be nowhere as flavorsome as their reputation might suggest. I find the dark field mushrooms most appealing. If you want a bigger burst of flavor use a few chopped dried porcini mushrooms. Rehydrate the mushrooms, and strain the reconstituting liquid into the stock. With risotto it's easier to use cup measurements as you need a volume of stock to rice. This is one of the reasons why risotto is easy to cook for 500 to 600; the recipe is so easy to work out!

INGREDIENTS

- 24 flat field mushrooms, left whole
- olive oil
- 2 cloves garlic, crushed
- flat-leaf parsley, chopped
- sea salt
- 60 g (2 oz) unsalted butter, cubed
- 60 g (2 oz) grated Parmesan
- 1.25 litres (2.5 pints) Chicken Stock (page 122)
- 30 ml (1 fl oz) olive oil
- 1 small onion, finely diced
- 2 cloves garlic, chopped
- 375 g (13 oz) Arborio rice
- 125 g (4 oz) dry white wine
- sea salt and freshly ground pepper

METHOD

Preheat a grill or barbecue. Brush the mushrooms with olive oil and grill to impart a lovely smoky flavor. When the mushrooms are cool, slice and add a little more olive oil, garlic and parsley. Or, slice and sauté them in a pan with olive oil. When cooked place them in a bowl so that none of the juices are lost (they are very important to the final flavor of the risotto). Add a little more olive oil, garlic and parsley.

Have around the stove the mushrooms, butter and cheese. Place the stock at the back of the front burner you intend to use and bring it to a simmer. Place a heavy-based saucepan at the front and add the olive oil. When it is hot add the onion and garlic, stirring until they soften, but not colored. Add the rice and stir. The rice will start to stick as the starch comes out. Once that happens add the wine and continue to stir until the wine is completely absorbed. Add a ladleful of stock to just cover the rice. If you drown it the risotto will lose some of its unctuous quality and if it's too dry it will stick and retard the creaminess of the finished dish. It is important to keep stirring at this early stage or the rice will sink to the bottom and stick.

As the stock is absorbed, add another ladleful of stock; the rice will be very thirsty at the beginning and start to slow down as it absorbs more and more liquid. Continue to add ladle after ladle of stock. (Don't be tempted to take the easy way out and pour lots of stock on.) After between 15 and 18 minutes the rice should be ready for the last stage. Bite into a grain — it should be soft on the outside and firm in the middle. Add a little more stock, the butter, cheese and mushrooms with their juices to the pot, and stir through. Put a lid on and remove from the heat. After 3 to 4 minutes take the lid off and stir. Test by biting into a grain. It should be cooked through but have a nice resistance in the middle, a smooth bite that is firm and supple. Grind over some pepper and serve in bowls. Buon Appetito!

KING SHRIMP RISOTTO WITH CHILI JAM

SERVES SIX AS AN ENTRÉE AND FOUR AS A MAIN COURSE

This dish used to feature on the Rockpool menu at the beginning, and is one that I still love to cook at home. The flavor of prawn stock and rice work richly together. The chili jam can be replaced with fresh chilies, added with the onions, but the rich, thick jam gives the finished dish body. I use chicken stock to moisten the shells; to me fish stock takes on strange flavors after it is made. In the Rockpool kitchen chicken and veal stocks are used for all fish dishes — fish stock has never been on the stove in all the time we've been open. The recipe for chili jam will make enough to keep. Just refrigerate in a sealed jar and bring it out when barbecuing fish or poultry. It's also a knockout on fried eggs and couscous for breakfast.

INGREDIENTS

- 24 x 80 g to 100 g (2.5–3 oz) Yamba king prawns or any other fresh king prawns, shelled and deveined
- 30 ml (1 fl oz) olive oil
- 1 small onion, finely diced
- 2 cloves garlic, crushed
- 6 coriander (cilantro) roots, crushed
- with 2 teaspoons sea salt
- 375 g (13 oz) Arborio rice
- 125 g (4 oz) dry white wine
- 60 g (2 oz) unsalted butter, cubed
- 60 g (2 oz) grated Parmesan
- 12 fresh baby corn, halved
- 250 g (8 oz) blanched fresh peas (optional)
- 12 fresh water chestnuts, sliced
- 125 g (4 oz) chopped coriander leaves

Chili Jam
- 1.5 litres (3 pints) vegetable oil
- 3 Spanish onions, peeled and chopped
- 4 red capsicums (peppers), seeded and chopped
- 6 long red chilies, seeded and chopped
- 10 small Thai red chilies, chopped
- 10 cloves garlic, sliced
- 2 knobs ginger, peeled and sliced
- 2 punnets cherry tomatoes
- 500 g (8 oz) castor sugar
- 375 ml (13 fl oz) fish sauce

Prawn Stock
- olive oil
- prawn (shrimp) heads and shells
- 1 small onion, finely diced
- 1 clove garlic
- 1 small carrot, finely diced
- 250 ml (8 fl oz) dry white wine
- 4 vine-ripened tomatoes, blanched, skinned, seeded and chopped
- 1.5 litres (3 pints) Chicken Stock (page 122)

METHOD

To make the Chili Jam, in a heavy-based saucepan large enough to hold all the vegetables comfortably pour in the vegetable oil and heat it until it starts to smoke. Put in the onions, capsicums, chilies, garlic and ginger, and cook until they start to turn golden. Stir. Add the cherry tomatoes and continue to cook and stir until they go a very dark brown. When the vegetables start to go dark golden brown they will blacken very quickly, so be careful. If the vegetables are not taken to a dark enough color the jam will be too sweet. Add the sugar and caramelize. Add the fish sauce. Remove from the heat and blend. The oil will come to the top as it settles — leave, as it helps preserve the jam in the fridge.

To make the Prawn Stock, heat up some olive oil in a medium-sized pot. Add the prawn shells and stir. After 5 minutes, add the onion, garlic and carrot, and cook for a further 5 minutes. The shells should be bright red, and the color and flavor compounds should be going into the oil. Add the wine and reduce until almost gone. Add the tomatoes and the stock, and bring to a simmer. Skim off any scum that rises to the surface and turn down to a simmer. (If the shells are boiled for the hour the stock will end up with a bitter flavor.) Leave for 1 hour and strain.

Heat up some olive oil in a heavy-based frying pan and sauté the king prawns for 2 minutes on each side. Remove and drain on kitchen paper. Bring the prawn stock to a simmer at the back of the stove. Place a pot with 30 ml of olive oil on the front burner. Add the onion, garlic and coriander roots, stir until soft but not colored. Put in the rice and stir continuously until the rice starts to stick. Add the wine and allow it to all reduce. Pour in ladle after ladle of stock and stir; be careful not to drown the rice or let it dry out, the starch must continually bind the rice and stock into a sauce. Continue this process for 15 to 18 minutes until the rice grains are soft, but with a firm bite. With the last 2 ladlefuls of stock, add the prawns, butter, cheese, corn, peas and water chestnuts, and stir through. As the liquid starts to come to the boil again put a lid on and remove from the heat. After 4 minutes remove the lid, stir through the coriander leaves and place in bowls. Top with chili jam and serve.

PIZZA

Pizza is a popular fast food that always seems to be consistently done in the wrong way, like hamburgers and fried chicken. They seem to be just commodities to be consumed; taste is not important, just convenience. Fast-food pizza is often laden with saturated fats and salt, and a soggy base. Prepared properly, so that it has a thin crust and light topping, however, and served with a nice salad and a glass of red wine, pizza can be healthy convenience food.

The most important step to making good pizza is not to put on too much topping. It's easy to get carried away and to think that you're being generous, but all that does is make the pizza heavy and soggy. Make your own tomato sauce and use full-flavored cheeses. Cook the pizza at high heat so it seals quickly and allows the base to stay crisp. A pizza stone, available from good cooks' supply stores, is terrific for this and for making bread.

BASIC PIZZA

MAKES 5 X 12 CM (8 IN) PIZZAS

INGREDIENTS

Pizza Base

- 1.5 kg (3 lb) plain flour, sifted
- 2 tablespoons sea salt
- 3 tablespoons honey
- 500 ml (1 pint) water
- 30 g (1 fl oz) fresh yeast
- 50 ml (2 fl oz) extra-virgin olive oil

Tomato Sauce

- 500 g (1 lb) tomatoes, halved
- 200 ml (5 fl oz) olive oil
- 200 g (5 oz) onion, chopped
- 2 cloves garlic, chopped

METHOD

To make the Pizza Base, combine the salt with flour. (This helps to dilute the salt as yeast hates it.) Mix the honey and water together and warm to blood temperature. Add the yeast, crumbling it with your fingers. Don't overheat the water or the yeast will die.

Tip the flour and salt into a bowl and make a well in the centre. When the yeast is foaming, after about 10 minutes, add the water and honey, and olive oil to the flour. Mix the liquid into the flour. When it forms a mass turn it out onto a bench and knead. Continue kneading for 8 minutes until the dough is strong and elastic.

Place the dough back in the bowl and allow it to prove in a warm place until the dough doubles in size, about 1 hour. At this stage it can be knocked down for use or refrigerated until needed (it must be allowed to come back to room temperature a couple of hours before use).

Preheat the oven to 180°C (350°F).

To make the Tomato Sauce, place the tomatoes in the preheated oven for about 20 minutes until they soften. Put through a food mill or sieve. Heat up some olive oil in a saucepan and fry the onion and garlic. Add more oil to the pan to make up a cup. Pour in the blended tomato and continue frying for about 1 hour, until you have a paste. Use this on the pizza base, and any leftover oil on salads or to dress the pizza.

Preheat the oven to 200°C (400°F).

After the dough has risen, knock back and knead for 2 minutes. If you have a pizza stone the best way is to cook the pizza straight on the stone. Alternatively, lightly flour the bench and break off enough dough to fit your pizza tray; 70 g (1.5 oz) makes a nice pizzetta for one. Roll the sectioned dough into balls and start to roll the dough in quarter turns, making sure it's nice and thin. Add your toppings — don't go overboard. Lightly flour a pizza paddle and slip it under the pizza and quickly slide it onto the stone or tray with a jerk of the wrist. Cook for 5 minutes in the preheated oven until the base is crisp and golden brown.

PIZZA IDEAS

When I first opened Rockpool I wanted to serve food in the bar, so Trish and I decided to invest in a little pizza oven. It was great fun and everyone enjoyed playing around with it. It also helped out with a lot of staff meals. That oven now lives in the MCA café and produces pizzettas, to be eaten as you watch the ferries come into Circular Quay. Pizzas are a terrific vehicle for some very diverse toppings, and the sky's the limit. However, please don't put satay sauce on one, or red curry of chicken on another — Asian flavors and pizza don't mix; there's something unholy and immoral about those kinds of combinations. It's my feeling that people who perpetrate such sins be shot on sight. Here are a few ideas that are popular at Rockpool.

KING SHRIMP, RED PEPPER AND PESTO PIZZA

Select spanking-fresh prawns (shrimps) and peel, devein, and half lengthwise. Grill some red capsicum (peppers). Peel, slice finely and marinate them in olive oil and garlic. Make up some pesto and grate some fontina cheese. Fontina has many of the same properties as mozzarella when cooked, but a much richer, nuttier flavor, and I particularly like it with prawns. Roll out the pizza base, spread with tomato sauce, sprinkle with a small amount of cheese, and place the pepper slices and prawn halves on. Slide into the oven and cook until the base is golden brown. At this point the prawns should be just cooked. Remove from the oven, drizzle with pesto and serve.

SMOKED SALMON AND MASCARPONE PIZZA

You'll need some quality light smoked salmon; tomato sauce; washed young rocket leaves and extra-virgin olive oil. Season some mascarpone with lemon juice, salt and pepper. Roll out the pizza base, spread on some tomato sauce and slide the pizza into the oven. When it's nicely browned remove and top with smoked salmon and rocket. Spoon on the mascarpone, drizzle with olive oil and grind over some pepper. Serve.

SALAMI, PUMPKIN AND PARSLEY PIZZA

Thinly slice some spicy salami, roast some cubes of butternut pumpkin until brown and grate some fontina cheese. You'll also need tomato sauce, picked and washed flat-leaf parsley, extra-virgin olive oil and fresh lemon juice. Roll out the pizza base, spread on some tomato sauce, and place the salami and pumpkin on top. Sprinkle with cheese, slide into the oven and cook until golden brown. In a bowl toss the parsley with the olive oil, lemon juice, sea salt and a grind of pepper. Place the salad on the pizza and serve.

TOMATO, OLIVE AND HERB PIZZA

Choose beautiful ripe tomatoes. If you can't find good tomatoes pick another topping. You'll need plump oven-dried olives from Italy, tomato sauce, and grated fontina cheese. For the herb salad pick individual leaves of tarragon, dill, coriander, chervil and mâche. Use extra-virgin olive oil and a good sherry vinegar for the dressing, and season with sea salt and freshly ground pepper. Roll out the pizza base and spread on some tomato sauce. Slice the tomatoes and ring around base. Sprinkle with a very small amount of cheese, place a few olives on top and slide into the oven. Cook until the base is golden brown. Toss the herbs with the dressing, place on the pizza and serve.

CALZONE

Calzone is really a pizza sandwich, and can be filled with any variety of fillings. Although they are usually cooked in an oven like pizza, they can also be fried. Armando Percuoco, who runs one of Sydney's best Italian restaurants, Buon Ricordo, tells me that the fried calzone comes from Naples in Italy. The dough is rolled out, stuffed with cheese, one of which is mascarpone, and folded onto itself to form a half circle to seal. It is then fried in olive oil. Armando serves it with a beautiful tomato sauce. So simple, but so delicious!

SWEET THINGS

Desserts have always been of paramount importance at Rockpool. I have always maintained that a good ending is as important as a good beginning, from the time the door opens to the time petits fours are served and goodbyes exchanged. To do this means running a big kitchen brigade and floor team, and making substantial investment in the pastry section.

The head pastry chef would also have to be someone with similar ideas about food as I and someone I could work closely with. Lorraine Godsmark used to be the manager at Perry's, but really wanted to learn to cook, so she used to come in and work some mornings with me. Together, we'd make puff pastry, brioche, cakes, bavarois and stocks. When I opened the Bluewater Grill at Bondi, I asked Lorraine to come and look after the pastry section and do some other cooking for me. She dived in at the deep end and took the job. I especially wanted to bring cheesecakes of quality back to Sydney restaurants, an idea that Lorraine pursued with a vengeance. Her passionfruit and banana cheesecakes soon became legendary. She left after a while to pursue cooking in other directions when I left for overseas.

When I came back to Sydney and Rockpool got underway I didn't have to look far for my pastry chef. Lorraine accepted my offer of a job, and I believe she is the very best pastry chef in the country. She has taught herself everything there is to know about pastry, and how all its elements behave.

The desserts in this book go back as far as Barrenjoey House. Some are from the Bluewater Grill, Rockpool and Wockpool. Most of them are fairly simple and can be made in advance. All are wonderful ways of finishing a meal.

PASTRY

Well-made pastry is the foundation of good desserts in any restaurant, and it's very achievable in a domestic kitchen. I tend to rate a restaurant on the quality of its tarts and desserts made out of puff pastry because puff pastry not only requires skill, but care. Many desserts exhibit skill, but the understanding of flavor and the love of produce are not there. One can easily become mechanical as a pastry chef, since everything needs to be weighed and precise. It's easy to overlook the human element that centres first on the taste and texture, care and nurture. Fortunately for Rockpool Lorraine is always thinking about taste, and its complementary effect on the rest of the meal.

Be gentle but firm when making pastry. Don't overwork, or it will be tough and dry. Don't be scared either; knead it, turn it and handle it firmly without being rough and you will be rewarded.

PUFF PASTRY

Puff pastry is made of water, flour and butter. When it cooks the water turns to steam, the butter lubricates the layers of flour and allows them to rise. So if you don't break the layers of flour with the butter during rolling you should get an even rise. The trick with puff pastry is to have the butter and base dough at the same temperature. This way the harder butter won't break the layers of pastry, nor would the softer butter push through the layers during the rolling process.

I first made puff pastry after I bought my second cookbook, *Cuisine Gourmande* by Michel Guerard. I would venture to say that there is not a good chef working in Australia cooking around 1980 who wasn't influenced in some way by this great man. I have never used a better recipe and, after all these years, there are just a few rolling method changes.

Puff pastry is often thought of as time-consuming, and although the results are not as good if rushed, the actual time taken up in the rolling process is minimal. It is very easy to go about your business in a kitchen, stopping every now and again to complete the pastry. You will be surprised at how little time it takes when you become proficient. Don't be too hard on yourself if your first attempts are not perfect, it takes a little while to become confident with pastry.

INGREDIENTS

- 250 g (8 oz) plain flour
- 1 teaspoon sea salt
- 50 g (2 oz) unsalted butter, softened
- 125 ml (4 oz) ice-water
- 250 g (8 oz) unsalted butter, for rolling

METHOD

Place the flour, salt and soft butter in a food processor. Add the water and process for 30 seconds until the dough comes together and forms a ball. Remove and knead lightly on a floured bench for 1 minute. Pull the dough into a ball then flatten it slightly with the palm of your hand. With a sharp knife, make a crisscross pattern on top with four cuts each way (this helps release some of the elasticity). Wrap tightly in plastic and place in the fridge for 2 hours to rest.

Beat the butter with a rolling pin between two plastic sheets to make it pliable and easier to roll. Roll out to a 15 cm (6 in) square. It should still be cool to the touch.

On a lightly floured bench roll out the base dough to a 25 cm (10 in) square. Place the butter in the centre of the dough and fold over the base dough to completely envelope the butter. Seal the edges carefully. Lightly flour the dough and turn it over so that the seams are on the bottom. Roll the pastry away from you in the same direction (never side to side) until it is of even thickness and twice as long as it is wide. Be careful not to break open the pastry.

Fold the bottom and top third of the pastry towards the middle to form 3 layers. Fold the pastry in half again. This is known as a 'book fold', and the first fold of the pastry. Turn the pastry 90 degrees and roll out gently to a similar-sized rectangle as before. Again do a book fold. This is the second fold of the first turn. There will be 4 more folds and 2 more turns before the pastry is finished. Wrap the pastry in plastic again and rest in the refrigerator for 30 minutes. Remove the pastry from the refrigerator and give the pastry another full turn. Rest again. After 30 minutes, remove and complete the last turn. Return the pastry to the refrigerator and rest for at least 30 minutes before use. Roll out according to the recipe.

SWEET SHORTCRUST PASTRY

This pastry is ideal for making custard and fruit tarts. It can be made in advance and will keep in the refrigerator for a week. It also freezes well. The recipes yields 1 x 28 cm (11 in) tart case or several smaller ones.

INGREDIENTS

- 250 g (11 in) plain flour
- 75 g (2.5 oz) unsalted butter, cubed
- a pinch of sea salt
- 90 g (3 oz) icing sugar, sifted
- 55 ml (2 fl oz) milk
- 2 egg yolks

METHOD

Place the flour, butter, salt and icing sugar in a food processor and process for 20 seconds. Add the milk and egg yolks and process for a further 30 seconds until a mass forms.

Turn out to a lightly floured bench and knead lightly for a few moments. Flatten on the bench and form a ball. Wrap in plastic and place in the refrigerator for 1 hour.

Roll out the dough with a rolling pin according to the recipe. Refrigerate until needed.

BRIOCHE

MAKES A LOAF

INGREDIENTS

- 125 ml (4 fl oz) milk
- 50 g (2 oz) castor sugar
- 1 tablespoon fresh yeast or 1 teaspoon dried yeast
- 3 egg yolks
- 250 g (8 oz) plain flour
- ½ teaspoon sea salt
- 80 g (2.5 oz) unsalted butter, softened
- egg wash

METHOD

Pour the milk and sugar into a pot and bring to blood temperature. Add the yeast and stir. After 15 minutes add the egg yolks.

Place the flour and salt in the bowl of an electric mixer. Affix the dough hook and mix at a medium speed for 1 minute. Add the yeast mixture and process for a further 3 minutes. Add the butter in small chunks, adding more after the first lot is absorbed. Once all the butter has been incorporated mix for 10 minutes, until the dough is smooth and elastic. Put in a bowl, cover with food wrap and leave in a warm place to prove until doubled in size.

Preheat the oven to 180°C (350°F).

Take the dough out of the bowl and knead on a lightly floured bench for 2 minutes. Place in a bread tin spread with Pure and Simple, glaze the top with a little egg wash, and allow to prove in a warm place until doubled in size.

Place in the preheated oven and cook for 40 minutes until the brioche is puffed and browned. Remove and turn out onto a cake rack to cool.

FINE APPLE TART

SERVES FOUR

This dessert was the first on the menu at Barrenjoey House when I took over the kitchen in January 1983. The year before I had worked with Jenny Ferguson at You and Me. I like Jenny's food a lot, it's very feminine and each dish is very important in the whole scheme of things. She also displays a real sense of generosity to her clients from start to finish. This involves going to the markets and getting the best produce, building up a terrific wine list, and working with the floor staff to create a truly wonderful restaurant. Jenny's restaurant in the heart of the city is sorely missed today. I have a theory that her heart was broken by another chef who criticised her in a review that he had no business being involved in, a chef who should perhaps have spent more time getting his own house in order. Or perhaps he was unaware of the gross injustice of his actions, but I can't help getting angry every time I think of her story.

I first tasted this tart at You and Me and it was my inspiration for many years after. The best time to make this is in autumn, when the Golden Delicious apples are around.

INGREDIENTS

- 300 g (10.5 oz) Puff Pastry (page 220)
- 6 Golden Delicious apples
- juice of 1 lemon
- 180 g (6 oz) softened unsalted butter
- 180 g (6 oz) castor sugar
- plain flour for rolling

- vanilla bean ice-cream
- 9 egg yolks
- 200 g (7 oz) castor sugar
- 500 ml (1 pint) milk
- 2 vanilla pods
- 300 ml (10 fl oz) cream (35 per cent butterfat)

METHOD

To make the Vanilla Bean Ice-cream, place the egg yolks and sugar in a bowl and whisk until pale and creamy. Pour the milk into a pot. Cut and scrape the vanilla seeds into the milk, place the cut pod in as well. Bring to the boil.

Pour the milk over the egg mixture, whisking all the time. Return to the pot and continue stirring with wooden spoon. Cook the custard over a moderate heat until it coats the back of a spoon. Pour the mixture into another bowl that has been set over ice. Allow to cool in the refrigerator, remove the vanilla pods and pour in the cream. Churn in an ice-cream machine and freeze

Roll out the pastry to a 20 cm (8 in) square and place on baking sheet. Cut a border 10 mm from the edges and 1 mm deep into the pastry. Refrigerate the pastry for 20 minutes.

Peel the apples, cut in half and core. Toss them in lemon juice to stop them from discoloring. Place an apple half on the bench and cut the ends off so they are flat. Cut into 2 mm thick slices. Repeat with the other apple halves. Take the pastry out of the refrigerator and carefully overlap the apple slices along the top of the pastry. Do the next row, overlapping the top row slightly as well. Continue until the apples at all used up.

Preheat the oven to 220°C (425°F).

Dot 50 g (2 oz) of softened butter over the apples and sprinkle on 50 g (2 oz) of sugar. Place in the preheated oven and cook for 20 minutes. Add the rest of the butter and sugar and cook for another 20 minutes. The pastry should be crisp and cooked and the apples caramelized. Remove the tart from the oven and place on a cake rack to allow the air to circulate and to stop the pastry from sweating. Cut the tart into four 20 cm x 5cm (8 in x 2in) rectangles and place on large white plates. Serve with vanilla bean ice-cream.

CHOCOLATE CAKE

SERVES EIGHT

I am sure most people in the world love chocolate, it has powers that turn many into addicts. If it's not overdone chocolate has a great pure flavor. For me the best way to have it is in a simple cake or chocolate tart. I don't like fussy combinations of chocolate desserts, and avoid at all costs anything called death by chocolate.

This is really like a chocolate souffle, and it behaves like one, meaning it rises and falls, so don't freak out when it drops in the middle, as there is no flour to hold it up. The cake keeps well for a couple of days out of the refrigerator.

INGREDIENTS
- 6 egg yolks
- 100 g (3 oz) castor sugar
- 50 ml (1 pint) Cointreau
- 400 g (14 oz) couverture (Calletaut) or dark chocolate
- 6 egg whites
- 50 g (2 oz) castor sugar
- 300 ml (10 fl oz) cream (35 per cent butterfat), whipped to firm peaks
- icing sugar, for dusting
- cream (35 per cent butterfat), whipped

METHOD
Preheat the oven to 140°C (290°F).

Cut a piece of greaseproof paper to fit a round 20 cm cake tin. Spray with Pure and Simple and put the paper in the tin.

Beat the egg yolks and the 100 g of sugar together until pale and creamy. Add the Cointreau and continue beating. Melt the chocolate over hot water, don't leave boiling water in the pot or you will scald the chocolate. Cool the chocolate to room temperature.

Whisk the egg whites separately in a very clean bowl and, when soft peaks start to form, add the 50 g sugar slowly. Whip until very firm.

Add the cooled chocolate to the egg yolks and stir until completely incorporated. Take a quarter of the whipped cream and egg whites and fold through the chocolate mix until well incorporated. Add the rest of the cream and egg whites and fold through carefully. Pour the mixture into the cake tin, place the tin in a bain-marie filled to halfway up the mould with hot water, and bake in the preheated oven for 1 ½ hours. Turn off the oven and open the oven door, wedge it with a wooden spoon and allow the cake to cool in the oven for 2 hours.

Run a knife around the edges of the tin. Dip the cake tin in hot water for 20 seconds and turn it over onto a plate — it should slide out easily. Cut into 8 serves and place on white plates. Sprinkle with icing sugar and serve with whipped single cream.

RASPBERRY AND VANILLA BAVAROIS

SERVES EIGHT TO TEN

I created this dish for a Christmas lunch in 1985 to get away from the Christmas pudding on a 35°C day, to great success. Raspberries and vanilla make a beautiful marriage. The sweet and tangy raspberries and the creaminess of the bavarois come together and need no other player on the plate. Cook out the sabayon properly so that the gelatine is not left to hold up the dessert by itself. This method calls for less gelatine and produces a softer-textured bavarois.

INGREDIENTS

- 5 egg yolks
- 200 g (7 oz) castor sugar
- 3 vanilla pods
- 500 ml (1 pint) milk
- 4 leaves gelatine
- 600 ml (1.1 pints) cream (35 per cent butterfat)
- 1 cm (0.5 in) thick Génoise Sponge (page 228)
- 3 punnets raspberries

METHOD

In a bowl whisk the egg yolks and sugar together until pale and creamy. Cut the vanilla pods lengthwise and scrape the seeds into the milk. Bring to the boil. Pour the boiling milk over the egg yolk mixture, whisking all the time. Place the bowl over simmering water and whisk vigorously for between 8 to 12 minutes, until the sabayon thickens and the whisk leaves a trail as it goes through. Remove the bowl from the heat and set over a bowl of ice.

Soak the gelatine in cold water and when it is soft squeeze out any excess water and place it in the warm sabayon. Continue whisking until the gelatine is fully incorporated.

In another bowl whip the cream until firm peaks form. When the bavarois mixture is completely cold and starting to firm up fold the cream through, until completely incorporated.

Line a 20 cm (8 in) springform tin with the sheet of gènoise sponge. Put in a punnet of raspberries, then pour in the vanilla mixture. Refrigerate for 30 minutes. Remove from the refrigerator and sprinkle the remaining 2 punnets of raspberries on top and chill again. The raspberries will sink down into the bavarois but not right to the bottom. Refrigerate for at least 3 hours.

To serve, dip a knife in hot water and run around the inside of the tin. Unclip and remove the springform. Cut into 8 or 10 portions and serve as is or with raspberry coulis.

PASSIONFRUIT MIROIR

SERVES EIGHT TO TEN

This, along with passionfruit soufflé and passionfruit cheesecake, is one of my favorite desserts. The beautiful creamy texture of the tart, with the sweet, acidic flavor of passion-fruit is uniquely Australian, and makes a knockout dessert. If you omit the glaze and forget about the génoise sponge base, the miroirs can easily be made in dariole moulds and served with either extra passionfruit juice or créme anglaise. When making this dessert cook out the egg yolks in the passionfruit juice until the mixture is well thickened, the gelatine alone will not hold its shape when turned out. You'll need a 23 cm (9 in) springform tin for the génoise sponge and a 20 cm (8 in) springform or hoop to set the bavarois.

INGREDIENTS

Gênoise Sponge
- 8 x 55 g (2 oz) eggs
- 250 g (8 oz) castor sugar
- 250 g (8 oz) plain flour
- 30 g (1 oz) unsalted butter, melted

Passionfruit Bavarois
- 300 g (10 oz) castor sugar
- 5 egg yolks
- 500 ml (1 pint) strained passionfruit juice
- 4 leaves gelatine
- 600 ml (1.1 pint) cream (35 per cent butterfat)

Passionfruit Glaze
- 100 ml (3 fl oz) passionfruit juice
- 100 g (3 oz) castor sugar
- 70 ml (1.5 fl oz) water
- 2 leaves gelatine

METHOD

To make the Génoise Sponge, preheat the oven to 180°C (350°F) and grease a 23 cm (9 in) springform tin. Beat the eggs and sugar together in a stainless-steel bowl until pale and creamy. Place the bowl over a pot of boiling water and simmer, stirring continually for 8 to 10 minutes. When the sabayon thickens remove from the stove and continue to whisk for another 5 minutes. Gently sift the flour on top and fold in. Add the melted butter and fold through. Pour into the prepared tin and bake in the preheated oven for 30 minutes. Test by sticking a skewer into the sponge — it should come out dry. Remove from the oven, run a knife around the edges and remove the springform. Cool the cake on a cake rack. Slice across into four 1 cm layers. Trim one layer to fit a 20 cm (8 in) hoop or springform tin. (Refrigerate or freeze the rest.) Press the sponge into the base of the tin.

To make the Bavarois, place the sugar and egg yolks in a stainless-steel bowl and beat until white and creamy. Add the passionfruit juice and continue to incorporate. Place over a pot of simmering water and start whisking. Continue to whisk for between 10 and 12 minutes, making sure that the eggs don't scramble and that the juice reaches about 85°C (185°F) (use a sugar thermometer). At this stage the mixture will be thick and the whisk will leave a trail. Remove from the heat.

Soften the gelatine in some cold water. Squeeze out the excess water and stir the gelatine into the passionfruit custard. Place this over a bowl containing ice and stir until it cools to room temperature.

Whip the cream until firm peaks form and fold through the custard. Return to the ice. Leave for another 10 minutes, stirring from time to time, then pour into the hoop or springform tin with the gênoise sponge and refrigerate for at least 3 hours.

To make the Passionfruit Glaze, boil the juice, sugar and water together. Soak the gelatine in some cold water. Squeeze out any excess water and stir into the passionfruit mixture. Pour into a bowl that has been set over another bowl of ice. As the glaze starts to firm up and is completely cold pour over the bavarois. Refrigerate for a further hour.

To serve, run a warm knife run around the hoop or tin and remove. Heat a knife slightly in hot water and cut the miroir into wedges. Place in the centre of a large white plate and serve.

PASSIONFRUIT TART

SERVES EIGHT

This tart should be to Australians what lemon tart is to the Poms. If one fruit stands out in my mind as Australian it would have to be the passionfruit. Its intensity sets it apart from other fruits, and it is an ideal partner for cream and eggs. We have cooked the Roux brothers' luscious lemon tart for many years at Rockpool, and this tart draws its inspiration from that. Chris Manfield who ran the Paramount Restaurant in Sydney with Margie Harris, and makes a terrific passionfruit tart from a pastry shell filled with passionfruit curd. The food at the Paramount is extremely creative and delicious; Chris cooks in her own unique style and is one of the very best contemporary Australian chefs, but she is at her best and most creative when it comes to desserts. I see no need to serve cream with this tart. You will need a 26 cm tin.

INGREDIENTS

- 9 x 55 g (2 oz) eggs
- 350 g (12 oz) castor sugar
- 300 ml (10 fl oz) double cream (45 per cent butterfat)
- 350 ml (12 fl oz) passionfruit juice, strained
- plain flour for rolling
- 500 g (1 lb) Sweet Shortcrust Pastry (page 222)
- a little egg wash for glazing
- icing sugar for serving

METHOD

Make the passionfruit mix the day before you wish to bake the tart (resting it in the refrigerator helps avoid splitting). Whisk the eggs in a bowl. Add the sugar and continue to whisk until well incorporated. While stirring gently, pour in the cream. Add the passionfruit juice and continue to stir until well blended. Cover and refrigerate overnight.

Spray a 26 cm (10 in) tart tin with oil. Lightly flour a bench and roll out pastry until it is 2 cm (1 in) wider than the tart case. Roll the pastry over a rolling pin and gently ease into the tart case, pushing the sides in gently so that it takes the fluting. Refrigerate for 30 minutes.

Preheat the oven to 180°C (350°F). Line the tart case with foil, place rice in the foil and bake blind for 20 minutes. Remove the rice and foil, brush the tart shell with egg wash and cook for a further 10 minutes. Remove from the oven and lower the temperature to 140°C (290°F). Return the tart case to the oven.

With the case sitting in the oven, carefully pour in the passionfruit custard. Fill the tart right to the top with a cup or a small dariole mould. Bake for 40 minutes. Check — the tart should be halfway set but still be wobbly in the middle. If you take it out too soon it will not set and run when cut; if you leave it in too long it will set too firmly and lose its elegance. Through experience you'll find the optimum set for the tart in your oven.

Remove the tart from the oven, balance on a cup and remove the sides. Put on a cake rack and, with a palette knife, slide the base off the tart tin. This will allow the tart to cool and the pastry to crisp up rather than sweat. Invert the pastry ring back onto the tart to help hold the sides in as it cools and sets. Allow to cool for 1 hour. Carefully cut with a serrated knife and place in the middle of large white plates. Dust with icing sugar and serve.

FROZEN ESPRESSO CAKE

MAKES TEN TO TWELVE SERVES

This is one of the great ice-cream cake tastes, developed back in 1985 at Perry's. I subsequently took it to the Bluewater Grill and Leo Schofield fell in love with it, as did everyone who tasted it.

Barry McDonald was starting to bring up King Island dairy cheeses and creams back in 1985, before he turned his hand to fruit and vegetable providoring in 1986 with the opening of the Bluewater Grill. He was in the kitchen, telling me about the crème fraîche that was coming up (before this all the chefs made their own), and asked if I could make a dessert out of it and give him an angle to push it to cooks who didn't use it in sauces and such. Lorraine had made me a great strawberry sorbet and vanilla ice-cream birthday gâteau out of Lenôtre's book, which had been delicious. The wonderful textures of the birthday cake kept springing to mind so I went for the combination of coffee and sour-tasting cream, but what sour-tasting cream! I still make this cake for some functions, and it still tastes as beautiful now as it did then.

INGREDIENTS
Meringue
- 100 g (3 oz) egg whites
- 100 g (3 oz) castor sugar
- 100 g (3 oz) icing sugar

Coffee Ice-Cream
- 9 egg yolks
- 200 g (7 oz) castor sugar
- 500 ml (1 fl oz) milk
- 125 g (4 oz) ground coffee
- 300 ml (10.5 fl oz) cream (35 per cent butterfat)

Crème Fraiche Ice-Cream
- 9 egg yolks
- 200 g (7 oz) castor sugar
- 500 ml (1 pint) milk
- 600 ml (1.1 pint) crème fraîche

METHOD

To make the Meringue preheat the oven to 110°C (235°F) Whisk the egg whites in a clean bowl. As they stiffen add 2 tablespoons of the castor sugar and beat until stiff peaks form. Fold in the sifted sugars and transfer to a piping bag.

Draw 2 x 25 cm (10 in) circles on a piece of greaseproof paper that has been placed on an oven tray. Starting from the centre and working outwards in a spiral, pipe out 2 x 25 cm (10 in) meringue disks. Place the meringues in the preheated oven for 1½ hours.

To make the Coffee Ice-cream whisk the egg yolks and sugar together until pale and creamy. Boil the milk and ground coffee, and allow to infuse for 10 minutes. Put through a fine strainer. Pour the coffee-flavored milk into the egg mixture, whisking all the time. Place the mixture in a heavy-based pot and cook the custard to 85°C (185°F) or until it coats the back of a spoon (be careful not to scramble the eggs).

Pour through a sieve into a bowl and set over ice to cool. When it is cold add the cream and churn.

To make the Crème Fraiche Ice-cream whisk the egg yolks and sugar until pale and creamy. Bring the milk to the boil and pour over the egg yolks, whisking continually. Cook the custard until 85°C (185°F) or until it coats the back of a spoon. Strain into a bowl over another bowl of ice, and allow to cool. Add the crème fraîche and churn.

To assemble cut the 2 meringue circles to fit a 23 cm (9 in) springform tin. Place a meringue on the bottom, half fill with coffee ice-cream, followed by another meringue. Fill with crème fraiche ice-cream, smooth over the top and place in the freezer. To serve remove the ice-cream from the refrigerator, run a hot knife around the sides and remove the ring. Cut the cake into wedges and place in the middle of large white plates and serve.

MILLEFEUILLES OF FIGS

SERVES FOUR

As a child I used to be very fond of a pastry called matches, a basic pastry and pastry cream sandwich with little squiggly lines of icing on top. After my first trip to France in 1984 I realised that these little treats were modelled after their Napoleons. Watching the French waiters carve slices off great slabs of pastry is so inspiring; the pastry crisp, and the cream, melt-in-the-mouth. It's difficult to imagine anyone not loving these desserts. Sydney restaurants have long since embraced millefeuilles, especially in summer, when they turn up in all manner of stone fruit and berries. The two main players are the pastry and the cream, so get them right and your dish is assured, there is nothing worse than tough pastry. Inspired by France, fig became a regular starter on the menu at Barrenjoey House whenever it was in season. Lorraine also uses it now and again in this dessert. She interleaves the pastry with slices of fig instead of enclosing them. It makes a spectacular visual impact since the fig slices are so attractive.

INGREDIENTS

- 350 g (12 oz) Puff Pastry (page 220)
- plain flour for rolling
- 8 figs
- icing sugar

Pastry Cream

- 6 egg yolks
- 130 g (4.5 oz) castor sugar
- 40 g (1 oz) plain flour
- 500 ml (1 pint) milk
- 1 vanilla pod
- 200 ml (7 fl oz) cream (35 per cent butterfat)

METHOD

To make the Pastry Cream put the egg yolks and sugar in a bowl and whisk until pale and creamy. Sieve in the flour and continue to whisk until well incorporated. Pour the milk into a heavy-based pot. Cut vanilla pod in half, scrape the seeds into the milk and add the pod. Bring to the boil, then slowly pour into the egg mixture, whisking continuously. Pour the mixture back into the pot and bring to the boil, stirring with a wooden spoon continuously. Once it comes to the boil cook for 5 minutes, stirring well all the time. Pour into a bowl and put cling wrap on the surface to stop a skin from forming. When the custard is cool, put the cream into a bowl and whisk until firm peaks form. Fold a quarter of the whipped cream through the custard. Once it is well incorporated add the rest of the cream and gently fold through. Cover and refrigerate until ready to use.

Preheat the oven to 200°C (400°F)

Lightly flour a workbench and roll out the pastry to a 30 cm square. To hold the pastry down a little when it cooks you must dock it by pricking it all over with a fork, then place on a tray and refrigerate for at least 2 hours. The pastry needs quite a bit of resting or it will shrink considerably during cooking. Place the pastry sheet in the preheated oven and bake for 30 to 40 minutes. You may have to turn the oven right down to allow the pastry to dry out completely. Remove and cool on a cake rack. When the sheet is cool carefully cut it into 3 strips, then cut each strip into 4 to give you 12 rectangles of pastry. Cut the top and bottom off the figs and slice into 3 mm thick rounds.

Preheat the oven griller or salamander. Select the 4 nicest looking pieces of pastry and sprinkle with icing sugar. Place on a tray and put under the grill until the sugar caramelizes. Put a little dot of pastry cream in the middle of 4 large white plates to stop the pastry from sliding around. Place a piece of pastry on each plate and put a spoonful of pastry cream on. Line the slices of fig so they overlap on the pastry cream. Put a little more cream on top, top with a piece of pastry and repeat. Finish off with the piece of glazed pastry and serve.

MILLEFEUILLES OF MANGO AND COCONUT CREAM

SERVES FOUR

This variation on Millefeuilles of Figs (page 234) brings together mango and coconut, a delicious partnership that works particularly well with Asian-inspired meals.

INGREDIENTS
Coconut Pastry Cream
- 125 ml (4 fl oz) sweet white wine
- 40 g (1 oz) castor sugar
- 1 lime
- 1 vanilla pod
- 350 g (12 oz) Puff Pastry (page 220)
- plain flour for rolling out
- 2 large mangoes
- icing sugar

METHOD

To make the Coconut Pastry Cream, substitute coconut milk for milk in the recipe for Pastry Cream (page 234) and omit the vanilla pod.

To make the sauce put the wine, sugar, lime zest and juice, and split vanilla pod in a pot and bring to the boil. Simmer gently for 10 minutes, remove and allow to cool to room temperature.

Lightly flour a workbench and roll out the pastry to a 30 cm (12 in) square. Dock the pastry by pricking it all over with a fork. Place on a tray and refrigerate for at least 2 hours to minimise shrinkage.

Preheat the oven to 200°C (400°F). Place the pastry sheet in the oven, and bake for 30 to 40 minutes. You may have to turn the oven down to allow the pastry to dry out completely. Remove and cool on a cake rack. When the sheet is cool carefully cut it into 3 strips, then cut each strip into 4, to give you 12 rectangles of pastry.

Peel the mangoes and cut into 5 mm slices. Preheat the oven griller or salamander. Select the 4 nicest looking pieces of pastry and sprinkle with icing sugar. Place on a tray and put under the grill until the sugar caramelizes. Put a little dollop of coconut cream on 4 large white plates to stop the pastry from sliding off the plate. Place a piece of pastry in the centre of each plate and spoon over some coconut cream. Top with slices of mango and then a little more cream. Add the next layer of pastry and finish with the glazed pastry. Pour some sauce around the plate and serve immediately.

GINGER CUSTARD

SERVES SIX

This was a big winner on the Wockpool menu from day one. It's also wonderful with fresh fruit.

INGREDIENTS

Brandy Snaps
- 150 g (5 oz) unsalted butter
- 125 ml (4 fl oz) golden syrup
- 150 g (5 oz) castor sugar
- juice of ½ lemon
- 30 ml (1 fl oz) brandy
- 130 g (4.5 oz) plain flour
- 1 teaspoon finely grated ginger

Ginger Custard
- 3 tablespoons peeled and chopped ginger
- 60 ml (2 fl oz) water
- 150 ml (5 oz) double cream (45 per cent butterfat)
- 300 ml (10.5 fl oz) cream (35 per cent butterfat)
- 9 egg yolks
- 1 x 55 g (2 oz) egg
- 60 ml (2 fl oz) Stone's ginger wine
- 100 g (3 oz) castor sugar

METHOD

Preheat the oven to 140°C (290°F).

To make the Brandy Snaps, melt the butter and syrup in a heavy-based saucepan over low heat. Add the sugar and stir until it dissolves, add the lemon juice and brandy. Keep cooking until the mixture caramelizes. Remove from the heat and whisk in the flour and ginger. When cool enough to handle, divide the dough into walnut-size pieces and place on a greased baking tray (ensure they are well spread out). Bake in the preheated oven for 10 minutes. Remove from the oven and place over a rolling pin to curl. Store immediately in an air-tight container until ready to use.

Preheat the oven to 120°C (250°F).

To make the Ginger Custard, blend the ginger and water, then strain the juice through a fine sieve. Combine the two creams. In another bowl mix the egg yolks and whole egg together. Add the creams to the eggs and mix gently. Add the ginger wine and juice, and add the sugar. Stir together and pass through a fine strainer.

Take 6 custard or brulée moulds and pour the mixture right to the top. Place in a bain-marie and fill until halfway with hot water. Cover the moulds loosely with foil and bake in the preheated oven for 25 to 30 minutes. Remove and refrigerate overnight. The tops of the custards can be lightly covered in castor sugar and caramelized before serving if you like.

LIME SOUFFLÉ WITH LIME ICE-CREAM

MAKES FOUR SOUFFLES

The flavors of lime can carry not only the flavors of fish sauce, chili and palm sugar, but also the flavors of eggs, cream and sugar. This makes it a perfect partner for a souffle. We serve it with a passionfruit ice-cream that I adapted a long time ago from a recipe shared with me by Damien.

Lorraine has worked long and hard to make sure that every souffle stands up and is as good as the last. She spends a lot of time teaching people how to whisk egg whites until they are just right. I used to think that egg whites had to be at soft peaks stage to rise, and not overstretched. Lorraine, however, whips them to very firm peaks and gets terrific results. I've since been converted.

You'll need four soufflé ramekins for this dish. The souffles will be soft and creamy in the middle, I don't like souffles that are cooked firm all the way through.

INGREDIENTS
- unsalted butter, softened
- castor sugar for the moulds
- 2 egg yolks
- 90 g (3 oz) castor sugar
- 8 egg whites
- extra castor sugar for egg whites
- 130 ml (4.5 fl oz) freshly squeezed lime juice

Lime Ice-Cream
- 6 egg yolks
- 300 g (10.5 oz) castor sugar
- 300 ml (10.5 fl oz) freshly squeezed lime juice
- 600 ml (1.1 pints) cream (35 per cent butterfat)

METHOD

To make the Lime Ice-cream, place the egg yolks in a bowl and whisk in the sugar. Beat until pale and creamy, add the lime juice and mix. Place the bowl over a pot of simmering water and cook the lime mixture, whisking all the time until the sabayon thickens and falls off the spoon in ribbons. Remove and set over a bowl of ice to cool. When cold add the cream and churn. Place in the freezer until ready to use.

Preheat the oven to 190°C (375°F).

With a brush or finger coat the moulds with the butter, then half fill one mould with castor sugar, and with a circular motion tip the sugar into the next mould, coating the entire inside of the mould. Repeat. This is important so the soufflé rises evenly and caramelizes on the inside to give a pleasant crust.

Put the egg yolks in a bowl and whisk well. Add the sugar and whisk until pale and creamy and the sugar has dissolved. Place the egg whites in a very clean bowl and start whisking very gently for 1 minute. As it starts to foam start whisking more vigorously in a circular motion, lifting the egg whites to aerate them. When soft peaks start to form sprinkle some castor sugar over the egg whites and continue to whisk until firm and stiff.

Add the lime juice to the yolk mixture. Add a quarter of the egg whites to the yolk mixture and fold through to incorporate completely. Add the rest of the egg whites and fold through very gently. Spoon the mixture into the moulds, filling until it's a little over the rim. Run your thumb around the rim of the ramekin — this makes it easier for the soufflé to rise straight.

Place the ramekins in a bain-marie filled with hot water and cook for 14 minutes. Remove from the oven and dust with icing sugar. Place the ramekins on a plate and put a little lime ice-cream in a little bowl on the side. Serve immediately.

CONVERSION CHARTS

METRIC UNITS ARE USED THROUGHOUT THIS BOOK.
The approximate equivalents are as follows.

dry weights

10 g	$1/3$ oz
50 g	$1\frac{3}{4}$ oz
85 g	3 oz
100 g	$3\frac{1}{2}$ oz
112 g	4 oz
170 g	6 oz
225 g	8 oz
450g	16 oz (1 lb)
500 g	1.1 lb
1 kg	2.2 lb

oven temperatures

100°C	210°F	Very slow	
125°C	240°F	Very slow	
50°C	300°F	Slow	Gas Mark 2
180°C	350°F	Moderate	Gas Mark 4
200°C	400°F	Moderately hot	Gas Mark 6
220°C	450°F	Hot	Gas Mark 7
250°C	500°F	Very hot	Gas Mark 9

liquid weights

1 metric teaspoon	5 ml
$\frac{1}{2}$ metric tablespoon	10 ml
1 metric tablespoon	20 ml
1 US teaspoon	5 ml
1 US tablespoon	15 ml
$\frac{1}{4}$ metric cup	62.5 ml
$\frac{1}{2}$ metric cup	125 ml
1 metric cup	250 ml
4 metric cups	1 litre

Note: The US cup is slightly smaller than a metric cup.

length

1 cm	$1/3$ in
2 cm	$3/4$ in
2.5 cm	1in
5 cm	2 in
10 cm	4 in
20 cm	8 in

INDEX